A
Peaceful and
Working People

"La Familia" by José Clemente Orozco.
(Photo courtesy of the New School for Social Research.)

A
Peaceful and
Working People

Manners, Morals,
and Class Formation
in Northern Mexico

William E. French

University of New Mexico Press
Albuquerque

Library of Congress Cataloging-in-Publication Data

French, William E., 1956–
A peaceful and working people: manners, morals, and class formation in
northern Mexico / William E. French.—1st ed.
p. cm.
Includes bibliographical references and index.
ISBN 0-8263-1683-2
1. Social classes—Mexico—Chihuahua (State)—History.
2. Working class—Mexico—Chihuahua (State)—History.
3. Middle class—Mexico—Chihuahua (State)—History.
4. Social values—Mexico—Chihuahua (State)—History.
I. Title.
HN120.S6F74   1996
305.5'0972'16—dc20   95-32446
CIP

First paperbound printing, 2008

Paperbound ISBN: 978-0-8263-4581-3

13 12 11 10 09 08   1 2 3 4 5 6 7

Contents

Tables

Maps

Acknowledgments

While this acknowledgment reads a little like the story of my life, I, nevertheless, want to take this opportunity to thank many people. The journey that eventually resulted in this book began at the University of Calgary, where a fine program in Latin American history kindled my interest in Mexico. Since that time, I have enjoyed the friendship and encouragement of Chris Archer and Herman Konrad; a timely suggestion by Graham Knox helped me decide my future. I am thankful for their support and that I often find myself back in Calgary.

At the University of Texas at Austin I accumulated many debts, both personal and academic. In their respective seminars, Richard Graham helped show me what history could be about while Dr. Nettie Lee Benson provided an unsurpassed example of passionate commitment to the study of Mexico. I can think of no one I would rather have had supervise my dissertation than Alan Knight, and I am grateful for his quick responses and insightful comments on my work at that stage. I also thank the staff of the Benson Latin American Collection, an institution that seemed like a home away from home for a number of years. Above all, though, my greatest debt is to those with whom I lived the experience of graduate school—especially Frank de la Teja and José Fernández. I miss our conversations.

A University Fellowship from the University of Texas at Austin provided funds for research in archival collections in Mexico and the United States. In Tucson, I thank Mr. Andy Coumides for access to the American Smelting and Refining Company archives and Gilberto Ramírez for allowing me to use his couch. In Los Angeles, Janet Fireman offered hospitality, encouragement, and friendship (and a memorable trip to Venice Beach). In Washington, the staffs of the National Archive and the Washington National Record Center were helpful.

Although I did consult archival collections in Mexico City, most of my research was carried out in northern Mexico, especially in Chihuahua. I began almost every research trip in El Paso, Texas, where Richard Baquera and his family made me very welcome. They have invited me into their home each of the many times I have returned to El Paso over the last ten years. In Ciudad Juárez, the Universidad Autónoma de Ciudad Juárez has provided a forum, the Congreso Internacional de Historia Regional, where I have been able to present some of my work and also hear the work of a number of young historians of Chihuahua, including Carlos González, Ricardo León García, Noé Palomares, and others. In Ciudad Chihuahua, Licenciado Orozco and others at the Centro de Investigaciones del Estado de Chihuahua (CIDECH) were instrumental in facilitating access to local archives. Jesús Vargas, also of CIDECH, helped organize archival collections in Parral and shared his research on and enthusiasm for Chihuahua's history.

I first arrived in Parral under the most fortunate of circumstances. Expecting a few boxes of documents in a local collection (as indicated in a guide I had consulted in the AGN), I instead stumbled into a room literally full of archive boxes, neatly arranged and sorted by year. A team under the direction of Robert McCaa with funds from the Tinker Foundation had spent a year cleaning, organizing, and archiving this collection. Without their work it would not have been possible to write this book. Indeed, Bob McCaa continues to locate and help preserve judicial and other archives in Parral. But that was not all. In Parral, I was taken in off the streets by Carolyn Sexton Roy, also involved in this project of rescate and in her own graduate work. In addition to accommodation, she offered good humor and an introduction to almost everyone in town. Rosa María Arroyo Duarte has also long been involved in organizing and carrying out research in Parral's archives. She facilitates my use of the archives each time I work there. Municipal authorities from a number of administrations have also supported the project of rescuing and archiving numerous district and judicial collections.

The first draft of this manuscript was written in Logan, Utah, where the Department of History provided a secret office in the Utah State University Press facility to a junior faculty member in hopes that he would finish his dissertation. At a critical juncture, Linda Speth, then-director of the press, prevented a painting crew from throwing a drop cloth over the entire project, for which I remain sincerely grateful. A lively faculty made Logan an interesting place to live and work and I thank Len Rosenband, in particular, for sharing his command of bibliography with me. The dissertation became a book over the course of three summers of writing in my basement in Dewdney, British Columbia, and numerous trips back to Chihuahua. I thank the University of British Columbia for supporting my research and my colleagues there in the Department of History for making it a great place to work. I have also benefited from the comments and concern of many people over the years, especially Bill Beezley and Roderick Barman. Parts of Chapter 4 appeared as an article entitled "Prostitutes and Guardian Angels: Women, Work, and the Family in Porfirian Chihuahua," in the *Hispanic American Historical Review* (November 1992).

During the course of researching and writing this book, Evan and Leah were born. Although they now know that Dad goes away to conferences and to do research in Mexico, they may not yet understand what this has meant for Mom. I do. Thanks, Jan.

Dewdney, British Columbia
May 1995

A
Peaceful and
Working People

Introduction

Leaving his home in Gomez Palacio—located in the Mexican state of Durango—to ride the rails in search of work, Catarino Jurado landed in Parral, Chihuahua, in late 1910. After spending the day wandering around town looking for a job, he passed the evening under a bridge on the outskirts of the city with a woman he had met while eating *tamales* and drinking *atole* near the market. At one in the morning, bidding his new friend farewell, he returned to the city center to eat *menudo,* only to be shot and wounded by police. In the investigation that followed, Jurado revealed that he was forty-five years old, married, and an artisan, a shoemaker by trade; as this was his first visit to Parral, he knew no one who could vouch for him or support his statements. While Jurado's fate is unknown, his story, in general terms, is not unique. During the rule of Porfirio Díaz (known as the *Porfiriato,* 1876–1911), members of a *población flotante* (floating population), comprised of unemployed and marginalized artisans, *campesinos* deprived of their land, rural and urban laborers drawn by the prospect of higher wages, and others, roamed northern Mexico much like Jurado. They provided the labor force for a Mexico bent on material progress.[1]

Like their counterparts in many regions of the world, workers and their families in northern Mexico experienced the abrupt changes inher-

3

ent in the transition to what might be called the culture of capitalism. In this setting, as in others, the arrival of railroads, foreign investment, and capital-intensive industries, among other things, wrought transformations that touched the lives of all but a few. Not only did this process entail changes in patterns of land use and ownership, the nature and organization of work, and the ability of the state to extend its influence, it also mandated the creation of subordinate and suitably motivated workers and peaceful and working citizens. While the struggle to inculcate these values in populations in Europe and the United States has been analyzed, such is not the case with Mexico, where tension over work habits has been an important factor in shaping history for at least the last one hundred years. This book begins to fill this gap.[2]

Waging this struggle over work habits and values in northern Mexico were members of a growing and vocal middle class—the self-proclaimed *gente decente*—on the one hand, and, on the other, a young, mobile, and overwhelmingly male workforce of diverse origins. While each of these groups has attracted the attention of historians, only rarely has the relationship between the two formed the primary object of study. A major contribution of this book is to show that both the middle class and the working class constructed themselves reactively, that is, in relation to each other.

Central to this process of class formation were manners and morals. The *gente decente* disparaged both the aristocracy and the workers: while they labeled the former as idlers who were of no use to a developing Mexico, they condemned the latter as undisciplined and vice ridden. Rather than discuss class conflict and the economic conditions of workers, they pointed to what they regarded as the moral degeneracy of the working class, best symbolized for them by the figure of the prostitute. In contrast to the prostitute, they posited an idealized guardian angel who was to reign over the Porfirian family. The *gente decente*, to reform the working population, called on the state to regulate brothels, *cantinas,* and gambling, and asked workers to vacate public space and return to their homes. Although much of the middle-class emphasis on morality and domesticity was an attempt at self- and class-definition that cast the working class as the social "other," these ideals also appealed to certain workers, especially those with skills, who strove to be included in so-called decent society.

In *Domination and the Arts of Resistance,* James Scott notes that elites in peasant societies often hold up a model for "civilized" behavior that the rest of the society lacks the cultural and material resources to emulate. Whether this is speaking and dressing "properly," having certain table manners and gestures, or affecting distinctive patterns of taste and cultural consumption, peasants are asked to "worship a standard that is impossible for them to achieve."[3] The case of northern Mexico at the turn of the century illustrates that Scott's conclusions can also apply to societies experiencing the transition to capitalism. Whether it was the "proper" role of women, moral behavior, Sunday clothes, or cultural activities, the *gente decente* held up a model to which the working class did not, could not, measure up.

Scott also points out that subordination is often expressed in manners and gestures. Even seemingly small acts—a refusal to bow, a defiant posture, castes in India starting to wear turbans and shoes—signal a public breaking of the ritual of deference. This same behavior is apparent in northern Mexico, often centering on the use of clothing. Working-class women, for example, by wearing fine clothing, violated middle-class notions of women's appropriate behavior, thus overturning the social hierarchy. Likewise, working-class men used Sunday clothing to proclaim their equality and celebrated weddings and other ritual occasions with great expense, displaying what the *gente decente* considered irrational behavior. Through these acts, both men and women asserted for themselves an equality that their social superiors were quick to deny.

In emphasizing the role of manners in class formation, this book points to the importance of two subjects that have been left relatively unexplored in Mexican history.[4] The first is the central role played by moral or "cultural," rather than economic, criteria in dividing society into groups. I suggest that the most important social division or fault line in Mexican society during the Porfiriato was not the one separating "workers" from their employers, but rather the one that divided those who proclaimed themselves decent or respectable, the *gente decente*—which would include some artisans and public employees—from those who were not, a group that would include most mine workers. This division adheres more closely to the way contemporaries identified themselves and others. The second subject is the investing of urban space with notions of morality. During the Porfiriato, city streets, vacant lots, municipal centers, fairs, and brothels, among other areas, became part of a moral geography—contested terrain, in effect, upon which the struggles between social groups were mapped out.

The Mexican state supported the moral aspirations of the middle class. In Chihuahua, state officials mandated new, more limited hours of operation for brothels and *cantinas,* and attempted to drive vice away from city centers. Government representatives at the district and municipal levels regulated or closed circuses, fairs, public spaces, and popular celebrations. My study of moral reform underlines the complicated relationship that exists between power and morality. For the state, the language of moral reform had long afforded a cultural framework within which it could affirm its power and advance its claim to rule. For the *gente decente,* morality was the key not only to self-definition but to transforming the "lower" orders into compliant and productive members of society. Finally, for workers, morality offered a medium through which the dominant culture could be resisted or refashioned, while it provided them with a means to assert their own agenda.

One important aspect of this struggle over values was the formation of class. Labor historians have come increasingly to focus on issues like morality when discussing the factors shaping class consciousness. Rather than essentialism—the notion that capitalist wage relations should necessarily lead to particular forms of working-class thinking and behavior, undertaken by a self-conscious proletariat in opposition to other classes—labor historians now are as likely to study politics, popular culture, or precapitalist values in order to explain the creation of a sense of a labor "us" against a capital "them."[5] In northern Mexico, class formation did not follow inevitably from the foreign investment and economic changes that were taking place during the Porfiriato. Rather than rely solely on laboring for a wage, a substantial number of workers retained their ties to the land and maintained their loyalties to rural communities. They utilized wages earned in the mines and railroad camps of northern Mexico and the southwestern United States to supplement a subsistence existence on land they owned or worked; these men clung stubbornly to preindustrial values. Managers complained bitterly of their transience and their propensity to disappear during peak periods of the agricultural cycle. Members of the *población flotante,* they were sharply divided from those—often those with skills—who came to depend completely on wage labor.

Likewise, values unconnected to one's position in the process of production informed the outlook and behavior of workers in the industrial enterprises of northern Mexico. Along with their dreams, workers like Jurado brought outlooks and customs that had helped them make sense of their daily experiences as landless laborers, residents of rural communities, artisans, wage laborers, peddlers, and beggars. Along with preindustrial beliefs, working-class Mexicans shared with many rural residents conceptions of the proper role of government and their inherent rights as citizens. Many were quick to cite the Constitution of 1857 or appeal to ideals of individual rights they associated with Benito Juárez—the Mexican liberal president who wrote some of the reform laws and triumphed over a foreign-imposed monarch earlier in the nineteenth century—when they were confronted with what they considered to be the arbitrary acts of governmental officials or foreign managers. To legitimate their claims, workers drew from a tradition of popular or folk liberalism that was forged in the liberal–conservative struggles of nineteenth-century Mexico and fashioned by villagers to fend off a centralizing state. During the Mexican Revolution, they translated the rhetoric of middle-class reformers, who demanded effective suffrage and no reelection, into terms more appropriate to their lives: one man, one job; no bad bosses.

Gender also determined the way individuals experienced the process of class formation.[6] A young, mobile, and overwhelmingly male workforce gathered in the mining, railroad, and timber camps of northern Mexico. Women also migrated: although some took charge of rural properties while their fathers, husbands, brothers, and lovers temporarily labored for a wage, others accompanied their families to the new work sites. Corporate policy often encouraged this practice, for many companies preferred to hire "men of family," rather than single males, and to provide them with housing, schools, and hospitals in the belief that these amenities would reduce worker mobility. Managers also stressed the crucial role of wives in maintaining a household in which husbands, sons, and boarders, all working for the company, could recuperate. In addition to providing unpaid domestic labor, women also worked for wages as domestic servants and as factory workers; they sold goods and ran *cantinas* and brothels; they began to purchase sewing machines and other items of capitalist material culture and to orient themselves toward urban centers they associated with wages and consumer goods. In short, women, along with men, underwent working-class formation.[7]

What follows is a study of class formation, a process that has been more acclaimed than analyzed. Much has been made of the role of industrial workers in heralding the end of the old order under Porfirio Díaz and ushering in the new. Mine workers especially, who were supposedly imbued with the teachings of anarchism, have been placed at the forefront of the Mexican Revolution, heroically resisting American imperialism while bolstering Mexican nationalism. Their apparent class consciousness and class behavior seem to follow from their status as workers, while other potential sources of identity—popular culture, gender, peasant or artisanal—are hardly considered to be relevant. I begin with

UNITED STATES

LEGEND

— District
   Boundary
╫╫╫ Railroad
● City, Village

N

El Paso
(Texas)

Ciudad Juárez

GALEANA

Janos
Candelaria
San Pedro
Corralitos

WESTERN RAILWAY

Villa
Ahumada

Lago de Patos

BRAVOS

MEXICO NORTH

Casas Grandes
Galeana

MEXICAN CENTRAL

Rio Bravo del Norte

Madera
Namiquipa

GUERRERO

Dolores
Temósachic

Ciudad
Guerrero

Ocampo

RAYÓN

Chínipas

ARTEAGA

San Andrés
Ciudad Chihuahua
Cusihuiriachic

BENITO

JUÁREZ

Santa Eulalia

Rio Conchos

Ojinaga

ITURBIDE

CAMARGO

Naica

Carmargo

COAHUILA

Rio Conchos

ANDRÉS

Batopilas

DEL RÍO

HIDALGO

Tecorichic

MINA

Guadalupe
y Calvo

Hidalgo
del
Parral

Santa
Bárbara

PARRAL AND DURANGO

JIMÉNEZ

Jiménez

Bolsón de Mapimi

DURANGO

SINALOA

CHIHUAHUA

MEXICO

PACIFIC
OCEAN

GULF
OF
MEXICO

SCALE
1:5,000,000

50   0   50   100

in kilometres

Map 1: Chihuahua by District, 1910

the premise that the relationship between work experience and conscious-ness of class is not a given, but a matter for study, in which preindustrial traditions, popular values, and relationships with other social groups also matter.[8]

Such an approach has critics. Charles Bergquist, for one, warns that the insights of the so-called new social and labor history may distort im-portant influences shaping the lives of Latin American workers. While such methods may be appropriate to "advanced" capitalist societies, and to their level of economic, technical, institutional, and human resources, they are not suitable, he warns, to those of "underdeveloped historical fields and societies." In his opinion, social and labor historians studying Latin America need to be careful lest they "founder in a sea of primary information."[9] Others have shared Bergquist's concern about the uncriti-cal application of theories devised in the industrial world to Latin America.[10] While it is well advised to use caution when employing in Latin America methods developed elsewhere, there are a number of rea-sons that argue in favor of such a research strategy. First, it emphasizes the daily life or lived experience of social groups and classes not previ-ously considered. Second, analysis focuses on how these groups, espe-cially workers, acted and expressed themselves rather than how they were supposed to act. And finally, it facilitates comparative study.

Although this struggle over manners and morals was taking place throughout Mexico, it was particularly apparent in the North. It was in this region, with its dynamic economy shaped by mining and the haci-enda, where the middle class was most developed. Moreover, the North was also the site of a massive influx of foreign investment during the Porfiriato, especially in mining; in Chihuahua, more foreign capital was invested in nonrailroad enterprises than in any other state. Foreign in-vestment led to the growth in the number of workers in export produc-tion, a category that Charles Bergquist has identified as central for the study of labor in Latin America.[11] In the North, then, especially in Chi-huahua, middle-class Mexicans confronted growing numbers of workers in the mines, railroad camps, and cities of their state.

This book looks at the struggle over manners and morals as it was played out in Hidalgo District, located in the southern part of the state of Chihuahua, where it borders on the state of Durango (see Maps 1 and 2). Three reasons make this district particularly appropriate for study: First, in Parral, the administrative center of the *jefatura política* of Hidalgo District, Santa Bárbara, and Villa Escobedo, mining dates back to the very beginnings of Spanish economic activity in the North. Yet it was the

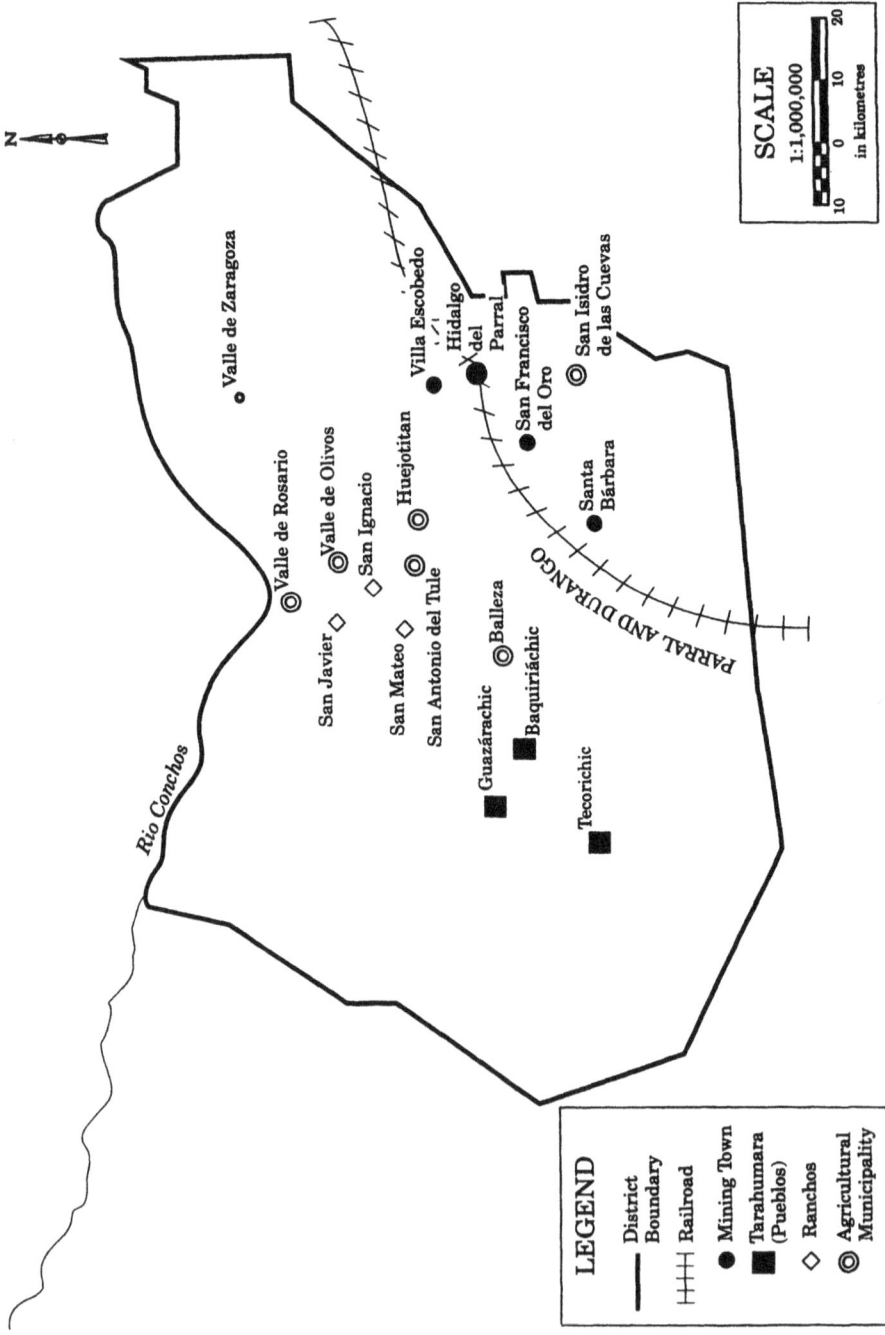

LEGEND

—	District Boundary
⊢⊢⊢⊢	Railroad
●	Mining Town
■	Tarahumara (Pueblos)
◇	Ranchos
◎	Agricultural Municipality

Rio Conchos

Valle de Zaragoza

Valle de Rosario ◎

Valle de Olivos ◎

San Ignacio ◇

Huejotitan ◎

Villa Escobedo ●

Hidalgo del Parral

San Francisco del Oro ●

San Isidro de las Cuevas ◎

Santa Bárbara ●

San Javier ◇

San Mateo ◇

San Antonio del Tule

Guazárachic ■

Balleza ◎

Baquiríachic ■

Tecorichic ■

PARRAL AND DURANGO

N

SCALE

1:1,000,000

in kilometres

10   0   10   20

Map 2: Hidalgo District

arrival of a spur of the Mexican Central Railroad in 1899 that stimulated the Porfirian-era mining boom. After this date, mining became a technologically advanced and capital-intensive proposition in Hidalgo District, as it did in other areas in northern Mexico, including Cananea, in Sonora, El Boleo, in Baja California, and Santa Eulalia, as well as in Chihuahua, to name only a few. Although the book focuses on Hidalgo District, comparisons will often be made to these towns and others in northern Mexico, including nearby Batopilas, Santa Eulalia, Cusihuiriáchic, and Candelaria, in the northwestern corner of the state. All these mining centers, although not company towns, came to depend on the operation of large-scale, usually foreign enterprises known as *extractories.*

The second reason for choosing to study class formation in Hidalgo District was the coexistence of mining- and agrarian-based communities. As in other rural settings in northern Mexico, residents of the predominantly agricultural municipalities of the district—including Balleza, Valle de Zaragoza, Valle de Allende, Huejotitan, San Antonio del Tule, and numerous smaller settlements—subsisted, produced agricultural goods for a market, and confronted the pressures brought about by the loss of their land and the lure of higher wages in the mining centers. They jostled with recent arrivals, including skilled workers from traditional mining centers further south and those without skills from all over the country, in the mines and mining camps dominated by foreign capital and advanced technology.

Finally, the district served as a gateway for workers going north, to the borderlands, and south, to the Laguna district, regions undergoing tremendous economic development. Because it so often represented but one more stop for a laboring population that "floated" in and out of both wage and subsistence work—as determined by circumstances and individual inclination—the conclusions reached here are more generally applicable. Studying the struggle over manners and morals in Hidalgo District, then, is to study the lives of workers and their families as they were lived throughout northern Mexico.

The organization of this book reflects its central concern with the struggle to inculcate the capitalist work ethic. Chapter 1 examines the changes in the nature and organization of mining that resulted from the application of capital and new technology to this industry. As well as setting limits and exerting pressures on those living and working in northern Mexico, these changes led to the need for a new kind of worker. The managerial practices designed to increase worker subordination and inculcate values of time and work discipline are discussed in Chapter 2.

Managers made use of incentive, including an employment package and the company store, as well as force in order to attract and keep workers. In Chapters 3 and 4, the campaign of the *gente decente* for moral reform and the ideal family is set out, as is the role of the state in implementing this program. In addition to representing self- and class-definition, these reforms were an attempt to domesticate and change the morals of workers. Chapter 5 deals with how individuals and families lived, accepted, reformed, and resisted the transformations accompanying working-class formation. A "moral economy," stressing the right of mine workers to earn a living, informed and justified workers' actions. In Chapter 6, the behavior of those in the mining community, including the response of mine workers to the Mexican Revolution, is discussed. Workers reshaped middle-class political rhetoric and applied it to their work situation. Finally, the last chapter evaluates the effects of ten years of revolution in Chihuahua. A conclusion follows.

Focusing on the struggle over work habits and values in the late nineteenth and early twentieth centuries adds a new dimension to Mexican historiography. It points to the central importance of manners and morals in the process of self-definition and class-definition then under way. People in northern Mexico, as in other times and places, expressed their ideas about self and society and gave meaning to their lives in moral terms. This book shows how these terms and their everyday expression, through manners, though they were often drawn from common cultural material, took on different meanings for different social groups. Thus, while the phrase "peaceful and working people" expressed those characteristics that the *gente decente* desired to inculcate in the working classes, it was also a term workers used to define themselves, providing them with a moral basis for asserting their own respectable status.

1
Ways of Working

The day for the amateur and the man whose capital is so far
behind him that he can never reach it, is past.

—*Mexican Mining Journal*, August 1909

. . . the peonage system of labor employment and the patio
system of ore treatment, and the rawhide system of ore extracting
all began to disappear at about the same time, with the advent of
up-to-date mining methods, machinery, standard American
mining tools, and the intelligence that was required
for their operation.

—American mine manager

In the closing decades of the nineteenth century, new mining methods
premised upon advances in the geological and chemical sciences revolutionized the extraction and treatment of metal-bearing ores. Smelting and
cyanidation replaced mercury amalgamation for deriving precious metal
from ore, making possible the profitable exploitation of ore bodies containing smaller amounts of precious metal per ton. In the mine itself, the
introduction of pneumatic drills, dynamite, hoists, and modern drainage
and ventilation equipment restructured the workplace. New ways of work
accompanied technological change. As mining became a capital-intensive
proposition presided over by geologists and engineers, it no longer depended on the skills of workers. For those without skills, the majority of
the workforce, mechanization meant the performance of one simplified
task within a well-defined hierarchy of jobs and at an increasingly faster
pace. Because the new methods of extracting and processing ore required
access to increasing amounts of capital, the bulk of mining came to be
carried out by large corporations. By the 1920s, most mine workers in
Mexico, as elsewhere in the Americas, worked in large industrial establishments known as *extractories*. The role of workers in the mining process, the productivity of their labor, and the means of controlling them

were becoming increasingly dependent on the amount of capital invested in the mining project.[1]

Yet technological transformation did not alter ways of working in the same manner everywhere. The impact of technological change in mining, as in other industries, depended upon the social context in which work took place as well as upon the response of workers. In the American West, for example, skilled miners of the preindustrial era resembled craftsmen in the way they controlled both their own workspace and the process of production; the new technology introduced after 1890 devalued many of their traditional skills, drove them into unskilled jobs, increased the proportion of unskilled workers, and led to a speedup with workers racing to keep pace with the new machines.[2] The same process of technological innovation characterized the operations of the St. John d'el Rey Mining Company, a British gold-mining concern in Brazil. Here, however, though mechanization led to a replacement and reorganization of labor and a transformation in the nature and structure of the workplace, it did not reduce levels of skill nor subdivide workers' tasks.[3] Finally, in Peru, the Cerro de Pasco Corporation introduced technological innovations, primarily the use of electric power in hoisting and operating air compressors, blowers, water pumps, and lights. These changes, however, did not radically alter the system of production. Rather, the company continued to rely on preexisting technology and labor relations for the extraction of ores. It employed peasant miners—at least until the 1950s—who retained links to their villages and viewed mine work as a temporary or seasonal occupation. The corporation operated profitably because it paid wages that were insufficient to provide subsistence to workers and their families.[4]

In Hidalgo District, the introduction of new mining and ore processing techniques in the early years of the twentieth century preserved the long-standing division between skilled and unskilled workers. Although unskilled workers formed an increasingly larger proportion of the mine labor force, managers continued to rely on skilled workers to drill ore, install timber, repair and operate machinery, and carry out a number of other jobs above and below ground. This does not mean, however, that they worked in exactly the same way as before. Many found their decision-making powers curtailed when they became wage laborers; even those forming independent work gangs, known as *cuadrillas*, working under contractors (*contratistas*), might be told how to perform their job. Workers in these gangs, who were paid by the task instead of receiving a daily wage, faced the problems inherent in mine work and assumed the risk, and consequent financial penalty, of delays. As the mining industry became more closely tied to the demands of smelters, world market silver prices, and the availability of capital, all workers found that the demand for their labor could disappear very suddenly through no fault of their own.

Smelters and the Mining Industry in Hidalgo District

In Mexico, the mining industry owed its rejuvenation in the late nineteenth century to the American demand for silver ore containing a high proportion of lead. To smelt efficiently, American smelter owners in Denver, Pueblo, Omaha, Kansas City, and San Francisco imported Mexican lead-silver ore to mix with ores, low in lead content, from the American West.[5] Faced with such competition, Colorado lead-ore miners succeeded in having a prohibitive duty, the McKinley Tariff, imposed on lead in 1890. As a result, American capitalists established the Mexican lead-silver smelting industry, building smelters at Monterrey, San Luis Potosí, Aguascalientes, Velardeña, Torreón, Mapimí, and a few years later, at Avalos, near Ciudad Chihuahua.[6] As in other mining regions, the particular geological properties of the ore helped shape the timing of its exploitation and the nature of work.

In Hidalgo District, the silver mining industry also benefited, at least initially, from the necessity of blending silver ores in the process of smelting. Ores in Parral and Minas Nuevas were silicious, that is, high in silica rather than heavy in lead, and required a smelting process in which the silica was discarded as slag while the silver adhered to a collector like lead. Mexican smelter owners, with access to ores high in lead content from mining centers near their smelters, required a source of silicious ores; and after completion of a spur of the Mexican Central Railroad between Jimenez and Parral in 1899 enabled the cheap transportation of ore to the smelters, mines in Hidalgo District served this purpose.[7] The arrival of the railroad marked the beginning of the era of modern mining. Within a year, American, British, and Mexican capitalists had invested in mines and built up-to-date mills and other reduction works, narrow-gauge railroads, and sawmills in the district. The *Engineering and Mining Journal*, in concluding that foreign capital and energy had lost no time in taking advantage of a promising situation, stated: "Parral is over 300 years old, yet it is not exaggeration to say that more ore has been mined since the arrival of the railroad than during the whole previous time."[8]

Although smelter owners initially sought silicious ore in Hidalgo District, their utilization of alternative sources for such ore devastated the mining industry after 1903. Mine owners who continued to ship ore to the smelters after this date lamented that there was practically no competition in the field; by late 1904, they described the district as financially dead because of the high smelter charges.[9] Mine owners in Hidalgo District began to join others in Mexico and the United States in complaining about their increasing dependence on the American Smelting and Refining Company (hereafter referred to as ASARCo). Formed in 1899, ASARCo represented an effort by the major smelter operators in the United States to divide ore markets and to eliminate the fierce competition that had resulted in low profit margins. Brought together to form the company were the Consolidated Kansas City Company, the Omaha and Grant Company, the United Company, and other companies in Colorado, Pennsylvania, Utah, and Illinois; between them, they had controlled about two-thirds of the nation's smelting and refining capacity.[10]

As ASARCo acquired control of the silver-lead smelting business, miners throughout North America cited discriminatory rates, ASARCo's refusal to buy ore, and the de facto confiscation of their mines as evidence of a so-called smelter's trust. The *Engineering and Mining Journal* warned of the possibility that such concentration might represent a great evil because it gave power to a "few men to dictate the policy to many, overriding individual inequalities, destroying freedom of action and increasing the chances of favoritism."[11] In 1901, the consolidation of ASARCo and Guggenheim interests led to an even greater concentration in smelting. By 1905, the Guggenheims, through ASARCo and other subsidiaries including the American Smelters' Security Company and the Guggenheim Exploration Company, blanketed northern Mexico with their smelters, fixing rates, establishing quotas, dividing the country into territories with other smelter operators, and thereby doing away with competition.[12]

ASARCo increasingly dominated mining in Chihuahua. The correspondence of A. S. Dwight, vice president of the Candelaria Mining Company (a company beginning to develop its property in San Pedro), reveals that small mine owners were in no position to stand up to the company. Dwight lamented that although the ores from its property were a "perfect godsend" for the smelter, he had been forced to accept long-term ore purchasing agreements on ASARCo's terms. Short of closing operations to enforce his point in negotiations—a tactic that was out of the question because the mines were not yet paying propositions—there was little he could do.[13] Dwight's complaints reveal that ASARCo could control min-

ing activity without direct ownership of the mines. From ASARCo's point
of view, outright ownership was not always desirable if the smelting department could secure the delivery of ore through a long-term contract.
In Hidalgo District, the local paper, *El Hijo del Parral,* condemned the
iron chains of the great trust that seemed to have shackled the local mining industry.[14] Although completion of a new smelter by the Madero family
in Torreón in 1902 initially promised competition for ASARCo as well as
better smelter rates for mine owners in Hidalgo District, a pooling agreement dashed these hopes.[15] By 1909, ASARCo alone accounted for more
than a quarter of the metals produced in Chihuahua and employed 15
percent of the mining workforce.[16]

Rather than lead smelters, however, it was the introduction of a new
technology for processing ore that eventually led to a renewal of mining
activity in northern Mexico generally and Hidalgo District in particular.
Cyanidation, patented in 1887, had proven its value in the gold mining
industry in South Africa, where the new technique for recovering precious metals had made possible the profitable exploitation of previously
uneconomical ore.[17] The process worked by crushing ore into a powder,
adding water and cyanide, and then agitating the mixture until the cyanide formed a compound with the gold and silver particles. The precious
metals precipitated out of the solution once zinc was added.[18]

Whereas mines in South Africa had shown the value of cyanidation in
the recovery of gold, metallurgical experts demonstrated in Mexican mines
that the process could also be successfully applied to the treatment of
silver ore. In 1904, the Creston-Colorado Mining Company in Minas
Prietas, in the neighboring state of Sonora, installed a plant to treat silver
ore with cyanide, which knowledgeable observers described as "the most
modern and complete plant in Mexico as well as one of the best plants of
its kind in the whole world."[19] Other mining companies in Mexico followed suit. In the old mining center of Guanajuato, for example, the new
system, combined with the availability of cheap electrical power, led to a
fourfold increase in the production of precious metals.[20] In 1906, engineers at the Dolores Mine in Chihuahua constructed the first plant in
Mexico to reduce all ore to slime for subsequent treatment with cyanide.[21] By building treatment plants at their mines, mine owners ended up
with a concentrate they could send to distant markets at a profit. The
cyanide process solved the problem of high transportation costs and eliminated the dependence of mine owners on the smelters. This simple method
not only revolutionized the process of mining silver, but saved Mexico's
silver mining industry. By flooding the market with large amounts of cheap

silver, however, it allowed only low-cost producers, large companies with plenty of capital, and miners working extremely rich ores to survive.[22]

The lack of cyanidation facilities in Hidalgo District, until near the end of the Porfiriato, led mine experts to describe it as technologically backward rather than modern. One correspondent to the *Mexican Mining Journal* concluded that mine owners in Parral were unaware that low-grade ores had been successfully treated with cyanidation at other Mexican mines; in early 1909, he described Parral as the most technologically out-of-date camp in the country.[23] Another observer added that the district's decline between 1904 and 1909 had been caused by the lack of adequate financial backing.[24] His comments illustrate that the need for cyanidation mills made mining—already a capital-intensive proposition—even more dependent on the large-scale investment of capital. The *Mexican Mining Journal,* in proclaiming the local treatment of ore to be an economically sound proposition, concluded that mining now required considerable capital and expertise: "The day for the amateur and the man whose capital is so far behind him that he can never reach it, is past."[25] In the first decade of the twentieth century, the greatest impediment to achieving modernity and development seemed to be the lack of capital.

In 1906, an American company, the Veta Colorado Mining and Smelting Company, began constructing plants to treat ore with cyanide in Hidalgo District. Unfortunately, for the company, a financial downturn in 1907 delayed completion of the project; and it was 1909 before new mine owners, armed with substantial financial backing, arrived to invest the capital necessary for the local cyanidation of ore.[26] In that year, managers of the newly incorporated Palmilla Milling Company sparked a wave of optimism in Parral by announcing that they would soon begin constructing a one-thousand-ton-capacity cyanide concentrating plant. James Hyslop, manager of a British-owned mine in San Francisco del Oro, was ecstatic: "It will please you to hear that I am now under the impression that Parral and district is on the eve of a 'boom.' The Palmilla mill is to be constructed at once. The Esmeraldo will build a small mill as also the Porvenir. These in combination with hydro-electric power from the Rio Conchos will start things running."[27]

Others shared Hyslop's optimism. The construction of cyanide facilities and the opening of new mining properties through 1910 prompted managers of the Parral and Durango Railroad to order new equipment to cope with the increasing business on the line.[28] Observers also expected

idle mines to resume operations, for it was now possible to treat ore lo-
cally rather than cede all profits to the smelter owners. Late in 1910, the
El Paso Morning Times predicted a great future for Hidalgo District:
"Thus Parral starts out in 1910 with a new epoch in mining and milling
industry and will take a rank well up among the great mining districts of
Mexico."[29]

As mining and milling became even more capital intensive, mine ownership in Hidalgo District came to be concentrated in fewer and fewer
hands. After 1904, companies with substantial resources, capable of weath-
ering economic downturns, viewed depressed conditions in the district as
a great business opportunity. As one mining investor concluded: "I am
sorry to hear how bad business is in your neighborhood. It is really a
great opportunity for men with money to step in and introduce modern
plant and machinery, modern methods, and such skilled exploitation of
ore bodies, which enables us to deal profitably with low grade ores even
under the present distressful conditions."[30] Economic downturn led to
the concentration of mine ownership, investment of capital, and the introduction of new technology—only in this way could profits still be made,
given the depressed price of silver and the low grade of ore found in the
district.[31]

Between 1909 and 1911, investors arrived to consummate big deals in
Hidalgo District. One takeover that caught the imagination of the border
press was the purchase of Pedro Alvarado's mine, the Palmilla, by a Texas
financial syndicate headed by A. J. McQuatters. Pedro Alvarado, referred
to (inaccurately) as a multimillionaire peon who had gone broke, was an
entrepreneur whose mining methods shocked American mining experts.
They expressed astonishment at the loose manner of record keeping and
the wholesale theft of high-quality ore by mine workers (they estimated
that workers had stolen as much as 25 percent of the total production of
the mine).[32] Alvarado also refused to mechanize his mining operations,
fearing that many longtime workers would be forced out of their jobs.[33]
In many ways, Pedro Alvarado's demise represented the end of one era
and the beginning of another. Gone were inefficient mining methods,
mining without up-to-date machinery, sloppy accounting practices, and
lax labor control. In their place arrived absentee ownership, oligopolistic
control, capital-intensive mining procedures, and bureaucratic methods
of managing labor.[34]

The concentration of mine ownership in Hidalgo District involved more
than the displacement of Mexicans by foreigners. The McQuatters syndicate also bought out foreign mining companies that had been in opera-

tion since the 1880s. In 1910, purchase of the Hidalgo Mining Company gave the syndicate control of some of the largest producing mines in the region. Managed for twenty-three years by James Long, this company had been built up slowly after beginning with a small property in the 1880s. Long had also organized and operated the Parral and Durango Railroad—the means of shipping ore and supplying timber, fuel, and supplies to much of the district—which also fell into syndicate hands. Other foreign companies acquired by the group included the Alvarado Consolidated Mines Company and the Palmilla Milling Company. For the business press, the transfer of the Palmilla company meant that "for the first time in the history of this wonderful mine," it was "being worked and developed in a modern way."[35] In 1910, the mining press reported that the syndicate, now named the Alvarado Mining and Milling Company, was spending the capital necessary to place it at the forefront of those who were introducing modern mining and milling methods to Mexico.[36]

But it was the American Smelting and Refining Company that took the greatest advantage of the economic downturn before 1910 and the instability caused by the Mexican Revolution, from 1910 to 1920, to consolidate its grip on mining in Hidalgo District. Between 1910 and 1920, ASARCo managers viewed the Mexican Revolution as a great business opportunity, and they sought to buy mines even though, at times, the board of directors thought otherwise. An indication of ASARCo's success in acquiring mines during the revolution can be gleaned from the fact that while five companies and approximately one hundred individual mine owners operated mines in Hidalgo District before 1910, only three companies and six individuals carried out mining operations after 1920. By the mid-1920s, ASARCo operated three distinct mining units in Hidalgo District.[37]

The concentration of mine ownership and the subsequent introduction of capital-intensive mining methods meant an increase in the number of mine workers laboring in large industrial establishments like those owned by ASARCo. In the municipalities and mining camps of Hidalgo District, *extractories*—defined by Ronald Brown as companies that owned smelters, concentrators, stamp mills, railroads, blacksmith facilities, and electrical generators as well as mines—came to dominate the industry.[38] In the mining camp of Los Azules, for example, one company, the El Rayo Development and Mining Company, employed half of the camp's population; in a similar fashion, the San Francisco del Oro Company dominated the town of the same name because it was the only large operation in the area. In another case, the Tecolotes y Anexas Company in

Santa Bárbara employed over one thousand workers in 1910. Other *extractories* in Hidalgo District included the Veta Colorado Mining and Smelter Company, the Alvarado Mining and Milling Company, and the Esmeraldo-Parral Mining Company.[39]

Capital-Intensive Mining
Methods and Labor

Managers investing in new mining technology believed it would reduce operating costs and increase profits by eliminating workers, a process characterized by *The Engineering and Mining Journal* as the substitution of American mining machinery for Mexican peon labor and by the border press as the definition of modernity itself.[40] The cumulative impact of the changes taking place resulted in traditional Mexican mining methods giving way to long-term mining strategies designed by geologists and engineers. Modern drills, high explosives, and expensive drainage and operating equipment required a systematic organization of mining that one engineer compared to laying out a great battle plan.[41] Armed with capital and the latest expertise, American mine managers disparaged Mexican methods. Rather than systematically working their mines, Mexicans—in the Americans' opinion—ransacked or gutted their properties in search of high grade ore that would enable them to get rich quick through a "bonanza," a process American mine managers derisively referred to as "gophering" rather than mining. In 1909, the general manager of ASARCo's mining department described Mexican methods as mining with no regular use of timbering and operating "so as to get the ore out as cheaply as possible, irrespective of the future welfare of the mine." By contrast, he considered his own efforts as rational, systematic mine development that would enhance the value of the property.[42]

In the American context, some historians have argued that the process of mining as undertaken in the large extractories created a substantially safer working environment than did the operations of smaller, less technologically advanced mining companies.[43] Likewise, historians of mining in Mexico maintain that mining became more tolerable, as pneumatic drills and power machinery freed peons from the exhausting work of dragging two-hundred-pound sacks of ore up ladders in suffocating temperatures, and that the utilization of electrical energy resulted in improved conditions for mine workers.[44] A recent study focusing on mine workers' diseases in the United States places these conclusions in doubt. By contrast, because the new machine drills and faster pace of work resulted in an increase in the inhalation of free silica, they led to more cases of silicosis, a disease that claimed more lives than all mining accidents.[45] Accident reports for mines in Hidalgo District between 1900 and 1920 (discussed in greater detail in Chapter 5) reveal a terrible carnage. Over the long term, however, silicosis must have exacted an even greater toll in workers' lives. In the 1920s, ASARCo officials confirmed that Parral's ores were a particularly dangerous source of silica. Moreover, air drills and dry surface crushing mills exacerbated the silicosis health hazard for mine workers throughout the district.[46]

Technological Change Underground

Between 1870 and 1910, within the mine itself, one age ended and another began as hand drilling with bar and sledge and blasting with black powder gave way to mining with pneumatic drill and dynamite. Other fundamental changes included the use of hoists to transport men and ore; the application of electricity to mining; and the development of mechanical ventilation and modern drainage equipment. Technological change in the extraction of ore led mine managers to demand a new type of mine worker who, according to the *Engineering and Mining Journal,* was far less efficient as an individual worker but worked as part of a system to deliver more tons of ore and at a lower cost than before. Not so intelligent, but obedient and industrious, the new worker was a more desirable employee to many companies than a man who could prospect, follow a vein, and make his own decisions in the workplace.[47] Mine managers in the American West, for example, had initially hired experienced Cornish miners because they possessed the latter attributes. By the turn of the century, however, company officials replaced Cornish miners with lower-priced Italian and eastern European workers whom they could train to perform specific tasks within the mining operation.[48]

In mid-nineteenth-century Mexico, mine workers, known as *barreteros,* working with picks, wedges, sledges, bars, and black powder—technology that had not changed much since the colonial period—drew on their experience to determine how mining would be carried out. They also controlled their own workforce. Pairs of skilled miners (*paradas*) hired unskilled labor according to the task at hand, often bidding on jobs and receiving payment for work accomplished rather than a daily wage. Rates for payment by the task (*destajo*) varied, depending on the work to be done and the conditions encountered. Other workers—including timbermen (*paleros*), whim and hoist operators (*palanqueros*), drainage-pump operators (*bomberos*), carpenters (*carpinteros*), and blacksmiths (*herreros*)—did likewise. These workers, their assistants, and apprentices organized themselves into hierarchies similar to those found in the workshop of a craft.[49] Such skilled workers constituted a minority of mine workers throughout North America. In mid-nineteenth century Mexico, for example, unskilled laborers (*peones*) organized into gangs made up from two-thirds to three-quarters of the total mining workforce.[50]

Before mining came to be characterized by capital-intensive methods, *barreteros* spent their time at work in pounding steel bars into rock with four- or eight-pound sledgehammers. A lone miner worked the four-pound sledge, or singlejack, with one hand while holding and turning the steel bar with the other. Teams of two mine workers doublejacked, for the eight-pound sledge required two hands to swing. Doublejacking mine workers regularly switched tasks to allow maximum effort while wielding the sledge. In noting the predominance of doublejack drilling in Mexico, American observers revealed their prejudices: the *Mexican Mining Journal* concluded that double-handed drilling allowed the *barretero* to loaf with a clear conscience for longer periods than with singlejacking; that *barreteros* could not be happy without companionship; that Mexicans, as a race, did not have the strength to work singlejacks; and that it was difficult to get Mexican workers to depart from customary work patterns.[51] Such opinions reveal an ignorance of the social dimension of double-handed drilling. In many Mexican mining camps, relatives—often a father and son—labored together on a drilling team to the benefit of both workers: while the father passed his mining skills to the next generation, the younger man prolonged the father's working life by spending more time in swinging the sledge. Working in teams also provided miners with a built-in safety system in case of emergency.[52]

Above all else, the industrialization of metal mining meant power drilling rather than drilling by hand. By the early years of the twentieth century, workers in North American mines operated compressed-air drills. In 1906, for example, hard-rock miners in Ontario, Canada, switched from recently introduced steam drills to lighter, piston and hammer-action pneumatic drills; then, in 1914, companies in Ontario increased productivity eight to ten times above that achieved with hand drills by introducing hollow steel drills, water-cooled drills, and hammer drills. This new equipment enabled the large Lake Superior copper mines to produce over 20 percent more copper with 20 percent fewer miners.[53] So effective were these drills that mine managers often announced the arrival of new air compressors and machine drills by laying off workers. The arrival of compressed-air drills meant that a mine could lay off three-quarters of its doublejack teams and still produce more tonnage than before.[54] By 1902, mine workers employing power drills extracted about three-quarters of the precious metal ores and six-sevenths of all copper ore in the western United States and British Columbia. As tools became lighter, faster, more durable, and more adaptable, mechanical drilling proved economically advantageous in an increasing number of circumstances.[55]

Between 1900 and 1910, mining managers introduced pneumatic drills into Mexican mines. In the Pilares Mine of the Moctezuma Copper Company in Sonora, for example, reporters hailed the installation of an Ingersoll-Rand air-compressor plant, enabling the operation of pneumatic stoper drills, as a form of liberation: because each drill could do the work of fifteen men with hammers, the company would no longer need to depend on its workers.[56] By 1920, air drills had replaced sledgehammers to such an extent that mining engineers in the copper camps concluded that only old-timers doublejacked. Similarly, in the hard rock of the San Pedro Mine in Chihuahua, "two little machines" could do as much work as twenty men.[57]

As mine managers in Mexico reached the same conclusion as managers throughout North America—that is, that pneumatic drills could increase productivity—they had little difficulty in making the decision to invest in the new drilling technology. In 1909, George Laird, the resident manager of the Candelaria Mines in Chihuahua, explained the bottom line to his board of directors in the United States. Because each drill could do the work of twenty men, he calculated that ten machines would be equal to two hundred men breaking ore during a shift. The savings resulted from the fact that the actual labor cost in mining with ten machine drills was the equivalent of only sixty men plus the increased cost of coal consumption in running the air drills, which Laird estimated would be the equivalent of forty men per shift. "In other words," he concluded, "we will get four times the results at half the cost if using only hand labor, or with not to exceed our present operating cost we should produce four times the amount of ore." As the initial outlay for the new drills was twelve thousand dollars, the switch to compressed-air drills increased the capital requirements of mining as well as the productivity of workers.[58]

In Hidalgo District, the low quality of the ore provided an added impetus to switch to machine drills. Because the key to treating such ores with cyanide was to extract large amounts, mines in Hidalgo District would only yield a profit if they were worked on a large scale. Large companies added machine drillers to their rosters because hand drillers could not provide the ore tonnages necessary for profitable mining. In the Minas Tecolotes y Anexas, in Santa Bárbara, for example, not one machine driller can be located among more than five hundred workers laboring in company mills and mines and on the railroad in 1900. By 1910, however, the company utilized both hand and machine drillers. Of approximately 300 men at work in the mines that year, 20 operated single hand drills, 55 doublejacked, and 65 operated air drills. In another case, that of the El Rayo Mining and Development Company, of 219 men at work in the mines in 1910, 20 used air drills, 19 doublejacked, and 3 operated a singlejack.[59]

In mining regions that have received more scholarly attention than northern Mexico, studies show that the introduction of air drills did not necessarily threaten established work practices or social and economic relationships in the workplace. In Michigan copper mines, for example, mine workers who perceived the Rand machine drill to be beneficial worked to help make the innovation successful. A number of reasons account for such cooperation between labor and management. First, managers did not attempt to use the drills to destroy the existing contract system of payment, but encouraged contract miners to try the drills. Second, the drill did not completely eliminate hand drilling, but it left to doublejack teams the task of working marginal deposits, inaccessible areas, and stopes containing ore after the air drillers had finished. Third, because two men were required to transport and operate the equipment, Rand drills preserved the tradition of men working together in teams. And fourth, because machine drills meant substituting short periods of heavy lifting and moving for longer periods of hard labor with a sledgehammer, most copper miners were quick to surrender their sledges for machines powered by compressed air. Larry Lankton chastises historians who, in failing to realize the coarse and arduous nature of mine work, write nostalgically about the independence and dignity of hand labor.[60]

The precise impact of the new drilling technology on *barreteros* in Hidalgo District is difficult to determine. Most singlejack and doublejack drillers in the district were experienced mine workers from traditional mining centers such as Zacatecas and Guanajuato. Even before the introduction of machine drills, however, the independence and decision-making powers characteristic of the mid-nineteenth-century *barreteros* had been eroded. The statements of mine workers to judicial authorities inquiring into mining accidents during the period between 1900 and 1925—although they were transcribed in the third-person format of official proceedings and undertaken for the purpose of establishing blame—offer a glimpse into the world of work as described by the workers themselves.[61] From their testimony, *barreteros*, rather than being self-employed experts shaping their own workplace and hiring unskilled labor for the task at hand, seem to have frequently worked set shifts, having nothing to do with the hiring process and waiting to be put to work in specific locations by a shift boss (*poblador*) employed by the company.

It is difficult, for example, to characterize the *barreteros* doublejacking with bars and hammers in the Clarines Mine in Santa Bárbara in 1906 as skilled craftsmen who determined their own conditions of work. After arriving for the night shift, *barreteros* waited for the *poblador* to give them tools and place them in the locations they were to work. Nor did they hire their own help or form their own work gangs; other than their drilling partner, they could identify by name no one else with whom they had been working.[62] Even in the Palmilla Mine, owned not by foreign capitalists but by Pedro Alvarado, *pobladores* assigned tasks to *barreteros*. Workers explained that the following procedures were the ones commonly followed in the mines in the district: after the drilling had been completed at the end of each shift, the drill holes (*barrenos*) would be measured (sometimes by a *medidor de barrenos*), the *barreteros* would leave, and the *poblador*, often accompanied by a blasting expert (*pegador*), would bring in the dynamite, insert it into the *barreno,* and, finally, set off the charge. The *poblador* would then wait until he had heard all of the *barrenos* explode, for a misfired or only partially fired hole still contained explosives and could (and often did) blow up in the faces of the next pair of *barreteros* to work there.[63]

Still, some decision-making power remained in their hands. *Barreteros* and *pobladores* agreed that they were equally responsible for inspecting the work site to make sure that it was safe enough to drill. Conveniently, this practice relieved the company of blame in case of an accident; yet it also indicates that *barreteros* possessed specialized knowledge about their task and their working environment.[64] In one of the few available accident reports involving the new air drills, from the Tecolotes Mine in Santa Bárbara in 1913, air drillers (*perforistas*) unanimously stated they understood that they themselves were obligated to have wooden supports installed in the stope, as called for by circumstances.[65]

Barreteros were also distinguished from other workers by the fact that they continued to be paid by the task rather than receiving a daily wage. (By contrast, the few company records that have been located reveal that *perforistas* were paid a daily wage.)[66] Payment by the amount drilled in a shift occasionally prompted *barreteros* (probably only the inexperienced ones and then probably only once) to take chances in drilling in already existing *barrenos*. As Ramón López, a twenty-seven-year-old mine worker from Durango working in the Hesperides Mine in Santa Bárbara, explained after an old *barreno* (called a *mocho*) had exploded and injured another pair of *barreteros,* he and the *poblador* had warned the pair not to drill there, but they had wanted to finish early and get paid for someone else's work.[67]

Further complicating an evaluation of the impact of the new drilling technology on *barreteros* is the fact that many different arrangements for accomplishing work existed simultaneously. In place of hiring workers and paying them a wage, companies could arrange with a contractor (*contratista*) to undertake specific tasks or the entire mining process. *Contratistas* were paid by the job, rather than a daily rate, and they assumed responsibility for forming and paying their own gangs of workers (*cuadrillas*).[68] Mine experts recommended that companies operating in Mexico place as many underground jobs as possible on a contract, or piecework, basis. Although these experts shared with other Americans the dominant negative stereotypes of Mexicans, they advocated contract work not because of the supposed "nature" of Mexican workers, but as the best means of controlling laborers regardless of their national or "racial" origin; after all, concluded the *Engineering and Mining Journal,* which laborer could beat the so-called American miner as a killer of time?[69] Managers found that they reduced costs to a minimum by breaking down all jobs into set tasks, often called *tareas,* and paying for the results obtained rather than for the time at work. They hoped that the task system would also provide an incentive to workers: when they had completed the stipulated amount of work, miners could come to the surface for a full day's wage regardless of how long it had taken them to accomplish the job.[70]

For *barreteros,* two general types of contract labor existed in the district. In the first, the company gave the contract to an individual who provided his own workers and supplies, loaded and removed all the ore, and was responsible to the shift boss for the progress of the work. The *Chihuahua Enterprise* reported that, in such cases, the *contratista* generally worked with his men and received only slightly more money than ordinary *barreteros*.[71] In the other form of contract, each pair of *barreteros* worked independently, under separate contract to the company, and received payment for the amount drilled in each shift. The *barreteros* working in the Palmilla Mine (discussed above) operated under the second type of arrangement. While the first type of contract might leave decision-making power in the hands of the *contratistas*—for many of them worked as *barreteros* alongside the other members of the *cuadrilla*—the second type of contract did not. Moreover, the insecurity inherent in both forms of contract could make such arrangements unpopular with workers; one of the first demands made by the mining union in the 1930s was for the elimination of the *contratista* system.[72]

Mining companies did not limit the *contratista* system to *barreteros*, but employed it to carry out many aspects of the mining process. As an ideal, experts advocated that all drifting, stoping, sinking, timbering, filling, tramming, track-laying, and even hoisting be done by contract. The following instances of contract work have been identified in accident reports. Gangs of workers organized and paid by independent *contratistas* dug tunnels and carried out developmental work; replaced old timbers with new; gathered and delivered lime to the mining companies; and broke ore in patios outside the mine.[73] In the San Diego Mine in Santa Bárbara, two *contratistas* and their respective *cuadrillas* carried out all mining operations, one during the day (from six or seven in the morning to five or six at night) and the other during the night.[74] A multitude of different arrangements was possible between company and *contratista*. In one case, a mining company paid fifteen pesos for each meter dug in a tunnel.[75] In some ASARCo mines in the mid-1920s, two distinct types of contract existed simultaneously: in one, the company gave explosives to *contratistas* to carry out their work, while, in the other, the company sold explosives to *contratistas*.[76]

Despite the possibility that *barreteros* might maintain control over the workplace through the *contratista* system, as the air drills enabled more holes to be drilled in a shift and often by fewer workers, they devalued the importance of the knowledge possessed by drillers. No longer referred to as *barreteros*, those operating air drills were known, instead, as *perforistas*. American mining engineers, in considering *perforistas* as skilled workers, reported that with training Mexican workers quickly became competent in working with the new equipment.[77] Moreover, accident reports suggest that each driller, rather than working as part of a team, often operated his own small pneumatic drill. Far from destroying the two-man system, however, workers reconstituted it underground. Although each man operated a separate drill, *perforistas* testified that they helped each other carry out work as the situation demanded.[78]

Technological Change and the Division
of Labor Underground

The new drilling technology also altered the jobs performed by other mine workers. In the American West, the increased pace of work resulting from the introduction of the new drills weighed most heavily on unskilled workers known as *muckers* and *trammers*. These men—who shoveled ore into cars (muckers) and pushed the cars full of ore (trammers/ *cargadores*) to chutes or cages—strained to remove the greater quantities of ore produced by dynamite and machine drills. In Nevada and Colorado, these unskilled workers increased as a percentage of the mining workforce, and many skilled workers found themselves forced into these unskilled positions.[79] Guadalupe Nava Oteo identifies this same trend for Mexico. He divides mine workers into two categories: a shrinking, well-paid group with skills and a growing number of poorly paid workers doing dangerous and heavy work.[80] Juan Luis Sariego Rodríguez also notes the difference between mine workers drawn from an agricultural background who possessed no skills—the majority—and a type of worker aristocracy made up of skilled miners, from areas such as Guanajuato and Zacatecas, and professionals, like blacksmiths, electricians, and carpenters, with experience in other industries. Both he and Raúl Santana Paucar, however, tend to downplay the effect of technological change on workers' skills. In treating the period from the turn of the century to the late 1940s as a coherent, unchanging whole—the so-called traditional model of the organization of mining work—they see, in place of de-skilling, an intensification of the manual efforts of workers.[81]

Evidence from Hidalgo District suggests that unskilled workers, including shovelers, rock breakers, ore sorters, car men, peones, and helpers of various sorts, formed an increasingly larger proportion of the total mining workforce. As early as the turn of the century, the local press had lamented the lack of training for workers. *La Nueva Era* pointed to the unskilled nature of most available mine work and demanded the establishment of a mining school to teach skills to workers, declaring that "our rudimentary mining instruction is so scarce and deficient . . . that it can be said in general terms that we still don't have miners."[82] By 1920, *perforistas* working for ASARCo in Santa Bárbara earned at least three pesos a day, making this wage the dividing line between relatively skilled and unskilled workers. Of the company's 1,136 employees, almost two-thirds made less than that amount. The single largest work category was that of *peones*, composed of 378 workers, who earned only a peso and a half per day.[83]

Cycles of Dependence

Workers, in addition to confronting changes in the ways of working, found that their labor was not always in demand. As the capital requirements of modern mining tied the Mexican mining industry more closely to business cycles in the United States and to changes in the world-market price of silver, workers came to experience this dependence as extreme fluctuations in the availability of jobs. The towns of Parral, Santa Bárbara, Villa Escobedo (formerly Minas Nuevas), and San Francisco del Oro, which were dependent almost entirely on the mining industry for their existence, expanded and contracted in rhythm with the mining cycle. Changes in the fortunes of the major mining companies reverberated through the regional economy: businesses failed, rents and property values dropped, and municipal treasuries evaporated when the mines closed. At these times, workers deserted the mining towns to search elsewhere for jobs; between 1900 and 1910, the population exodus reached as high as 40 percent in some of these municipalities. At all times, a fluctuating and floating migratory population (considered in more detail in the following chapter) troubled the district's more affluent residents.

Between 1898 and 1910, the nature and quality of ore in the district, as well as the needs of the smelters and the level of mining technology of individual companies, led to variations in the pattern of population fluctuation within the district. For their part, managers contributed to this instability by hiring only for the immediate task at hand, thereby encouraging high labor turnover. Company policies and economic criteria were not the only contributing factors, however. Workers prized their mobility (for reasons to be discussed in Chapter 5); they often chose to leave jobs to return to their fields during peak periods in the agricultural cycle, or to search for better-paying jobs in the United States. Still, such personal decisions paled in comparison to the economics of the mining industry as causes of the mass migration of workers and their families between 1900 and 1910. As the timing of population fluctuation differed within the district, this migration will be analyzed separately for each municipality.[84]

In Parral, local newspapers proclaimed a "new era" for the town and talked of a "mining fever" as the industry boomed from 1897, designated as the city's most prosperous year in the nineteenth century, until 1903.[85] As a consequence of the increased demand for workers, total population grew from 11,250 to 16,382 inhabitants between 1895 and 1900. The large influx of workers from other states, especially Zacatecas, prompted calls for the control of crime, drinking, and vice. The boom culminated in 1902, the most prosperous year for the municipality during the final decade of Porfirian rule. In 1903, a long period of decline began. So abrupt was the change that residents described their district as engulfed in a general crisis. The following year, *El Hijo del Parral* pleaded for the return of the American mining companies so that hundreds of workers could go back to work. Merchants characterized 1905 and 1906 as years of terrible crisis and of great decadence in commerce. Parral lost inhabitants: by the end of 1906, over five thousand people had left, reducing its population to less than twelve thousand. The worst was yet to come, however. In the last few months of 1907, business recession in the United States devastated the already staggering mining economy. According to the *jefe político*, stores were closing and the scarcity of work had forced workers to leave and search for mining work elsewhere. By 1909, less than nine thousand people lived in Parral. Unfortunately, it is difficult to determine if Parral shared in the mining recovery experienced by the rest of the district in 1910, for the yearly report, usually filed by the *jefe político* in January of the following year, could not be located. Midway through the year, however, merchants in Parral continued to complain of distressing economic conditions, and another resident lamented that he had been forced to cut in half the amount of rent he charged for his house.

Like Parral, Santa Bárbara grew in the final years of the nineteenth century to almost seven thousand inhabitants. In 1900, the municipal president requested permission from state authorities to double the municipality's police force to control the large, mobile labor force that had gathered in response to the new work opportunities. Between 1899 and 1901, the number of workers laboring in the mines of the municipality grew by one thousand (from twenty-five hundred to thirty-five hundred). The mining industry experienced a downturn in late 1902 and 1903, however, and merchants complained that economic hard times and a consequent lack of customers had reduced their business by 50 percent. Both property prices and population continued to fall in 1904 and 1905. In one particularly drastic blow to the local economy, the closing of the Tecolotes Mine in 1904, eight hundred men were thrown out of work. In his report for 1905, the municipal president stated that because the most important mines in the district had shut down, Santa Bárbara was in the midst of a mining crisis.

In sharp contrast to Parral, Santa Bárbara experienced an economic boom in 1906 and 1907, which was based on the recovery of the mining industry. During these two years, the city's population grew by three thousand inhabitants, culminating in a total population of over ten thousand inhabitants by September 1907. Local officials reported that the number of inhabitants increased daily as mine work attracted thousands of laborers to the municipality. The boom proved short lived, however. By mid-1908, the total population had decreased to between eight and nine thousand people; officials described 1909 as a year of crisis, and although the big Tecolotes Mine remained in operation, the rest of the mines had closed. In 1910, the mining industry in Santa Bárbara recovered, with the San Diego, Alfareña, and Cabrastante mines all hiring workers and the increasing demand for labor driving wages up slightly. This was a sharp departure from the practice of the mining companies between 1907 and 1910: most had taken advantage of the economic downturn to reduce wages.[86] By November of that year, over twelve thousand people lived in Santa Bárbara. Another indication of recovery occurred in nearby San Francisco del Oro, where the San Francisco del Oro Mining Company began hiring mine workers and laborers to work on a new railroad spur; still another sign of improved conditions appeared when company managers offered to pay a monthly subvention to the municipal police, hoping to discipline their growing workforce by assuring themselves of a police presence.

In Villa Escobedo, the mining industry also enjoyed a recovery in 1910, with the villa's total population finally equaling that of 1900, the previous peak in mining activity. Although the town had grown to over five thousand inhabitants in the late nineteenth century, the economic downturn that characterized much of Hidalgo District during the late Porfiriato had hit first in the mines around Villa Escobedo. As early as 1901, local officials described mining as suspended and the population as diminishing. Despite a brief recovery in 1904, the next three years were bad and 1908 was dismal; by the end of 1908, most workers had left the town. With recovery in 1910, over five thousand inhabitants populated the town, and local officials reported that economic conditions had improved.

Conclusion

In the final years of the nineteenth century, the mining industry in Hidalgo District owed its rejuvenation to the arrival of a spur of the Mexican Central Railroad and the need for silicious ores. After 1903, mine owners in the district suffered when smelters turned elsewhere for ore; they complained bitterly of the smelter trust and campaigned for the establishment of a smelter in Parral. Although none was built, the cyanidation process promised to deliver local mine owners from their dependence on the smelters. Low silver prices and an economic downturn in 1907, however, delayed the construction of cyanidation facilities until 1909 and 1910, when new investors discovered Hidalgo District. By then, technological innovation enabled companies with plenty of capital to mine the low-grade silver ore of the district at a profit. Despite the extreme fluctuations in the demand for labor occasioned by these changes before 1910, by the following year one mine manager compared Parral to a bustling New England manufacturing town.[87]

The concentration of ownership accompanying the investment in new mining methods meant that mine workers would now labor in *extractories*. In these organizations, a shrinking, relatively well-paid group with skills worked alongside a growing number of poorly paid, often temporary, wage laborers. As *barreteros* became *perforistas*, the importance of drilling and blasting skills diminished and mine workers lost control over the workplace. Outside the *contratista* system, they also lost control over the hiring of unskilled mine workers. The division of labor and an emphasis on a hierarchy of unskilled jobs left this latter group with menial, often dangerous work and no prospect of acquiring mining skills. These men formed part of a floating population, combining mine work with subsistence agriculture and other wage-labor opportunities. The next chapter considers the efforts of managers in transforming them into suitably motivated, and subordinated, workers imbued with the time and work ethic of industrial capitalism.

2

Managers and the Inculcation of the Capitalist Work Ethic

Despite technological innovations in mining methods, the rhythm of the agricultural cycle continued to dictate the pace of work in the northern Mexican mining industry at the turn of the century. Laborers, rather than adhere steadily to mine work, returned to their fields to plant and harvest their crops, or they quit work when their immediate needs had been met and often looked elsewhere for jobs. In the opinion of managers, however, ways of working based on the task and on seasonal cycles needed to be discarded in favor of a culture of work that entailed the inculcation of new values and a new time discipline. Managers utilized both force and economic incentive to transform peasants and transient wage laborers into docile, reliable, and disciplined wageworkers. Newly created state and district police forces, supported with company funds, patrolled Hidalgo District in an effort to guarantee order and to facilitate company operations; at the same time, by offering higher wages, bonuses for attending work regularly, and company-sponsored housing, medical care, schools, and food, managers hoped to reduce worker absenteeism.

In northern Mexico, as elsewhere, the inculcation of suitable work habits took time, even generations. In the mining region of Carmaux, France, for example, the task of transforming peasants into miners took

sixty years of daily struggle. In another case, in the southern United States
at the beginning of the present century, Piedmont textile manufacturers
attempted to teach the virtues of thrift, reliability, and industrial discipline to recent arrivals from the countryside surrounding their mills. They
aimed to turn millhands into worker citizens who would adopt regular
work habits, accept their employers' authority, and believe that in the
mills there was nothing to be lost and everything to gain. Herbert Gutman
generalizes this phenomenon in arguing that recurrent tensions over work
habits shaped the American national experience in the nineteenth and
twentieth centuries. E. P. Thompson, in making the same argument for
England, has shown that fines, bells, clocks, money incentives, preachings,
schooling, and the suppression of fairs and sports led to new labor habits
and a new sense of time discipline in the English working class. In these
areas, as in northern Mexico, the attempt to inculcate the capitalist work
ethic—entailing the spurning of one culture and the absorption of another—was a dominant characteristic of the transition to industrial capitalism.[1]

The technological change that accompanied capital-intensive mining,
rather than reducing the need for suitably motivated workers, exacerbated the so-called labor problem in northern Mexico. Once again, the
parallels with other areas undergoing industrialization are striking. Even
on the assembly lines of the Ford Motor Company in the United States—
the symbol of the triumph of machines and of machine-paced work in
twentieth-century factories—managers grappled with a workforce that
lacked what they regarded as acceptable work habits. The failure of machine-paced work to curtail the need for suitably motivated workers,
coupled with a massive influx of predominantly southern and eastern
European peasants, forced Ford officials to devise additional means to
shape men into workers who displayed proper attitudes and habits for
factory work. Ford managers, in borrowing the strategies used by early
industrialists in eighteenth-century England, brandished the proverbial
stick and dangled the proverbial carrot to create a new ethos of work
order and obedience.[2]

Mine managers in Mexico, like Ford officials and employers elsewhere,
followed the example that had been pioneered by British factory owners.
Their efforts to inculcate the capitalist work ethic in a preindustrial population are examined in this chapter.

Land and Labor

The nationwide concentration of landownership that occurred during the rule of Porfirio Díaz forced peasants off the land and into the wage-labor market. Across Mexico, as land became a commodity to be bought and sold, a landgrab of unprecedented proportions led to the concentration of landownership and a corresponding condition of landlessness for most Mexicans. Mexico's post-1884 economic boom ushered in the greatest catastrophe since the massive Indian mortality of the sixteenth and seventeenth centuries; villagers, who had held on to their lands under Spanish rule, now lost them to hacendados, speculators, and wealthier members of their own communities.[3]

In Chihuahua, the concentration of economic and political power in the hands of the Terrazas clan facilitated their acquisition of land. Luis Terrazas, in serving as state governor for much of the period between 1860 and 1884, and again after 1903, used his position for economic gain; by the end of the Porfiriato, his extended family controlled some fifteen million acres of the state's most fertile and best-watered land. Enrique C. Creel, Terrazas's son-in-law, regarded communal property as an obstacle to economic development and, shortly after becoming interim governor, decreed the Municipal Land Law of 1905. The law, allegedly designed to allow the poor to obtain land, served as a pretext for the transfer of communal lands to large landowners and speculators. Creel also supported new legislation mandating the replacement of elected mayors with appointed officials, thus imposing political centralization, which prompted aggrieved communities to complain that they had been deprived of both their elected officials and their landed patrimony. The concentration of landownership also drove formerly independent agriculturalists into the wage-labor force.[4]

In Galeana District, Chihuahua—the region where this process has been studied most thoroughly—members of the ruling oligarchy and foreign capitalists stripped agrarian communities of their lands. These two groups took advantage of the Municipal Land Law of 1905 to end corporate control of village land in the district.[5] Similarly, in Hidalgo District, local officials reported abuses in the denouncing of municipal lands under the 1905 law that, in most cases, deprived the poorer classes of access to land. In 1906, for example, Pedro Alvarado, owner of the Palmilla Mine, and his partners confronted residents of Rancho de Las Animas and attempted to seize for themselves land owned by the community.[6]

Land was a contentious issue in the predominantly agricultural communities of Hidalgo District. As few agriculturalists grew crops around the mining towns of Santa Bárbara, Villa Escobedo, and San Francisco del Oro, residents of Zaragoza, San Antonio del Tule, San Isidro de las Cuevas, Huejotitan, and Balleza supplied the mining centers with food and basic necessities. The paucity of agricultural production in the mining towns can be surmised from the high price of food as well as from the statements of local officials. Whereas the *presidente municipal* in Villa Escobedo estimated annual mining production in the *municipio* to be worth six million pesos in 1903, in that same year he evaluated agricultural production—excepting livestock (there were some eighty-five hundred head of cattle in the region)—at a mere three thousand pesos. The *jefe municipal* in Santa Bárbara reached similar conclusions: he noted that livestock was not very abundant and that agriculture really could not be said to exist in the area under his jurisdiction.[7] The demand for agricultural commodities in the mining towns was so great that the resulting export of food led to shortages in the municipalities where it had been produced. Despite the fact that the 1908 harvest was barely sufficient to feed residents of San Antonio del Tule, landowners there sold their crops in the mining regions for higher prices. In Valle de Zaragoza, even in bad years, 30 percent of the corn and bean harvest was exported to other markets. Similar practices took place in San Isidro de las Cuevas, where landowners grew fruit and vegetables for export to Santa Bárbara, and in Huejotitan, where they shipped corn to the mining towns.[8]

Distinct types of land conflict emerged in the municipalities given over primarily to agricultural production. In the least populated municipalities, San Antonio del Tule, Huejotitan, Valle de Olivos, and Valle de Rosario, agriculture predominated, with livestock raising occurring on a small scale and commerce remaining insignificant. Although all were classified as municipalities, in the opinion of the *jefe político* they were not large enough to merit that designation.[9] In 1902, residents of the Hacienda de San José de Gracia, near Valle de Rosario, discovered that their best irrigated land had been surveyed by a company associated with J. Macmanus, Enrique C. Creel, Antonio Asúnsolo, Juan Terrazas, and Ramón Guerrero, and subsequently sold to someone else. Operating under federal legislation passed in 1883, the Ley de Terrenos Baldíos, companies surveyed vacant public lands, receiving one-third of the land surveyed in compensation for their work. These entrepreneurs—active as well in Galeana District, where abuses also occurred—had declared privately owned land to be vacant. Petitioners from the hacienda declared themselves to be under invasion and on the verge of being thrown out of their homes.[10] Although the role of survey companies in the alienation of communal land here and elsewhere in Mexico is now a matter of some dispute, in this case the predatory activity of a survey company can be documented even though it retained no land in the transaction.[11] Rural residents of this region, like many others, were forced to eke out a living elsewhere, perhaps incorporating wage labor in the mines and railroad camps as part of their strategy for survival.

Different problems emerged in Balleza, one of the most populous agricultural municipalities in Hidalgo District. Although the local *presidente municipal* considered the climate suitable for raising a variety of crops, he blamed what he regarded as the lack of progress in his district on the ignorance of local farmers, the lack of modern implements, and the absence of rapid means of communication with commercial centers.[12] After the *jefe político* visited the region in the summer of 1906, he added that taxes in Balleza weighed most heavily on those least able to pay; while the poor and working people suffered, rich landowners received exemptions. According to this official, the failure to divide village common lands, or *ejidos,* into individually owned parcels paralyzed progress and entangled authorities in constant wrangling.[13] This was especially so in Tecorichic, Baquiriáchic, and Guazárachic, the Tarahumara pueblos within the jurisdiction of Balleza.

After the turn of the century, the survey of land and its subsequent expropriation provoked these Indian communities to barrage municipal and state officials with petitions. Especially aggrieved were the inhabitants of Guazárachic, led by their *gobernadorcillo* José Pallan, where a new effort to survey and divide up communally held property took place in 1902–3. According to petitioners, local officials and their families had conspired with the engineer in charge of the land survey to defraud the Indians of their best property. They demanded that the land be distributed to Indians and not remain in the possession of the self-proclaimed *gente de razón,* who had acquired it illegally.[14] The Tarahumara, however, were lamenting a well-established trend rather than a recent development. In his travels through the Sierra Madre in the 1890s, Carl Lumholtz observed that Indian lands had been appropriated by Mexicans, leaving the Tarahumara with only the least desirable properties.[15]

Non-Indian inhabitants of Guazárachic countered with petitions of their own. Characterizing the Tarahumara as "lazy" and "unwilling" to cultivate properly the land they possessed, they maintained that the Tarahumara wished to eliminate their presence merely to avoid vigilance and proper prosecution for their indulgence in vice and crime. Mexicans also exerted pressure on local and district officials for access to Tarahumara land by arguing that they would face starvation if their petition were denied.[16] While sympathetic municipal officials lamented Tarahumara "obstinancy" and "capriciousness" in denying land to Mexicans, the Tarahumara were more likely acting out of experience, for a decade earlier Lumholtz had concluded that once they rented land to Mexicans, Indians rarely regained ownership. By late 1908, the *jefe municipal* in Balleza reported that the measurement of land by a state-appointed engineer had spawned a revolutionary movement among the Indians of Baquiriáchic, Guazárachic and Tecorichic.[17]

Inhabitants of these pueblos were not the only ones to lose land to Mexican neighbors. Tarahumara petitioners from Tecorichic, San Javier, San Pablo de Balleza, San Mateo, San Ignacio, San Juán de Atotonilco, and Baquiriáchic uniformly decried the loss of their land to *gente de razón* and the connivance of local authorities in this process.[18] As the *jefe político* of Hidalgo District did not sympathize with Tarahumara claims, state directives ordering him to intervene on their behalf did little to halt the process of land alienation. In his opinion, the Indians desired merely to pledge or sell their newly acquired land only in order to complain later of being robbed by the *gente de razón*.[19]

Similar problems emanated from municipal jurisdictions without a Tarahumara presence. In Valle de Zaragoza, the center of livestock production in the district (containing nineteen haciendas and some twenty-five thousand head of cattle in 1907), distribution of the community's *ejidos* to individual owners prompted bitter disputes pitting residents against each other. This process, begun in 1894, continued to divide inhabitants ten years later. Likewise, in San Isidro de las Cuevas, increasingly impatient *vecinos* were still waiting in late 1902 to acquire legal title to land they had denounced between 1894 and 1899.[20]

Even those managing to obtain land often found prohibitive the capital outlay necessary to work it. In general terms, the district can be divided into three geographical zones: mountainous regions, low-lying hills separated by river valleys, and fertile floodplains. While the first zone was unsuitable for agricultural production, in the valleys and on the floodplain *campesinos* grew corn and beans, typically on unirrigated land, and wheat, on land with access to water; the hills also provided excellent forage for livestock. Both the value of the land and the capital required to produce a crop varied primarily according to the quality of the land and its location. In Valle de Zaragoza, for example, a plot suitable for growing wheat fetched between 2,500 and 3,000 pesos; for beans, land valued between 250 and 300 pesos was sufficient. In Balleza, a hectare (2.47 acres) of irrigated land (*labor de riego*) sold for 200 pesos while the same amount of unirrigated land (*de temporal*) cost 50. Sowing 1 *fanega* (about 2.5 bushels) in this municipality required the landowner to invest from 20 to 30 pesos from sowing to harvesting, while the same quantity of wheat demanded 30 pesos and corn required 90.[21] In the face of these expenditures, many turned to sharecropping or worked as agricultural laborers during peak periods in the agricultural cycle.

Personal and collective misfortune also drove men into wage labor on a seasonal or permanent basis. With only three seasons in the Sierra Madre—the dry, from March until June, the rainy, from July until the end of October, and the winter, from November through February—the failure of the rains to arrive on time or an early frost could have devastating results. Without winter rains, drought could be expected in May and June and lead to a poor wheat harvest, while lack of precipitation in July and August reduced the amount of corn produced. Corn, planted at the beginning of the rainy season (in late June and July) and harvested in early November, was particularly susceptible to frost, which, if it arrived early enough, could mean the loss of the entire crop. When the cereal harvest was poor—as it was in San Isidro de las Cuevas in 1902, when the rains failed to arrive—*campesinos* migrated to other municipalities in search of work.[22]

In a number of cases, position in the family life cycle dictated migration patterns. The lack of jobs in agricultural production around Valle de Zaragoza in 1906, for example, prompted men without family obligations to search elsewhere for work. In this instance, these men were not the heads of families; therefore, it is unclear whether their actions formed part of a broader strategy for the maintenance of a rural household.[23] More typical was the behavior of those who served as *comisarios de policía*, a post usually occupied by a local resident who had been named by the *jefe político* to keep the peace in his *rancho* (sometimes to the detriment of his familial relationships). Rather than enrich themselves in this position, *comisarios*, in their frequent notes of resignation, stressed that economic necessity, debt, and the need to support their families forced them to leave their communities to search for jobs. Hardship was a rural experience they shared with many of their neighbors, as was the decision to become a wage laborer.[24]

In years when the rains came and frost did not, slack periods in the agricultural cycle enabled rural residents to eke out a living by combining subsistence agricultural with wage labor. In Galeana District, independent small producers grew their own crops in three months and spent the other nine working for wages, preferably in industrial jobs close to their own land. These were the semi-agricultural, semi-industrial migrants, or peasant workers, whom mine managers so disparaged for their failure to adhere steadily to mine work.[25] Peasant workers can be distinguished from other laboring groups by their characteristic integration of small-scale agrarian and wage-earning activities that serve to tie their rural households to the evolving wage-based industrial system.[26] In northern Mexico, during the course of any given year peasant workers tended to work in a great range of jobs in both the agricultural and industrial sectors, including the mines, railroads, and lumber camps of their own country and similar jobs in the United States. Like peasant workers in other geographical and temporal settings, they engaged in industrial work in the off-season, in winter, or in their so-called spare time.

Peak demand for agricultural labor in Hidalgo District occurred during the planting of wheat in the spring, the harvest of wheat and the planting of corn in July, and the fall corn harvest. Even though population in the agricultural municipalities grew at these times, it was still impossible to find workers; in Balleza, San Antonio del Tule, and Huejotitan, for example, entire families took part in the planting of corn in July.[27] In Balleza, the *jefe político,* faced with plummeting school attendance, had little choice but to submit to the agricultural cycle and cancel school until the first of August.[28] Many of the smaller *ranchos* in the district remained uninhabited for much of the year and came to life only during the rainy season, when the crop needed attention.[29] After these periods of intense agricultural labor, rural residents of Hidalgo District, like their counterparts elsewhere, sought jobs in nearby mines, railroad camps, and construction projects.

Many migrated to the United States in search of work. State officials lamented that the exodus of Chihuahua's lower classes to higher paying jobs in the United States posed a threat to progress and development in Mexico. Joaquín Cortazar, Chihuahua's secretary of the interior, instructed *jefes políticos* to refrain from issuing certificates authorizing such travel to prospective migrants. To deter migration further, Cortazar circulated reports from Mexican consuls in the United States purporting to describe the horrible conditions endured by Mexican workers in Arizona and California. According to these documents, the *enganchado,* or "hooked" Mexican worker, having been deceived by unscrupulous labor contractors, found himself out of work and stranded in a foreign country. The consul in Los Angeles concluded that the promise held out by labor contractors of higher wages was nothing but a big lie.[30]

Mexican workers knew better, however. Migrants from Chihuahua, and increasingly from other parts of the country, flocked to the mines and railroad camps of the American Southwest, lured by real wages almost double those they could earn in Mexico.[31] For many from central Mexico, migration proceeded in two stages: in the first, to the high pay and available jobs in the Mexican North, and in the second, on to the American Southwest. South of Chihuahua, in the Laguna region of Coahuila and Durango, for example, unskilled and landless migrants from central and southern Mexico labored as agricultural workers, as miners, and as unskilled laborers in growing industries. The small towns of the region served as employment centers where these migrants could obtain information about jobs as far away as central Mexico and the United States.[32]

After the extension of railroads to the border in the closing decades of the nineteenth century, mine managers in northern Mexico found themselves competing with railroad, mine, and construction companies in the United States for the same pool of unskilled laborers. According to 1908 estimates by the United States Bureau of Labor, between 60,000 and 100,000 Mexicans entered the United States each year. Two years later, the Dillingham Commission reported that Mexican nationals made up 7.1 percent of the total workforce in metalliferous mining and 12.8 of the western smelting and refining workforce. The figures in Arizona were 26.4 percent and 60.5 percent, respectively. Moreover, by 1912, Mexicans were the main source of labor for the railroads west and south of Kansas City.[33] While periods of economic growth meant that managers competed with higher paying companies in the United States for Mexican workers, during economic downturns thousands of these workers came streaming back across the border. Instead of jobs, they often found only the company of an increasing number of landless laborers.

A heterogeneous wage-labor force came into being in northern Mexico during the late nineteenth and early twentieth centuries. While the concentration of landownership, reduced access to communally held land, and the capital outlay necessary to undertake agricultural production forced many rural residents to depend exclusively on laboring for a wage, others—including peasant workers and independent small proprietors—combined subsistence agriculture with wage labor. In bad years, debt, poor harvests, and natural calamities could convince even the most committed agriculturalist to search for wagework. This did not always mean that men had to leave their communities: agricultural estates also needed short-term laborers during emergencies and peak periods in the agricultural cycle. Other rural residents accepted sharecropping and various rental arrangements. Despite these differences, however, most inhabitants continued to govern their lives according to seasonal cycles; even many of those migrating to the United States returned in the fall, after a summer of work, to harvest their corn.[34] Employers in the new industrial enterprises, on the other hand, required disciplined and suitably motivated workers who were willing to keep time to the new rhythm of industrial work.

The Proverbial Carrot

Managers complained bitterly about the quality of the floating population of landless migrants and peasant workers who provided the unskilled labor in the mines of northern Mexico. In their opinion, workers migrated back and forth between farm and smelter; they worked only long enough to satisfy their immediate needs; they would quit when they got a little ahead, only to return when they needed food; they did not take a serious interest in mining; they would not stick to their jobs; they might quit at any time when there was a "bag of beans and a pot of corn meal" in the house; and after the rainy season began, it was very difficult to retain workers, for they disappeared into the hills to prepare a little plot for planting corn.[35] In the mining town of Batopilas, older workmen always took a week off to plant their crops, and they moved to the plot with their families when it was time to harvest.[36] Managers of the Candelaria Mining Company, in anticipation of the seasonal migration of the Yaqui Indian laborers who worked the company's mines, ordered workers to break all the ore possible so that the remaining Mexican laborers could be kept busy bringing ore to the surface until the Yaqui returned. Non-Indian workers at the Candelaria, who also retained links to the land, returned to their *ranchos* with the onset of the planting season.[37] These examples, along with the constant complaints of managers, betray the extent of peasant participation in the wage-labor force.

According to managers, mobility prevented workers from attaining maximum proficiency in their jobs in the mines, limited the development of their problem-solving capabilities, and disrupted production schedules. Peasant workers saw wages as purely instrumental, and as a result, they considered work performed in the industrial setting as a means to gather income before returning to subsistence agricultural production. Such workers, distancing themselves from industrial work, sought to sustain a family-based agrarian holding rather than maximize their earnings.[38] Like the peasant workers in northern Mexico, migrants from central Mexico also lacked the dedication to work desired by managers. The transient nature of this population was revealed most starkly on occasions such as one in 1902, when news of a new railroad project in a neighboring state provoked a hasty exit of workers from Parral, shocking managers and causing middle-class observers to speculate about the imminent collapse of their town.[39]

How, then, was regular work attendance to be fostered? One way was to offer high wages to attract and retain workers. Before the turn of the century, the relative scarcity of labor had led to wages that were higher in northern Mexico than in the central and southern parts of the country. After 1900, the increased demand for workers in the Mexican North and its proximity to the American border forced employers to pay even more. Managers of mining companies in Chihuahua offered better wages to lure skilled mine workers from Zacatecas, and unskilled workers were paid two to three times what they could earn as agricultural laborers. Whereas agricultural wages in Hidalgo District rose from 37.5 centavos to as high as 75.0 centavos during periods like the wheat harvest, when the demand for agricultural laborers was at its peak, unskilled mine workers regularly earned as much as a peso and a half a day.[40] Moreover, managers of the mining companies that arrived after the turn of the century exerted even more upward pressure on wages by offering wages higher than those paid by existing companies.

This tactic, however, could backfire. Mine managers throughout Sonora complained bitterly when William C. Greene doubled miners' wages at Cananea. According to one disgruntled manager, Greene's policy, based on misplaced generosity, merely served to make it more difficult to obtain workers. As the average Mexican miner worked only long enough to satisfy his immediate needs, doubling the wage resulted in miners now working only half as long as before. In this manager's opinion, such behavior justified the standard company practice of not paying workers enough to permit them to save money. Another manager rationalized low wages as a positive development for workers: he felt it made them happier because it gave them less opportunity to drink and gamble.[41] (The self-serving nature of this rhetoric is discussed further in Chapter 4, where the role of drinking and gambling in popular worker culture is considered.)

As a general rule, high pay failed to accomplish the results desired by managers. Migrants and peasant workers were target earners; thus, increases in the daily wage often served only to reduce the number of days they were willing to work. Consequently, managers in northern Mexico experienced the same frustrations as their counterparts elsewhere during the transition to industrial capitalism. In the Asturian coal mines of northern Spain, for example, managers could not understand why workers would not respond to monetary incentives; likewise, in France during the first half of the nineteenth century, the incentive most logical to managers—higher pay—failed to secure reliable workers.[42] In northern Mexico, as in Europe, workers failed to respond to the wage stimulus in ways that managers predicted, and managers sought additional means of disciplining them.

One such strategy was to hire "family men." Managers on both sides of the border considered men with families to be more faithful workers; they believed that the presence of wives and children made it more difficult for workers to pack up and leave at any time. The *El Paso Morning Times*, for example, reported that the Mexican "hombre" with a family was at a decided premium, as men without families were prone to drift elsewhere after working for a few days.[43] Railroad and mining companies in Mexico and the United States employed this tactic, as did mining companies in nineteenth-century France. In the French case, mine owners rewarded workers who were family men because it obviated the need for them to compete for labor on the open market.[44]

Others turned to the bonus system in order to ensure a steady supply of reliable workers. Beginning in the late nineteenth century, ASARCo, one of the biggest employers in northern Mexico, offered workers a peso per day provided that they attend work regularly. ASARCo officials implemented this policy only after failing to obtain suitable workers by other means. Initially, the company had imported Chinese laborers only to find that the entire contingent had disappeared into the United States within a few months. Imported Italian workers proved equally disappointing. Finally, despite the protestations of skeptical managers, Willard Morse, head of ASARCo operations in Mexico, instituted a bonus system that guaranteed double pay for regular attendance. Company officers reported, after a short period of adjustment, that average monthly attendance had climbed from eleven to twenty-four days and that they were experiencing no difficulty in obtaining workers. On the basis of these results, ASARCo established the bonus system in all of its plants and mines throughout northern Mexico.[45] Other companies soon followed suit. In Cananea, for example, all workers who labored twenty-six days or more per month received a premium of twenty-five centavos (later increased to fifty centavos) per day. Whereas Mexican laborers at Cananea averaged less than fifteen days of work per month before managers instituted this system, 70 percent of the workers soon qualified for the premium.[46] Throughout the North, the bonus system promoted steadier employment.

Many mine managers also believed that by creating new needs, laborers could be enticed to work regularly. James Douglas, an American mine owner, blamed worker indolence on the climate, declaring that Mexican miners shared with all tropical and semitropical inhabitants an aversion to steady work. Luckily, according to Douglas, the effects of climate could be overcome by good example: exposure to the higher living standard of American workers would lead Mexicans to ape their lifestyle and "discard sandals and wear shoes." Douglas, along with other managers, concluded that the subsequent need to earn money to maintain this exalted position would convince Mexican mine workers to abandon their erratic habits and to work steadily.[47] In coaxing workers to become consumers, the company store (*tienda de raya*) played an important role. One mine manager described how he kept the company store at his mine well stocked with goods of all grades and paid particular attention to their attractive appearance. As a result of his efforts, he discovered that workers gradually bought better clothes and a higher grade of furniture and, of greatest importance, became more efficient and worked longer. In recognizing the link between consumption and steady work, managers encouraged workers to develop new desires and to covet new material goods.[48]

The Company Store

Usually regarded by historians as the bête noire of workers throughout North America, the company store often served to attract and retain suitably motivated workers. The traditional view of miners owing their souls to the company store has been called into question in the United States. P. V. Fishback concludes that in Virginia the company store formed part of the employment package offered by coal companies to workers in what seemed to have been a relatively competitive labor market. Here, miners usually were not indebted to the company store, nor did the store charge higher prices than nearby independent stores.[49] In the case of mill villages in the southern United States, two recent studies present contradictory conclusions: in contrast to Jacqueline Dowd Hall's argument that worker indebtedness to the store was a strategy utilized by mill owners to maintain a stable workforce, Cathy L. McHugh views the store as part of

a comprehensive welfare system aimed at developing a disciplined workforce.[50] In his recent work, Ramón Eduardo Ruiz reaffirms the dominant
interpretation of the company store in Mexican historiography. He describes the store as the "cornerstone of mining company dominance" and
as the means by which managers added to company profits; for him, the
relationship of workers to the company store was a "bastardized version
of debt peonage."[51]

Such was not the case, however. Mining and railroad companies in
northern Mexico often subsidized prices in the company store to attract
workers to isolated regions. Managers of the Mexico North Western
Railway, for example, offered goods in the company store at Madera,
located in the Sierra Madre between Ciudad Chihuahua and Ciudad
Juárez, at prices comparable to those prevailing in the state capital. In
effect, the company assumed the cost of transporting goods from major
distribution centers to its area of operations. This subsidy formed part of
an employment package that included housing, schools, and churches
designed to attract workers.[52] D. E. Woodbridge, in a rare study of labor
in northern Mexico during the early twentieth century, compared employee purchases in one company store to total wages. He concluded that
a relatively small proportion of total wages, less than 20 percent, returned
to the company through employee purchases in the store. This percentage may well have been higher in smaller, more isolated camps.[53]

In Hidalgo District, most large foreign mining companies, rather than
operate their own company store, granted local merchants the right to do
so. A detailed contract specified the obligations of both parties. The mining company agreed to provide the building and deal exclusively with the
merchant operating the store as long as the merchant remained open from
six in the morning until eight at night and sold all that was necessary for
the sustenance of those working for the company. In San Francisco del
Oro, for example, the San Francisco del Oro Mining Company contracted
with G. C. Beckmann, of Parral, to open a company store there in 1910.
Workers purchased goods in the following manner. Each morning the
company submitted a list to the store indicating how much each worker
had earned; workers were permitted to "spend" up to 75 percent of that
total on store merchandise. Workers, then, were not advanced goods on
credit, but given the opportunity to purchase goods from wages they had
already earned but had not yet been paid. On payday, the company settled
its account with the store in cash, less a 5 percent discount, and agreed to
give preference to Beckmann in the shipping of material, machinery, and
metals. No deductions of any kind were made from the balance paid to

workers. For his part, Beckmann promised to charge fair prices by adopting as his standard those charged in the Parral market.[54] As mining in San Francisco del Oro was just beginning to recover from the 1907 recession, such an arrangement may have been the only way the company could ensure the availability of goods for its workers. In other words, the company guaranteed a monopoly in order partially to offset the great risk and expense of doing business in a mining town. A similar policy prevailed in Los Azules, where the Saldaña brothers, local merchants, ran the company store of the El Rayo Mining and Development Company.[55]

In the single case of abusive practice involving a company store encountered in local archives, a store owner without such an arrangement with a mining company coerced workers into buying his goods. Managers of the Veta Grande Mining Company, the only company operating in Villa Escobedo in mid-1908, permitted workers, upon their request, to purchase goods on credit from a store run by Juan N. Baca. Local authorities reported that prices in Baca's store were identical to those in other stores in town, and only about half of the company's workforce had opted to purchase Baca's merchandise. This left the other half free to establish credit in any of the other businesses located in town. The company, on bimonthly paydays, deducted the amount spent from each worker's paycheck. Unfortunately for the miners, Baca was also the *encargado* in charge of the operations of the Veta Grande Mining Company. Police reported that he hired mine workers only if they agreed to purchase all of their merchandise and food from his store, firing those who shopped elsewhere. In this instance, the dire economic conditions prevailing in Villa Escobedo (where mining was almost completely paralyzed and many workers had already left town) contributed to Baca's predatory behavior. His actions not only abused workers, but also threatened the very existence of other local merchants. The case reveals not debt peonage—Baca's prices were identical to those charged in other stores—but the abuse of the office of the *encargado*. Baca's power to dictate to workers where they could shop derived from special circumstances—an economic downturn and Baca's position as *encargado*—rather than from a contractual relationship between the store and the mining company.[56]

Elsewhere in the state, in the mining district of Santa Eulalia near Ciudad Chihuahua, mine workers complained that their inability to obtain credit forced them into unsatisfactory relationships with company stores whose prices were often higher. In a petition to the governor in 1907, three hundred mine workers pleaded for relief from the system of company stores, called *aviadoras* by the miners. Mining companies in Santa Eulalia usually offered their workers credit in one local store for work already accomplished; as in Hidalgo District, each day the company would deliver to the store lists of workers and their earnings, from which the purchasing power of workers could be determined. According to one local newspaper, such practices meant that true company stores did not even exist in the district. By the same token, the paper's argument that store owners deserved to charge an extra 7 or 8 percent because of the risk they took that they would not get paid was invalid—miners could not spend in advance of what they earned, so no risk existed. For their part, mine workers demanded two changes: first, the liberty to spend their wages where they pleased; and second, payment in cash to new workers during the first few days at work to offset the hardships at this critical time, when they had not yet established credit in local stores. Although low wages rendered mine workers susceptible to the abusive practices of store owners, this was hardly a means by which mining companies added to company coffers.[57]

While it is not known how the governor responded to the petition sent by workers, state authorities did proscribe other tactics used by mining companies to reduce workers' independence. In mid-1905, district officials in Parral received notification from the capital that substitution of company scrip, known as *fichas, tarjas,* and *planchuelas,* in place of legal tender would no longer be tolerated. Although state authorities had to prod the *jefe político* in 1908 to enforce this prohibition, the following year they congratulated local officials for their role in reducing the use of scrip in the district.[58] Despite the fact that mining-company records contain few references to this practice, it had not been eliminated. During the years of the Mexican Revolution, managers of the Mexico North Western Railway, for example, resorted to the issuing of scrip to control labor as workers tended to remain on the job when the company owed them money.[59]

Still, despite the use of scrip and the predatory behavior of some stores, no "bastardized form of debt peonage" existed. All merchants in Hidalgo District expected to benefit from bimonthly paychecks issued to workers. Local merchants in Santa Bárbara and Parral refused to close their shops early on Sunday afternoon or on national holidays if mine workers were to be paid on those days. Municipal officials, to ensure Sunday store closings, extracted promises from mining-company managers that workers would not be paid when stores were closed. Also, new rural mounted-police units (discussed later in this chapter) regularly escorted shipments of cash to mines throughout the district. Every two weeks, workers spent these earnings in company stores as well as in stores that were not owned, operated, or affiliated with the mining companies.[60]

The Employment Package

In addition to company stores, many mining companies offered housing, schools, and hospitals as part of an employment package designed to attract and retain workers. Self-interest motivated companies to provide these amenities, with managers acting on the assumption that any measure that improved the hygienic condition of workers increased their efficiency. Although workers in the United States often rejected employer health programs as a paternalistic infringement on their prerogatives, managers encountered no such resistance in Mexico.[61] ASARCo, an early believer in such self-interested corporate beneficence, established schools and hospitals, staffed with company physicians, at its mines and smelters. According to managers of the copper company in Cananea, company provision of schools, housing, and health care, along with high wages, had led to the development of the most efficient body of Mexican workmen in the country.[62] Other companies deploying the same tactics were not so cheered by the results. For example, managers of the Moctezuma Copper Company, despite providing low-cost housing, with light and water, town sanitation, adequate school buildings, salaries for teachers, and a first-class hospital, failed to note a corresponding increase in worker efficiency.[63]

For most of the large foreign mining companies investing in Hidalgo District, the expense of building houses, schools, and hospitals was necessary to attract workers of high quality. The El Rayo Mining and Development Company, for example, spent twenty thousand pesos to establish a school and build houses for workers when it began its operations in Santa Bárbara. When increasing enrollment made it impossible for a single teacher to do all of the work, the company, along with the company store, contributed an additional fifty pesos per month to pay for the salary of another teacher.[64] In another case, the Moctezuma Lead Company diverted funds that it had formerly paid to a government inspector into a fund to pay a teacher's salary when it established a school in the mine workers' neighborhood, known as El Ultimo Esfuerzo, near the Tecolotes Mine. Although schools might attract the best workers, they did not necessarily reduce their mobility. ASARCo maintained two schools—one for boys and another for girls—at its smelter at Aguascalientes, paying higher salaries to get teachers to work there: whereas teachers in the nearby town received sixty pesos per month, teachers at the company school earned one hundred. Despite the high-priced help, few students attended beyond the fourth year, a pattern that managers blamed on the mobility of workers: "The student would hardly start his work in a given year before the father would move elsewhere, and thus the child would have to begin over again."[65]

Schools, as well as attracting workers and their families, also provided the setting to instill in future generations of workers values that were suitable to the new workplace, including those of reliability, punctuality, and deference to authority. Inculcating these values was a goal that managers shared with many middle-class Chihuahuans who made education a priority in their state. In Chihuahua, teachers served in the front lines of the struggle to impose order, progress, and the capitalist work ethic. In Parral, for example, a new system of School Banks was introduced in 1898. Every Monday, students, in front of their classmates, handed in their deposits to teachers, who recorded the entry in the students' bank card and deposited the money in the Miners' Bank. Even the children of those who were less well-off were expected to participate by bringing a few centavos to be deposited in the bank. The *Chihuahua Enterprise* expected the banking scheme to be "a great educator" as well as to prepare the way for savings banks on a larger scale.[66]

As Parral boomed after 1900, the number of schools increased along with the number of those attending them. Rodolfo Valles, the *jefe político,* proudly pointed to attendance records in his district: between 1902 and 1906 the average number of students attending Parral's five schools had grown from 526 to 1,480. According to Valles, in addition to inculcating a sense of order and love of country, the mission of educators was to make people realize that the school led directly to the workshop and, from there, home. At the end of a day's toil, the worker hurried back to a home sanctified by honor and hard work.[67] Officials like Valles shared with mine managers the common hope that education would create suitably motivated and disciplined workers.

During the first two decades of the twentieth century, new managerial concern for the health and safety of workers also came to be represented in the employment package. Although the attempt to eliminate accidents and hazards contrasted sharply with past performance, too much should not be made of this change: for most companies, attention to worker health and safety came after the Porfiriato. Neither, however, should companies be accused of treating Mexican workers in a different manner than they treated workers in the United States. The industrial-safety movement did not get under way in that country until 1906–7, and progress in eliminating industrial accidents came only after the First World War. Mining and smelting remained dangerous occupations well into the twentieth century until safety and workers' compensation legislation forced companies to eliminate hazards.[68] In other words, mining companies in the United States treated labor in much the same way as corporations in Mexico during the first decade of the twentieth century. In both countries, however, early critics of the brutalization of labor, including the Guggenheims, introduced health and safety policies in hopes of avoiding labor violence.[69]

In Mexico, ASARCo built hospitals and provided health care as part of the employment package. It took time, however, to convince workers that these facilities were actually intended for their benefit. Willard Morse remembered that when ASARCo first opened company hospitals, workers hurt on the job ran away rather than allow themselves to be admitted. Soon, however, Morse concluded that workers came to view hospitals as "part of their establishment."[70] The *Mexican Mining Journal* went further; in its opinion, hospitals represented one of the few "real blessings" bestowed upon the Mexican *peon*.[71] In Hidalgo District, four of the five doctors in Santa Bárbara had American medical degrees, as did five of the sixteen doctors in Parral. Within the district, company resources contributed to a dramatic improvement in the ability of the authorities to respond to public-health emergencies. During a smallpox epidemic in Santa Bárbara in 1909, the Tecolotes Mining Company provided facilities to isolate patients from the general population and paid all of the expenses incurred in exterminating the disease. In 1910, ASARCo managers opened the recently constructed company hospital in Santa Bárbara to all residents of the municipality, regardless of the nature of their illness. Agustín Páez, the *jefe municipal*, regarded the policy as beneficial for all inhabitants and agreed to contribute twenty-five centavos per day toward the cost of feeding each patient.[72]

Once company hospitals, schools, and housing had attracted the best workers, managers endeavored to transform them into loyal employees.

To do this, they cultivated paternalistic relations with their workers, hoping to wrest a moral and emotional commitment from them. Mine-owner Pedro Alvarado was successful in evoking such a response, and when Alvarado's wife died in 1905 the humblest workers from his mine, La Palmilla, carried her coffin to the cemetery.[73] So was the Shepherd family, owners of Batopilas. In Batopilas, Shepherd cultivated the belief that he personally took care of his workers and that all benefits originated with the *patron*. Members of Shepherd's family expected workers to reciprocate by rejecting unions, as illustrated in the following description of events that transpired when a union organizer arrived in camp:

> The Chief further instructed them [the workers] to let the cast-off union man know that their Patron was their friend; that he provided them with a good hospital; that he let them have money when it was needed in emergencies; that he charged them no interest, allowing them a long time in which to repay it; that unless this newcomer was in a position to duplicate or to improve these conditions he would do better to go away. This he did. That was the last as well as the first we ever heard of him or any other labor agitator. It was a joke for a long time among our men.[74]

Mexican mine owners and family-run companies were not the only ones to cultivate such bonds. Managers staffing modern corporations like ASARCo also engaged in symbolic acts calculated to reaffirm the personal links between patrons and clients. Willard Morse, for example, made a point of posing among the children and teachers in the class photos taken in company-sponsored schools.[75] As well as attracting the best workers, schools provided managers with another opportunity to display their personal interest in workers and their families. Such managerial behavior was not unique to Mexico: German industrialists also attempted to make their enterprises the focus of worker affections by using symbolic acts to emphasize the personal relationship that was supposed to exist between employers and workers. In both cases, personal interest was offered in exchange for loyalty to the company.[76]

For many managers, the supposedly inherent racial characteristics of Mexicans legitimized paternalistic treatment of the workforce. After all, explained Ralph McA. Ingersoll, Mexicans were like children: "The attitude of the larger companies is necessarily paternal; the people dealt with are children and must be looked after and guarded, to insure any production whatever."[77] Other managers believed that Mexicans aspired only to buy pictures and statues of saints and to show off their clothes to neighbors (especially their gaily decorated *sombreros*). Moreover, they were supposedly gossipy and passionately fond of music. This meant that foremen should take a "fatherly interest" in Mexican workers and be "the big parent of the establishment." Ingersoll wanted to transform Mexicans into Americans; that is, to teach them to bathe every day, sleep in clean rooms, and curb their voracious appetite for drink.[78] As well as justifying the paternalist impulse, race could legitimize abuse: T. Lane Carter concluded that one of the first things to learn in dealing with the *peon* is that it is "not safe to hit him, as it is a kaffir."[79]

In Hidalgo District, managers protected their paternalistic prerogatives by reacting sharply to any interference in company business. Early in the Mexican Revolution, for example, managers stated that they would rather quit mining than take orders from a former worker who was campaigning for municipal office on the platform of shorter hours and more pay.[80] Nor did they tolerate the "meddling" of local officials. When James Hyslop concluded that a local judge had interfered in the business of the San Francisco del Oro Mining Company, he used his influence with the *jefe político* to have him removed from office.[81] As in French mining and metallurgical firms, managers of mining companies in Mexico emphasized a worker's status of employee over that of citizen. Eventually, because this led to the perception that the companies were antinational, it made them targets of the postrevolutionary state.[82]

The Proverbial Stick

High wages, bonuses, company stores, schools, hospitals, and housing represented proverbial carrots. What of the proverbial stick? Managers advocated the use of force to create suitably motivated and subordinated workers, demanding that the Porfirian state provide the order necessary to carry out business that included the repression of striking workers. Foreign mining companies contributed extensively to new state and local police organizations created for these purposes, with managers expecting to enjoy political influence commensurate with their economic power.

And they did. Managers and political authorities fashioned a system of vigilance and repression that enabled them to observe a mine worker on his daily journey from home to work. Within each mine, an *encargado*, chosen by managers in consultation with municipal officials and subsequently approved by the *jefe político*, kept the best order possible. To this end, the *encargado* wielded both informal influence and formal political power: if his suggestions failed to reform uncooperative or drunken workers, he could have them thrown into jail.[83] In addition to the *encargado*, larger mines outside major towns fell under the jurisdiction of a police judge or *comisario*. Although mutually interested in preserving order, managers and *comisarios* occasionally clashed. In 1902, when a man claiming to be the new *comisario* showed up at the site of the Parral Mines Limited, an English company operating in the vicinity of Santa Bárbara, conflict erupted. Whereas the manager considered the current *comisario* to be entirely to his satisfaction and "in every way the kind of man who was needed there," he labeled the replacement as insolent, arrogant, and abusive. His interpretation is not surprising: after being told to "keep your hat off in my presence, Gringo," the new *comisario* and his men forced the manager, at riflepoint, to witness the changing of the *comisario*.[84] Although such confrontation was unusual, as attested by the publicity this incident received, workers were well aware of the activities of these officials. After 1910, mine workers struck to demand the removal of *comisarios* who had abused their power to administer fines, mete out corporal punishment, and send workers to jail.[85]

The influence enjoyed by managers extended beyond the workplace. Those employed by the most powerful companies took their concerns directly to the *jefe político*, if not to higher authorities in Ciudad Chihuahua; as illustrated by the behavior of Hyslop (discussed above), they could have uncooperative local officials removed. Company funding of municipal and state police forces provided them with additional leverage. In 1902, Tito Arriola, the *jefe político* of Hidalgo District, organized a new police force to operate in his district. The Cuerpo de Policía Rural, christened the new Acordada by the press, was to control brigandage and cattle rustling in the isolated *ranchos* and along the Chihuahua-Durango border.[86] Mine-company funds also ensured that the force would have a presence in the mining camps in the district. The new rural police escorted pay shipments to mines, maintained order during paydays, and attempted to reduce drinking, gambling, and other forms of vice in the mining towns.[87] Considering the Corps as an important means of labor control, managers made monthly contributions to maintain the force, with the amount varying according to economic conditions in the mining industry (see Table 2.1).[88]

In 1908, mining companies also began contributing to the funding of local police. Municipal police forces throughout the district expanded after the turn of the century, in response to the growth in population. In

Table 2.1
Monthly Contribution to Sustain Cuerpo de Policía Rural, 1903–1911

Contributor	Monthly Amount (pesos)
Moctezuma Lead Co.	30
Tecolotes Mining Co.	25
San Francisco del Oro Mines	25
Los Azules	25
Veta Colorada Mining and Smelter Co.	20
El Rayo Mining and Development Co.	20
Hinds Consolidated Mining Co.	15
La Union	15
United States Mining Co.	10

Santa Bárbara, for example, the increasing number of workers prompted the *presidente municipal* to double the size of his force in 1900. Three years later, he requested that funds be provided to hire six additional policemen. By 1907, the municipal police force there included one commander, one lieutenant, and sixteen policemen, all equipped with new weapons and mounts.[89] Although contributions from mining companies had not underwritten this expansion, the force patrolled day and night in the outlying mining camps. Depressed conditions in the mining industry beginning late in 1907, and the subsequent loss of municipal revenue, soon made it impossible for municipalities to maintain these forces. In 1908, the municipal police force in Parral was cut in half; in Santa Bárbara, the number fell from twenty to twelve.[90] That same year, managers of the three large American mining companies still operating in Villa Escobedo informed municipal officials that they would provide a voluntary donation of forty-five pesos per month to support the municipal police. The following year, managers of the El Rayo Mining and Development Company and the company store in Los Azules offered municipal authorities in Santa Bárbara seventy-five pesos per month to hire two additional policemen.

Fear of bandits persuaded managers to offer such voluntary contributions. For example, rumors of an impending attack on the company store in Los Azules, which was isolated from Santa Bárbara by distance and its mountainous location, prompted managers to offer funds to bolster the local police. Conditions were similar in other mining camps, with worsening economic conditions and the lack of jobs contributing to an out-

break of banditry throughout the district after 1908.[91] Early the following year, state leaders committed five hundred pesos to augment the
district's rural police in order to subdue bandit gangs operating between
Chihuahua and Durango. Local authorities were encouraged to cooperate with state and district police forces, and new regulations authorized
the pursuit of these gangs across political jurisdictions.[92]

Another reason prompted managers to fund local police forces: they
helped to control mine workers. Mounted municipal police increasingly
supervised paydays in mining camps located outside the district's populated centers. Paydays posed two problems for local authorities and managers: while increased scandal and indulgence in vice on the part of workers
during these times demanded an official response, paydays were also becoming days of confrontation between managers and workers. It was
during a payday in early August 1906 that carpenters at the Tecolotes
Mine in Santa Bárbara went on strike, refusing to return to work unless
they received a raise in pay. Having invested in police protection, managers demanded results. Although local officials reported that the strikers
were observing a peaceful and law-abiding attitude, managers petitioned
state authorities for an increased police presence. State officials promised
to augment the number of police and send a detachment of state or federal Rurales if necessary.[93]

After the strike, district officials regularly monitored paydays. Not only
did workers take this day to violate elite conceptions of morality; officials now feared that they might organize to upset the proper order of
society. *Jefes municipales* began to take note of worker-manager relations
in their reports to the *jefe político,* and local police stood ready to intervene in case of "disagreeable events."[94] In Villa Escobedo, mine-company
managers and local authorities met and agreed to standardize company
paydays. Instead of the seven-day pay period, all paydays would now fall
on the first Sunday following the fifteenth and the last day of each month.
The agreement forced workers who quit between pay periods to wait
until the next scheduled payday to collect wages they were owed. Managers of the Hidalgo Mining Company, Veta Colorada, Veta Grande y
Anexas, Sierra Plata, United States Mining Company, and La Industrial
agreed to adhere to the new pay schedule under penalty of a substantial
fine. The regularization of paydays enabled more efficient police supervision of workers.[95]

The *jefe político* also forced uncooperative workers into military service. While officials throughout the district held regular drawings to de-

termine who would be inducted into the army, the *jefe político* occasionally supplied recruits without resort to legal formalities: illegal forced conscription awaited those who did not qualify, in his opinion, as peaceful and working people. Rather than improving the moral character of the recruit, the army was perceived by most residents as a school for vice and immorality. One worker facing a future of forced military service petitioned the *jefe político* for mercy. While he believed that people of bad conduct deserved such a fate, he exempted himself from this category by pointing to his own adherence to work. This petitioner realized that Porfirian rulers, in cherishing the ideal of hard work, strove to use the state to punish those who did not share their views.[96]

Municipal officials also wielded power in the pursuit of order and progress. Their attempts to eliminate vice and moralize the working class will be considered in the next chapter; at this point, the enforcement of a state ordinance against carrying firearms is the focus of attention. This regulation, passed by the state legislature on October 31, 1906, mandated a ten-peso fine and the loss of weapon for anyone caught going about armed and without authorization. While municipal authorities enforced this statute where workers were concerned, mine-company managers experienced little difficulty in obtaining permission to pack their pistols in public.[97]

Occasionally, municipal officials founded mutual-aid societies in hopes of controlling the workforce. Officials and managers both feared the appearance of men they labeled as "trouble agitators." According to didactic articles on successful mine management in the *Mexican Mining Journal*, this was one of the worst problems that managers could face, for one such man could transform a hundred faithful workers into muttering enemies. It also seemed to justify the restriction of workers' mobility. One correspondent theorized that mine workers with a long experience of just treatment with a company would tend to disregard agitators.[98] Officially sponsored mutual-aid societies, like the one established by the *jefe municipal* in Villa Escobedo, provided an alternative to independent labor organization. Membership in this society, known as Protección del Hogar, entitled workers, in exchange for an initial contribution, to financial aid if they became ill or otherwise unable to work.[99] Middle-class organizations also founded associations to teach workers to read and write. In Parral, artisans formed the Sociedad de Obreros to provide adult night classes for workers.

Conclusion

A variety of circumstances forced peasants into the wage-labor force:
debt, poor harvests, and natural calamities, along with the concentration
of landownership, reduced access to communally held land, and the high
initial outlay required to grow a crop, were among the reasons peasants
became wholly or partially dependent on laboring for a wage. While some
combined subsistence agriculture and wage labor, sharecropping, or working small holdings during the rainy season and laboring in the mines or
on the railroads during the rest of the year, others without access to land
sought more permanent industrial jobs. Many—among them skilled mine
workers from Zacatecas and Guanajuato as well as unskilled laborers
from central Mexico—came from outside the state and soon moved on to
similar jobs in the southern United States. This growing, floating population posed problems for mine managers, and while some continued to
allow seasonal cycles to govern their lives, others constantly migrated.
Both groups failed to attend work regularly and lacked the discipline and
work ethic required by the new mining industry.

Managers utilized incentives and force in their struggle to mold suitably motivated and subordinated workers. In view of the failure of monetary incentives to accomplish this goal, they turned to other measures,
including bonuses for steady work, labor contracts, and the hiring of
family men. Company stores, housing, schools, hospitals, and churches
formed part of the employment package they designed to attract and
retain the best workers. In doing so, managers acted out of self-interest.
Such measures, in addition to providing tangible benefits to workers and
mining communities, gave managers an opportunity to forge symbolic
bonds with workers in an effort to elicit their loyalty. The self-serving
nature of this limited paternalism, with its goal of creating workers imbued with the proper work ethic, nevertheless afforded workers an attractive employment prospect that cannot easily be dismissed.

In difficult circumstances, paternalism gave way to repression. Managers funded newly created municipal and district police forces and kept
order in their mines with an *encargado*. They coordinated pay periods
with local authorities so that police could better supervise worker behavior. Heavily investing in police protection, managers expected state officials to control labor and provide conditions propitious for the profitable
operation of their businesses. They tolerated little interference in their
operations—whether from workers, union organizers, or district officials.
Their behavior eventually led, after 1910, to the perception that the large
mining companies were antinational institutions.

State officials did more than provide the force necessary to keep workers on the job. While managers implemented a more thorough division of
labor and offered money incentives, housing, company stores, hospitals,
and schools to create suitable workers, Porfirian officials attempted to
force workers to spurn aspects of a popular culture. Perception of the
need for moral reform has often accompanied the attempt to inculcate
the capitalist work ethic in preindustrial populations. The following chapter shows how officials, in subscribing to a developmentalist ideology,
regulated alcohol, gambling, prostitution and public space in the belief
that these measures would create peaceful and working people.

3

Moralizing the Masses

The last year, or a little more, has witnessed a wonderful decrease
in intemperance among the people in this state, and especially so
among the laboring classes. . . . The credit for this change is
wholly due to Governor Enrique C. Creel. . . . The result has been
the cleaning out of the cheap dives which were frequented by the
laboring classes, and, as a consequence, the great lessening of
drunkenness.

—*Chihuahua Enterprise,* 1907

During the Porfiriato, a nascent middle class sought to enlist the state
in the task of implanting the ethic of modern capitalism. The numerous
references to vice in middle-class discourse reveal its central role in this
struggle over values. The Mexican bourgeoisie hoped to eradicate vice
and inculcate values of thrift, sobriety, hygiene, and punctuality in succeeding generations of workers through state regulation of alcohol, prostitution, gambling, vagrancy, and public space. In short, members of
so-called respectable society, known as *sociedad culta,* subscribed to a
developmentalist ideology in hopes of turning a new, and feared, floating
population of rural and urban workers into patriotic citizens and peaceful, hardworking, and suitably motivated workers.[1]

In adopting an ideology stressing development and moral reform,
middle-class Mexicans were adhering to a well-established pattern. In the
first half of the nineteenth century, French industrialists also condemned
activities and attitudes that distracted workers from work and family.
They hoped to transform workers' morality by instilling selective middle-
class values: "from being ignorant the worker was to become educated;
from improvident, economical; from apathetic, ambitious; from drunk,
sober; from a philanderer, a devoted family man."[2] Industrialists asserted
their right to supervise this metamorphosis because they believed that

they already possessed the necessary virtues. Similarly, in the United States at the beginning of the twentieth century, Ford personnel managers attempted to inculcate middle-class values of the nuclear family, cleanliness in personal and domestic life, thrift, sobriety, traditional morality, family-centered recreation and entertainment, and, most of all, hard work in their workforce.[3]

Studies such as these point out that the values of what it means to be a patriotic citizen and a good worker must be inculcated, often in the face of a great deal of intransigence. As Corrigan and Sayer have shown in their work on England, capitalism necessitates the construction of an entire social, economic, and cultural edifice—a Great Arch. According to these authors, the construction of this arch is intimately linked to state formation, a process of cultural revolution by which means rulers moralize, normalize, and create individuals out of workers and build the cultural frame through which they claim their right to rule. Their work is premised upon Weber's insight that capitalism requires a specific and practical ethos.[4]

In Mexico, developmentalist beliefs provided an ideological underpinning for capitalism, as Protestantism had done elsewhere. According to Weber, the asceticism associated with the Protestant religion, leading to the disciplined and methodical organization of conduct, was an important factor motivating and legitimating continuous, rational economic enterprise.[5] Among the Mexican middle class, adherence to "American" values of hard work, thrift, hygiene, entrepreneurialism, and moral reform served the same purpose.[6] In addition, morality served as a symbolic shorthand around which concepts of citizenship, work, and race were clustered, allowing members of *sociedad culta* to mark off the respectable from the dangerous lower classes while, at the same time, providing themselves with a means of class and self-identification.

A History of Moral Reform

Attempts to impose moral reform and inculcate developmentalist values in Mexico occurred long before Porfirio Díaz became president. In the seventeenth century, mine owners hoped to discipline workers by bringing priests to their mines. A century later, viceroys attempted, with little success, to stop mine workers, whom they regarded as insolent, lazy, rebellious, and vice ridden, from drinking, gambling, frequenting taverns, and assembling in cemeteries.[7] These actions formed part of a more general campaign against popular culture carried out by the Bourbons in the final decades of colonial rule. Bourbon reformers waged a struggle that took place on many fronts, including the cleaning, beautification, and rationalization of city streets and buildings; reform of bullfighting, the theater, and other popular pastimes and celebrations; an attack on drinking, gambling and vice; and a campaign against religious "superstition." Such measures served both to educate the lower orders in the new values of the bourgeoisie and to provide them with a means of self- and class definition.[8]

Elites in newly independent Mexico continued to champion moral reform. As early as the 1820s, the liberal intelligentsia envisioned the creation of a homogenized modern society "dressed in European clothes and generally scrubbed and tidied up," in which the lower classes would be symbolically whitened through education, the influence of the press, and civilizing literature.[9] Municipal authorities in towns outside the nation's capital implemented measures designed to achieve these and related goals, a process of putting the basic principles of the Enlightenment into effect; they mandated that homeowners number their houses, build indoor toilets, regularly sweep the street and sidewalk in front of their properties, and remove all garbage. In addition, new regulations governed street entertainment and the sale of alcohol. By enacting these measures, authorities desired to ensure decency, a characteristic sign of a people governed by reason and amenable to it.[10]

During the Porfiriato, the emergence of a new and dangerous class, no longer under the sway of traditional authority, prompted northern Mexicans to emphasize moral reform. Especially after the turn of the century, middle-class Mexicans in Chihuahua perceived their society to be convulsed in social crisis. While they touted railroads as the primary example of Porfirian progress, they were appalled by the growing army of beggars, drifters, and workers who rode the rails into Chihuahua's cities and mining towns. Increased incidence of criminality was one sign of the supposed breakdown of order; idleness was another. Middle-class Chihuahuans described their state as inundated with a plague of men, women, and children, all supposedly sustaining idle lives by begging in the streets. Idleness itself was a symptom of moral and social crisis, with criminal behavior never more than a temptation away. Beggars, vendors, unemployed workers, and unskilled laborers shared one common characteristic: transience. All new arrivals, working or idle, unknown by the community and lacking permanent residences, were outsiders—people without a stake in the community. Many considered their presence to be a negative consequence of Porfirian growth and a threat to social stability.[11]

Middle-class Chihuahuans quickly condemned the behavior of this transient population. The municipal president of the mining town of Villa Escobedo reported frequent scandals in which drunken workers shot off their pistols at night. Paydays became occasions for egregious drinking and gambling. In San Francisco del Oro, another mining municipality, prohibition of liquor sales forced workers to journey to Santa Bárbara to purchase large quantities of mescal liquor. Then they frustrated local officials by drinking and stirring up scandals (singing loudly, shooting off guns, disturbing neighbors) inside their own homes. In the isolated railroad construction camps of the district, workers celebrated paydays with alcohol, horse racing, and cockfighting; on one occasion in 1904, the chief of public security arrived during a drinking spree and threw thirty-six workers into jail.[12]

The boom-and-bust nature of the mining economy added to the sense of a population in flux. Between 1895 and 1909 (as discussed in Chapter 1), Parral's population first expanded from 11,250 to 17,000, then contracted to less than 9,000. Similar dramatic fluctuations took place in Santa Bárbara and Villa Escobedo. Moreover, many migrants were simply passing through Chihuahua on their way to higher paying railroad and mining jobs in the United States. Forced off the land, searching for work, or supplementing agricultural income with wage labor in railroad and mining camps, these migrants swelled the *población flotante*.[13]

In addition to disparaging the floating population, the Chihuahuan middle class drew sharp boundaries between itself and the working class. Middle-class Chihuahuans were the literate, educated, propertied, and self-proclaimed respectable members of society. Teachers, journalists, and government officials, as well as merchants, shopkeepers, mine owners, and *rancheros,* fit into this category. In Hidalgo District, the Stallforth family was representative of the new middle class. Owners of a local mine, the Stallforths sponsored the building of an industrial school for young women. Also representative was Pedro Alvarado: his family connections and access to credit enabled him to persevere through bad economic times before his Palmilla Mine turned into a bonanza. Local officials such as Manuel G. Martínez and Agustín Páez were also members of the Chihuahuan middle class; they attempted to carry out moral reform in Hidalgo District's municipalities. By 1910, this literate middle class made up some 8 percent of Mexico's total population; in Chihuahua, its numbers had greatly expanded during the economic boom that had taken place in the early years of the twentieth century.[14]

Still, in the opinion of many members of *sociedad culta,* some workers might qualify as morally acceptable. For example, Rodolfo Valles, the *jefe político* in Hidalgo District, distinguished between the underclass and the working class. He condemned unwalled and undeveloped city lots as a threat to public health and security and as unworthy of the culture and beauty of Parral. Although owned by Parral's well-to-do, these lots provided safe haven for criminals and those addicted to vice. Valles specifically excluded lands owned by the working class from condemnation, stressing instead workers' commitment to improving their properties and aiding in the city's expansion.[15] On another occasion, *El Hijo del Parral* dismissed speculation about the town's impending collapse when a downturn in the mining economy prompted workers to leave the district for railroad construction jobs in a neighboring state. As far as the paper was concerned, this exodus of workers had little significance because they were not true members of the community, but merely part of the floating population carried along by the changing economic tides of late Porfirian Mexico: their arrival and departure coincided with that of the trains.[16] By means of the criteria of vice and transience, middle-class Chihuahuans clarified, in their own minds, the relationship between the dangerous and the respectable poor. Those who adopted middle-class values and lived permanently in their communities might qualify as members of the respectable working class.

Despite distinguishing between workers and the floating, vice-ridden population, many were troubled by the working class itself. Those in the middle class conceived of class boundaries in cultural terms, referring to themselves as members of cultured or refined society (*sociedad culta*) and to workers as representatives of the lowest orders (*gente baja*). One contributor to *El Correo,* for example, conceded that society accorded artisans derogatory and contemptuous treatment. This he blamed on the underdeveloped culture of workers, asking, "Will the working class be the only class that remains stationary and segregates itself from the rest?"[17] Other correspondents noted the weak sense of duty and patriotism among the working class. They appeared astonished that workers labored only in order to eat, not to improve themselves; working-class Mexicans did not seem to regard work as the means of obtaining independence, prosperity, or happiness. According to members of refined society, workers lacked civilization, justice, liberty, and a sense of duty: rather than ennobled, workers felt oppressed and enslaved by work.[18] As far as middle-class Chihuahuans were concerned, workers failed to measure up to the behavioral standards needed for inclusion in refined society; they refused to share in Mexico's progress.

The belief that one could obtain perfection through work formed part of a package of values promoted by adherents to the doctrine of what can be called social Catholicism. Indeed, *El Correo,* the reformers' forum, was an avowedly pro-Catholic publication. After 1891, with the publication and dissemination in Mexico of the Rerum Novarum proclamation, and especially in the final decade of Porfirian rule, social Catholics were preoccupied with what they referred to as the "social problem" or "corruption of the masses." They pointed to high levels of alcohol consumption, the common practice of cohabitation instead of marriage, the increase in prostitution, and the proliferation of illegal activities as evidence of the failure of progress in the moral and spiritual realm. In four national Catholic congresses held between 1900 and 1909, delegates considered, among other issues, measures to free workers from the grasp of vice, especially alcohol, and ways to ensure jobs that would pay a living wage to all workers. They also stressed the dignity of women and the sanctity of marriage, home, children, and family.[19] Yet this preoccupation with the perceived moral decadence of Porfirian society was not a uniquely social Catholic phenomenon. Nationally, the press of every ideological stripe lamented that material progress had not been accompanied by intellectual and moral advances. In Chihuahua, the liberal press, although it often identified the Catholic church as an obstacle to Mexican development, echoed the views of its Catholic colleague.[20] When it came to moral reform and the role of women, middle-class Catholics and liberals had more in common with each other than with their coreligionists among the *gente baja.*

The Vile Trinity of Vice

Members of *sociedad culta* lamented the effects on Mexican workers of alcohol, which they considered to be one of the greatest evils to afflict humanity. In their opinion, alcohol promoted worker absenteeism and poor work habits, and led to a loss of what they referred to as "productive wealth." What good is a drunk at work? asked *El Hijo del Parral.* He spends most of his energy in the *cantina* rather than in the shop; even worse, once he turns up at work he sleeps on the job or stops the rest of the workers from doing theirs. By behaving like this, the worker fails to fulfill his obligations, dishonors his trade, and discredits his workplace.[21] Another newspaper lamented that alcohol filled city jails with criminals and converted men's hands into instruments of brutality and crime rather than preparing them for useful duties and work.[22] This was a common refrain. Middle-class Chihuahuans, bemoaning alcohol's effect on contemporary public order, demanded restricted hours of *cantina* operation—especially Sunday-afternoon closing—to prevent drunken scandals and crime. Similar concern with crime led officials in Mexico City to make concerted efforts to enforce *pulquería* regulations there.[23] Common, too, was the preoccupation with utility. Porfirians of the *sociedad culta* measured themselves and their countrymen with the yardstick of usefulness to family and society. In their view, "useful" meant "working": by contrast, idlers, slackers, and the unemployed were the greatest social villains.

While, in the short term, drinking threatened to turn potentially productive workers into men useless to society or, worse still, criminals, its long-term consequences promised to be even more devastating. *El Correo,* claiming that its conclusions had been well proven by Charles Darwin, chronicled the generational effects of alcohol abuse: drunkenness and alcoholism predominated in the first generation, followed in the second by manic excesses and paralysis; hypochondriacal tendencies, suicidal ideas, and homicidal inclinations appeared in the third; finally, in the fourth generation, stupidity, idiotism, and the extinction of the "race" took place.[24] In accordance with the neo-Lamarckian assumptions of Latin American public health and medical practitioners (in which acquired characteristics could be passed on), alcohol, long viewed as a moral evil, also became an "enemy of the race." Not only was it thought to lead to crime, juvenile delinquency, prostitution, and mental illness; alcohol was also a "racial poison," portending permanent, hereditary degeneration capable of affecting entire populations.[25] Fear of racial degeneracy led middle-class Chihuahuans to demand strict compliance with regulations prohibiting minors from entering *cantinas* or consuming alcohol, and parents and governmental officials were expected to set a proper example for Chihuahua's youth.

Racial degeneration promised political consequences. Instead of becoming citizens imbued with patriotism and free will, subsequent generations might end up as a "shapeless," "rotten," "decayed," and "repulsive" mass. Such a population would find it impossible to stand up to oppressive despotism and tyranny at home or to protect Mexico's sovereignty against a foreign aggressor. In short, deformed future generations would be incapable of complying with the obligations of citizenship.[26] For many members of *sociedad culta,* then, campaigning against alcohol became a patriotic duty that rose above politics or religion. At stake were both the future of the country and the liberty of man.

Drunkenness also announced the end of virtue—liberty's natural ally. As they located virtue in the household and family, middle-class Chihuahuans sought to form a working-class home where all of the proper values could be passed on to future generations. As one newspaper explained, in the house of the honest and intelligent worker, a sanctuary of noble affections and purest enjoyment, children grew up to be docile, hardworking, and patriotic, while the wife concerned herself with the care of her husband. Such families did not contract debts or commit shameful acts; they lived without remorse, avoiding crime and poverty. Rather than spending money frivolously, they saved their paycheck. By turning to alcohol and forgetting his duties to family and nation, the nonvirtuous worker lost domestic peace, injuring man, family, and nation in the process. The newspaper concluded by stating that the best legacy a worker could leave his children was the example of his virtues: these children would be honorable, hardworking, and active citizens.[27] Drunkenness, in short, led to family breakdown, with society suffering the consequences.

It was, in part, the link between drinking and prostitution that caused moral reformers to turn their attention to the latter "vice." Bent on reducing drunkenness by limiting alcohol's accessibility, middle-class Chihuahuans began to criticize its sale and consumption in licensed brothels. For them, the union of alcohol and prostitution represented both a corruption of public morals and a source of criminality.[28] Because "enlightened" Chihuahuans considered public morality and good customs to be essential for order and the achievement of a cultured society, they demanded the prohibition of the sale of alcohol in brothels. Once they had accomplished this end (a new "tolerance regulation" was made law in Chihuahua City in the fall of 1903), members of *sociedad culta* campaigned for the prohibition's strict enforcement.[29]

Prostitution posed additional threats to morality and good customs. When petitioning city officials for the removal of prostitutes from their neighborhood, for example, five residents in Parral stressed that the immoral behavior of prostitutes negated the moral example they provided for their own children.[30] In another instance, *El Hijo del Parral* worried that the continual rubbing of shoulders between "ostentatious and luxuriously dressed fast women" (*mujeres alegres*) and those who lived by means of honest work might entice young women down the slippery slide into prostitution. In the event of such an occurrence, returning to honest life and moral living was deemed impossible, even if so desired, once the first peso changed hands. The newspaper concluded that prostitution was a cancer attacking the moral basis upon which society rested. Rehearsing many of the same arguments used against alcohol, *El Hijo* lamented that youths who frequented brothels were likely to become men useless to themselves and to society.[31] As in the case of alcohol, brothels promised to lead to the progressive degeneracy of the Mexican "race" by facilitating the spread of venereal disease and the corruption of minors.

Perhaps of greater significance for so-called respectable Chihuahuans was the location of brothels, especially those in the center of the city, allowing prostitutes to blend in and "confuse" themselves with honorable folk. They resented prostitutes attempting to make themselves equal to honorable people, and to solve this problem, they attempted physically to separate the categories of people they distinguished in Porfirian society. The desire to preserve social distinctions was often reflected in the very regulations governing brothels: prostitutes were required to be of the same social class as their clientele.[32] Such social segregation promised an orderly society in which everyone knew, and kept to, their place.

Reform-minded Chihuahuans, then, did not object principally to the existence of brothels or prostitutes (indeed, for many they were seen as a social necessity), but rather to their visibility and location. In the struggle to control public space, they coveted the city center for themselves and attempted to banish prostitutes to isolated neighborhoods. Lamenting the newly established presence of an immoral lodging house, residents of one Parral neighborhood campaigned to have the residents of the house thrown out of the city, "as is done in all cultured societies."[33] Shortly after the turn of the century, municipal officials in Chihuahua City proposed to locate all brothels in one neighborhood in what was then the outskirts of the city. Although supportive of the scheme in theory, *El Correo*—whose editor, Silvestre Terrazas, had identified the isolation of all prostitutes in remote neighborhoods as one of the most needed moral reforms—advocated a longer-term approach to the problems posed by prostitution. The newspaper concluded that, given the city's incessant growth and progress, this measure would merely postpone dealing with the problem. In its place, it proposed that city officials designate a yet more remote neighborhood—characterized by cheap land and no hope of increased population—in which to locate all brothels. It suggested that the new barrio be called "El Puerto de Cochinos."[34]

Middle-class Chihuahuans regarded gambling as the third component of the vile trinity of vice. For them, it was impossible to be both a gambler and an honorable man. In addition to being a social "cancer," gambling was described as a "gangrene of the social organism," which promoted the characteristics of avarice, jealousy, vengeance, depravity, and the loss of shame and riches and led to robbery, jail, the *presidio,* and even the scaffold.[35] Upon entering a gambling den, men trampled on their duties as fathers and husbands, sacrificing all they had at the altar of this vice. Much like alcohol and prostitution, gambling undermined cultured society, to the detriment of individual, family, and nation, and led eventually to the destruction of the family and the moral death of society.

As gambling represented wealth acquired through the ruin of other families or, perhaps worse, wealth that did not result from hard work, it was particularly repugnant to those who desired to inculcate the capitalist work ethic. Most middle-class commentators asserted that gamblers damaged society by robbing industry, commerce, and agriculture of hours that could have been spent working. In Parral, for example, *El Hijo* juxtaposed gamblers with hard workers: what was needed were working men for Parral's mines, not gamblers, who were characterized as idlers and slackers.[36]

Some reversed the causal relationship between vice and idleness, blaming the latter for increasing alcoholism, prostitution, and gambling. The mother of gambling is vagrancy, and the love of acquiring money without work the father, concluded *El Correo.*[37] Middle-class Chihuahuans invoked familiar themes to condemn idleness, citing loss of honor and virtue; the ruin of families, of future generations and the nation; and fear of increased crime. To begin with, slackers failed in their duty to family and nation; deprived of work's moralizing effect, they ended up as depraved, parasitic beings without shame or knowledge of human dignity. Moral reformers described idlers as a useless horde dedicated to robbery, deception, fraud, and swindling—to everything, in fact, except work, which would take from them a good part of their sweet leisure hours. Idleness also threatened Mexico's future by corrupting young people. In an initiative presented to the city council in Chihuahua, for example, one official urged action against the growing number of shoeshine boys on the city's principal streets. This rabble, as he described it, which was composed of young boys, had abandoned home and shop, becoming parasites who used shoeshining as a pretext to wander, freely living a life of idleness. These children were a threat not only to passersby (thus invoking the fear of increased crime), but also to the country's future, as they were the men of tomorrow.

While others focused on the effect of vice on work habits, these moral reformers, viewing work as a virtue in its own right, stressed its reformative power. "To work is to live," stated *El Hijo.* "Man, family and society develop and progress through work. . . . [Work] increases inventions, improves customs, conserves health, combats vice, provides riches, and maintains independence and liberty."[38] Rather than scorning the gambler and other "degraded" beings, *El Correo*—viewing work as essential to the process of moral and physical redemption—implored its readers to help in the task of regeneration. Moreover, according to the newspaper, the gambling problem was not an inherent evil, but a matter of interpretation: the gambler simply had to be made to understand that honest poverty was more worthy than wrongly acquired wealth.[39] For one contributor to *El Correo,* however, work alone was not sufficient to cure slackers. Like many nineteenth-century Mexican liberals imbued with utilitarian ideals, he believed that regeneration could only take place in the workshops of the penitentiary.[40]

The association of idleness with vice led middle-class Chihuahuans to demand state action against vagrants and idle men. *El Correo* directly linked vagrancy to vice: "The house of the slacker is the brothel, the gambling den, and the *cantina*. There he lives, there he is, and there he will be found at all hours, idle and satisfied."[41] The newspaper also criticized men who set up crates on streetcorners to sell cheap merchandise, instead of deigning to soil their hands with real work. Whereas these individuals were merely miserable, however, those in the first group, who were described as a stain on cultured society, were in need of state prosecution. During the last decade of Porfirian rule, middle-class Chihuahuans puzzled over why there should be labor shortages in the face of a seeming abundance of "vagrants." Drawing on the 1871 criminal code—which defined a vagrant as someone lacking property and income, and having no legitimate impediment, not exercising any skill, craft, or honest profession in order to subsist—they demanded state intervention to put such individuals to work.[42]

State officials agreed. In 1904, Governor Terrazas, describing vagrancy as one of the most noxious social evils, encouraged *jefes políticos* to pursue energetically and punish vagrants in order to return them to activity and work. In this instance, the labor shortages paralyzing mines in the state prompted official action.[43] That same year, the governor, in a letter to the *jefe político* of Hidalgo District, praised local efforts in regulating those who were not dedicated to honest work. Correcting vagrancy, he maintained, allowed companies to count on the availability of more workers.[44] A few years later, another governor, Enrique C. Creel, proposed that municipal lands on the north side of Ciudad Chihuahua be set aside for workers' permanent dwellings. The "Colonia de Obreros," as it was to be called, was to be "comfortable, pleasant, and sanitary"; to help ensure this, no *cantinas* were to be permitted.[45]

Distinguishing between vagrants and workers, however, posed something of a problem for those in the middle class. Writing in *El Correo,* Francisco Díaz blamed the precarious situation of the majority of artisans and workers on their poor work habits. In his opinion, instead of being dedicated to work and family, artisans, in growing numbers, swarmed the streets like true layabouts without credit or resources, confusing themselves with beggars. Most Mondays, he continued, they deserted their shops to squander their weekly wages with friends and to indulge in the degrading vice of alcohol. Díaz blamed artisans for their own plight: when workshops had made advantageous offers to workers, provided that they comply with their obligations in a full and exact manner, they had refused. In his opinion, their precarious situation would remain unchanged until they modified their conduct, complied with their duties, and learned to keep their word. At present, however, artisans lived in humiliation, playing a role little honored in society, and they were unworthy of public appreciation or social esteem.[46] Another writer, in demanding legislation to discipline unreliable workers, declared it was absurd that the public's rights and interests should remain at the mercy of lazy, capricious workers. He called for corporal punishment and prison terms to instill proper work habits.[47] All in all, in the opinion of middle-class Chihuahuans, a problematic relationship existed between vagrancy, vice, and the working class. Workers, already extremely mobile, became vagrants if they refused to comport themselves according to the standards of *sociedad culta.*

While these writers blamed workers for creating social confusion by missing work and indulging in vice, others used the criterion of vice itself to distinguish between social groups. For them, indulgence in vice served to mark off the dangerous from the respectable working class. "We have a veritable army of slackers that lives on top of the working classes," maintained *El Hijo del Parral.* In its opinion, slackers not only represented a criminal threat to society, but a heavy burden for the proletariat that sustained itself by hard work.[48] Others distinguished between frock-coated, middle-class, and lower-class idlers, often reserving their harshest comments for middle-class slackers. *El Correo* contrasted "frock-coated *léperos*" with lower-class drunks. Although each group occupied distinct drinking venues, upper-class drinkers were the most arrogant and scandalous, and thus deserved the heartiest condemnation because they bribed authorities to ignore *cantina* closing regulations. Reformers insisted that the authorities apply such regulations fairly.[49]

The Regulation of Vice

Many members of *sociedad culta* recognized the impossibility of eliminating vice and called, instead, for its regulation—the next best option in the struggle to moralize the masses. While they strove to reduce the consumption of alcohol to as low a level as possible, they favored a different strategy with regard to prostitution: as a necessary evil, even a benefit to society, prostitution would be conducted under state auspices in well-defined and properly invigilated areas. As for gambling, *El Hijo*, in commenting on popular Christmas fairs, admitted its inevitability, particularly since, in its opinion, gambling was the sole purpose of such fairs. How much better it would be, the newspaper concluded, to reform the law in a liberal and honorable sense, for regulating games of chance, as the state regulated prostitution and liquor sales, rather than making them illegal, would give more dignity to authority.[50] In the opinion of moral reformers, the mere passage of legislation outlawing vice, with no possibility of enforcement, served only to mock authority. By contrast, they anticipated that the regulation of vice would bolster citizens' respect for government. Middle-class Chihuahuans expected state and municipal officials to enforce reasonable moralizing measures.

Although prostitution and alcohol regulations existed before the turn of the century, the legislation of morals began in earnest when Luis Terrazas returned to the governor's chair in 1903, a position he had not enjoyed since the 1880s.[51] Before handing Enrique C. Creel that same office the following year, Terrazas enacted measures to regulate alcohol, prostitution, and gambling. Although such policies are commonly associated with Creel, many were begun under Terrazas. According to *El Correo*, Terrazas, in addition to dominating Chihuahua's economy and acting as a regional strongman, presided over a "moral and moralizing administration."[52]

Moral reform was also a municipal concern. In May 1903, Silvestre Terrazas presented Chihuahua City councillors with an initiative against alcohol and prostitution. Along with encouraging healthy public recreation, the initiative mandated increased taxes on alcoholic beverages, rigorous limitation of new *cantina* openings, reduced hours of operation, and penalties for *cantineros* who continued to serve intoxicated clients. Terrazas also called for a commission to be appointed to study the best means of combating alcoholism and prostitution and to designate a neighborhood for the establishment of brothels. Using statistics drawn from the operation of the jail in Chihuahua City to bolster his case, he concluded that these measures—especially the closing of *cantinas* early on Sunday—would significantly reduce crime and aid in the struggle to impose new work habits. Moreover, according to Terrazas, employers could do their part to improve the morality of the popular masses by changing paydays from Saturday to Monday, or to another day of the week, and offering a weekly or monthly bonus to dutiful employees.[53] In June, the interior secretary called for municipal councils throughout the state to enact *cantina* reforms. He hoped to reduce criminality and remove the bad moral example corrupting Chihuahua's youth, because he feared that future as well as formerly productive workers would be corrupted into becoming men useless to society.[54]

In July 1903, the state government approved *cantina* regulations submitted by Chihuahua City town councillors. Based on laws previously enacted in Mexico City, the new measure stipulated that liquor sales end at nine in the evening, Monday through Saturday, and that *cantinas* close at two in the afternoon on Sundays and during fiestas. It also required *jefes políticos* and *presidentes municipales* to license all establishments selling liquor, dividing such businesses into *cantinas,* on the one hand, and commercial outlets—such as cafes, candy shops, bakeries, restaurants, stores, and small shops—on the other. The measure distinguished between first-class *cantinas*, which were to be located in a central zone, and those in a second class, which would be situated throughout the rest of the city. While both types were subject to periodic inspection and had to meet hygienic standards, first-class *cantinas* also had to be constructed for easy cleaning, have tables and chairs of solid construction that were easy to keep clean, use glasses that were crystal, and offer a sufficient number of spittoons. Whereas *jefes políticos* had formerly been able to grant special permission for extended hours of operation, this right now became the prerogative of the state executive. A final article prohibited people from remaining in *cantinas* after closing hours.[55]

At the same time, Governor Terrazas directed *jefes políticos* to prohibit gambling in their jurisdictions, even during the traditional fiestas celebrated by each *pueblo*. The following year, in citing gambling's role in making men lazy and dishonorable, he issued gambling regulations that defined permissible games. Henceforth, chess, bowling, billiards, cockfights, horse racing, bicycle racing, foot racing, raffles, lotteries, dominoes, checkers, *conquian, brisca, escarte, tresillo, Panguin gui,* common poker, *paco, pelota, tiro al blanco,* and whist were to be permitted. All other games were prohibited. Under the new measure, clubs, casinos, and gaming establishments required a written license from the *jefe político* or the *presidente municipal.* Though games were not permitted in public plazas during fairs, gambling was limited to easily policed areas outside public view. Finally, the regulation prohibited gambling in brothels and ordered municipal and state employees to refrain from gambling.[56]

In September 1903, the state executive approved a Tolerance Regulation for Chihuahua City. The measure removed brothels from the city center, designating, as an alternative, three brothel zones, each with a different rate of taxation (those in the first zone were to be taxed at one hundred pesos per month). In addition to prohibiting gambling and liquor sales in brothels, the regulation required prostitutes to dress "properly" and not appear in the street in groups of more than two; it banned them from *cantinas,* billiard halls, restaurants, or cafes, and even from living in the first zone. Nor could they exhibit themselves from windows or balconies. Brothels could sport no external signs and were required to have opaque windows.[57] Such attempts to control public space and the bodies, even gestures, of prostitutes were common in Chihuahua. By dividing brothels into classes, middle-class Chihuahuans hoped to keep social groups from mixing in these establishments. They also intended to remove the example of vice provided by the prostitute from what they perceived to be increasingly promiscuous and vice-ridden city streets.

Taking office in 1904, Governor Enrique C. Creel continued the campaign begun by Terrazas. Upon assuming office, Creel reorganized Chihuahua's districts and replaced elected *presidentes municipales* with appointed officials known as *jefes municipales,* a move designed to strengthen state government at the expense of the municipalities.[58] He envisioned governing through a new breed of local official who would serve as a moral example in each *municipio,* and to back up his commitment to alcohol and gambling regulation, Creel mandated that henceforth state and municipal employees would be fired for drunkenness. Early in the following year, he reiterated his commitment to combat vice through the example of good government: state employees who did not contribute to the moralization of society faced dismissal—an order that Creel reaffirmed in June of that year.[59]

Under Creel, state and municipal officials focused on two hotbeds of vice: the billiard hall and the *cantina.* Members of *sociedad culta* reserved their harshest criticism for "mixed" commercial establishments—those that sold alcohol along with other goods and services—including billiard halls, restaurants, and grocery stores. Although some were willing to accept billiards as a legitimate form of recreation, most believed that the sale of alcohol and the gambling that took place in most halls turned them into dens of vice. Such businesses, described by the press as loci of immorality, proved especially difficult to regulate. Gambling regulations were also flouted in Chihuahua's *cantinas,* much to the disgust of *El Correo.* In mid-1905, the newspaper applauded municipal officials for finally enforcing these ordinances.[60] The year before, the *jefe político* had affixed notices to the doors of the city's *cantinas,* reminding *cantineros* that regulations prohibited minors from being on the premises or alcohol from being sold to minors, police agents, or those already inebriated.[61]

In mid-1906, at Creel's insistence, legislators passed a new law against intoxicating liquors. The regulation demanded official authorization for the establishment of new *cantinas* and reserved all rights of vigilance and control for state government. The law divided merchants into two classes: those who contributed to social well-being and those who made money through immoral enterprises. While members of the first group were to enjoy constitutional guarantees, those in the second became subject to the full force of the new law. Creel believed the law to be so advanced that it would not be surpassed by future legislation.[62] *El Correo,* however, remained unconvinced. It hoped that the regulation would not run up against the indolence, if not the complicity, of certain authorities. Believing that some aspects of the law were outside state jurisdiction and even unconstitutional in its curtailment of individual rights, the newspaper nevertheless wished Creel well in his campaign against alcohol—the cancer of modern society, in its opinion.[63] Finally, Creel's regulation also called for the formation of societies to work with state government to promote popular temperance.

The "Burning Morality" in Hidalgo District

One moral reformer, in an address to the Anti-Alcoholic League, praised the recently passed *cantina* regulations and pointed to the "burning morality" alive in Chihuahuan society. He also pointed to other social advances—laws that would make education available to thousands of Indians in the mountains; laws that would benefit workers and encourage their honor, patriotism, and thrift; and the worthy example of women workers. Without an open war on alcoholism, he declared, all these initiatives would remain a chimera.[64] In implanting the ethic of capitalism, progress required the elimination of alcoholism.

This "burning morality" extended beyond the seat of state government to the districts, municipalities, and mining camps of the state. Between 1900 and 1910, local officials in Hidalgo District regulated gambling, brothels, fairs, circuses, leisure activities, and the sale and consumption of alcohol. Perhaps none did so more keenly than the *jefe municipal* of Santa Bárbara, one of the district's most important mining centers. Concerned that working people should know the arrival and departure hours for mine work, Agustín Páez appropriated thirteen hundred pesos from the municipal budget to purchase a four-sided public clock. Despite the scarcity of municipal funds, he ordered the clock to be sent from Mexico City and arranged for expert supervision of its shipment and installation. Páez, supported by mine company managers and the town's principal residents, undertook construction of a ten-meter clock tower on Chapultepec Hill, dominating the village.[65] There could be no more visible example of the desire to impose time discipline on Mexico's laboring classes.

In Valle de Zaragoza, another municipality in the district, the *presidente municipal* exhibited a similar commitment to the developmentalist ethos. After observing that textile workers from Bella Vista were forced to miss a day's work in order to appear before him to register civil acts such as births and marriages, he requested permission to perform these acts after working hours and during holidays, either in the registry office or in workers' homes. Not only would this save a day's pay for the worker; it would boost the income of factory owners by keeping the machines running. Believing himself to be possessed of the same spirit that moved state government to regulate vice, he further proposed to register sites where suspected clandestine liquor sales took place. Failing to catch red-handed those involved in such illegal transactions, he favored aggressive regulation of certain areas of the municipality on the basis of his suspicions.[66]

Municipal officials, in advocating higher taxes and shorter stays for circuses, dramatic functions, operas, concerts, magicians, and somersaulters, drafted regulations for public amusements in 1903, prohibiting festivities that, in their opinion, would corrupt good customs and attack morality, especially certain dances introduced from the United States.[67] In striving to create a refined society by imposing high standards of public morality, they also justified the need for these measures by pointing to the losses suffered by local merchants, the poverty in which the needy classes remained after the circus left town, and the damage incurred by local mining companies. With prolonged festive periods, they maintained, workers stayed awake and were unable to report to work at the proper hour. Recognizing that mining companies needed a regular supply of punctual laborers, they sought to foster reliable work habits through regulation of public amusements.

District officials also regulated gambling. In 1904, Governor Terrazas congratulated Rodolfo Valles, the *jefe político* in Hidalgo District, for his efforts in controlling gaming in district *cantinas*. The governor was applauding Valles's initiative requiring *cantina* owners to apply for gaming permits—licenses granted only to those who ran games approved by the state.[68] In Santa Bárbara, the municipal chief lamented that the limited powers granted to him by law did not allow him to punish severely enough those caught indulging in games of chance. As a solution, he proposed that, upon discovering gambling, he close the establishment and remit to Parral those caught taking part. There, the *jefe político* himself might deal properly with the transgressors.[69]

Other officials in Hidalgo District were imbued with a similar commitment to moral reform. In April 1900, town councillors in Hidalgo del Parral attempted to control prostitution in their city by passing a Tolerance Regulation. They designated several city blocks as the area where brothels were to be located—called the *zona de tolerancia*—and prohibited prostitutes, who now had to be registered, from leaving the zone during the hours specified by the act. A new municipal official, the *agente de sanidad,* was charged with recording and regulating the whereabouts of prostitutes, who were required to submit to weekly medical examinations, to dress and behave "decently," and to refrain from encouraging business by standing in doorways, windows, and balconies, or through signs, signals, and words. Every brothel fell under the care and vigilance of a woman at least forty years old, this advanced age supposedly being sufficient guarantee against her participation in the trade itself.[70] The regulation, like those elsewhere in the country, was modeled on the French system, which rested on three goals: to create an enclosed milieu for prostitution, invisible to women, children, and other members of society; to impose constant supervision of the authorities in such a location, the first tier of which was the matron running the brothel; and to prevent the mixing of age groups and classes in such establishments. In Parral, as in France, vice was meant to be concentrated in one spot, and thus purged from the rest of the community.[71]

In June 1903, on his own initiative, the *presidente municipal* in Santa Bárbara established a well-defined brothel zone on the outskirts of town, giving resident prostitutes a week to leave their current lodgings and move to the area. This local official justified his action as the best means of imposing police vigilance in brothels and thus avoiding scandals, which was a very difficult task because prostitutes lived scattered throughout the town and along the street running to the train station. He asked the *jefe político* in Parral to approve his measure.[72]

Initially, regulations did not prevent the sale of alcohol in registered brothels. A 1902 register reveals the existence of four brothels in Parral housing some sixty-nine women, differentiated into first- and second-class prostitutes, with the former paying three pesos per month in municipal taxes and the latter two. Octaviana Ruiz, owner of the city's largest brothel, complained of excessive taxation: not only did she pay eight pesos each month in city taxes as well as taxes for weekly at-home medical examinations for every woman working for her, but she faced an additional monthly levy of ten pesos because her brothel had also been classified as a *cantina*. This she bitterly denied, maintaining that she sold only soda water in her establishment.[73]

By mid-1903, *cantinas* and brothels could no longer legally coexist. Responding to demands of the local press, complaints of mine managers concerning working-class alcoholism, and the suggestion of state officials that municipalities enact their own alcohol reforms, the *jefe político* prohibited alcohol sales in brothels and ordered *cantinas* to close during specific hours. On Sunday, *cantinas* located in neighborhoods were to close at two in the afternoon, while those in the center of town could remain open until four. The rest of the week, closing time was ten o'clock and midnight, respectively. "Mixed" commercial establishments were also to adhere to this schedule for alcohol sales, even if they remained open to sell other merchandise. Those violating the new regulation faced heavy fines and the loss of their license.[74]

Other officials in municipalities under Parral's jurisdiction quickly followed suit. In Santa Bárbara, officials ordered *cantinas* to close at ten o'clock, except those situated in the city center, which could remain open until midnight. The *presidente municipal* in Huejotitan, in blaming alcohol for the frequency of violent crime, issued regulations making merchants who sold alcohol responsible for preserving order in their establishments. Especially problematic were the groups of inebriated singers who caroused through the *pueblo* bothering peaceful citizens, exhibiting a lack of morals and civilization, and carrying on drunken scandals. According to this official, since workers, who made up the bulk of the population, were unable to attend to their tasks on the day following drinking, all liquor outlets would henceforth close each night at eight o'clock.[75]

As an integral aspect of the 1903 reform drive, state officials ordered *jefes políticos* and *presidentes municipales* to submit crime statistics so that the effect of the new regulations on the crime rate could be measured. Less than a month after regulating liquor sales in his jurisdiction, the *presidente municipal* in Santa Bárbara reported magnificent results:

whereas only 92 men had been arrested for crimes motivated by drunkenness since 12 July 1903, the day the new measure had gone into effect, in an equivalent period before passage of the regulation 157 had been detained on similar charges.[76]

Dramatic changes were not so apparent in other jurisdictions, especially in municipalities dominated by agriculture rather than by mining. In San Isidro de las Cuevas, for example, the *presidente municipal* noted no difference; all people in the community were docile, he explained, and had always been dedicated to their work. In Valle de Zaragoza, however, the absence of police and the alarm caused by the new regulations made compliance impossible. Because *cantina* owners refused to close, the *presidente municipal* found himself confronting a large number of drunken scandals. Maintaining that the layout of the town prevented proper police vigilance, he asked the *jefe político* for a corporal and two additional policemen to enable him to enforce the regulations.[77]

The *jefe político* had to rely on *presidentes municipales* to arrest and fine those indulging in alcohol-induced scandals and ensure that *cantinas* closed during restricted hours. Yet attempts to enforce the 1903 law in several municipalities met with the resistance of these very officials. Many supplemented a grocery or clothing business by selling liquor. To comply with the regulations, they were required to install blinds to prevent liquor sales from being observed from the street; they complained that not only would this prevent customers from seeing their goods, more serious still was the possibility that no respectable woman or family would dare enter their premises once blinds separated the shop from the public view. Municipal officials in Balleza petitioned the *jefe político* to overlook this aspect of the reform.[78]

Local records reveal a new concern with regulating the sale and consumption of alcohol in Hidalgo District after 1903. After the passage of regulations governing *cantinas* in that year, the presence of the police became the most important criterion when officials made decisions regarding liquor sales and the establishment of new *cantinas*. Police vigilance became critical to reform, and its absence prompted *presidentes municipales* to prohibit the sale of alcohol, even in closed bottles, in stores removed from the main centers of population and in isolated *ranchos* and *pueblos* throughout the district. In Santa Bárbara, for example, the *presidente municipal* explained to an unsuccessful petitioner that liquor sales would no longer be permitted in company stores in areas without police supervision. In late 1903, this became policy for all mining companies operating within his jurisdiction.[79]

Police-imposed vigilance also became a prerequisite to obtaining ap-
proval for the establishment of new brothels, for permission to host fairs
and circuses, and for the right to run lotteries. Members of *sociedad culta*
contrasted vigilance with clandestinity, and in the terminology of the day,
unregistered prostitutes became clandestine as did liquor, its illegal sale,
and the location of such transactions. Gambling and gambling dens fell
into the same descriptive category. While historians have emphasized the
police role in imposing order during the Porfiriato, they have not addressed its role in implementing and enforcing moral reform: police agen-
cies were to keep watch over moral reform, combating clandestinity with
their vigilance.[80]

In 1906 and 1907, alcohol regulation and enforcement acquired new
momentum in Hidalgo District. Frustrated by their inability to control
alcohol sales in "mixed" establishments, district officials closed such outlets in many areas of the district and imposed new closing regulations in
those that remained open. In Parral, the police commander and the *jefe
político* energetically enforced laws mandating Sunday drinking hours
and closing times for *cantinas*. In January 1907, the *jefe político* introduced a new regulation governing the sale of intoxicating beverages, which
reflected his concern with a new danger to public health posed by alcohol. Not only did alcohol promise the generational debilitation of the
Mexican race; the poor quality of liquor and its adulteration at the hands
of unscrupulous small vendors posed an immediate health hazard. In the
mining areas, including Villa Escobedo and Santa Bárbara, local officials
carried out measures to combat this menace.[81]

Despite this program of moral reform, a degree of hypocrisy charac-
terizes the rhetoric and actions of moral reformers and state officials in
Chihuahua who seemed more concerned with preserving the outward
appearance of order than with actually changing behavior. As was the
case with Puritanism in seventeenth-century England, such hypocrisy derived from the reluctance of the multitude to accept discipline: those in
sociedad culta could do little more than make men "visibly" rather than
"truly" religious.[82] They advocated vigilance rather than the elimination
of vice: the isolation, especially, of prostitutes in prescribed zones removed
from city centers, where they could not rub shoulders with or provide a
bad moral example for decent, honorable people; and opaque windows
and Persian blinds to keep families safe from viewing corrupt interiors.
Middle-class Chihuahuans stressed the outward appearance of confor-
mity rather than the creation of true believers in the developmentalist
ethos.

Increasingly, governmental officials became the targets of reformers' wrath as indulgence in vice seemed unabated in the state. In perceiving the police to be a part of the problem rather than part of the solution, members of *sociedad culta* called for new standards in police recruitment and the establishment of a police training school to improve the quality and morality of policemen. They stressed that society did not need new regulations, but rather proper enforcement of the existing morals laws. Despite state efforts to enforce higher standards for state and municipal employees—including threats to fire those who did not set a "moral example" for the masses—moral reformers lamented the duplicity of the police and governmental officials in vice.[83] They complained that political authorities were not active enough in imposing the new discipline, the new sense of the necessity of labor, upon the mass of the population. Disappointment in the slow pace of reform and outright governmental involvement in "immoral" acts turned many reformers against Terrazas-Creel rule.[84] Rather than less government, these Chihuahuans demanded more, better, and responsible government.[85]

Conclusion

Members of *sociedad culta* struggled to impose a new developmentalist ethos on the masses. They meant to create suitably motivated workers and patriotic citizens through state-enforced discipline, vigilance, supervision, and control. As vice jeopardized the inculcation of time discipline, habits of thrift and saving, and proper work patterns, all progress would be for naught without its regulation. Immorality posed even greater threats to Mexican society. Subscribing to a belief in racial and biological causation, middle-class Chihuahuans feared that uncontrolled alcoholism, prostitution, gambling, and vagrancy threatened the degeneration of the Mexican race. Although alcoholism and venereal disease represented the greatest evils, "degeneracy" could be moral as well as physical. Moreover, unregulated vice destroyed virtue, provided poor moral examples for the youth of Chihuahua, and created men useless to society. The struggle to impose morality thus transcended politics and the workplace to become a patriotic duty—at stake were the future of the country and the race itself.

In stressing the importance of moral reform and the preoccupation of middle-class Chihuahuans (including governmental authorities) with the inculcation of the developmentalist ideology, more than a simple functionalist model of social control is implied. Faced with a new, floating, and working population no longer subject to "traditional" rural authorities, members of *sociedad culta* contested for control of city space. They sought to differentiate between the dangerous and the respectable poor, and to distance themselves physically, by removing vice from city centers, and socially—as honorable members of society—from this new mass. Profession of a moral lifestyle reveals as much about their attempts at self- and class definition as it does the need for social control.

In their struggle to regenerate the Mexican masses, members of *sociedad culta* identified the stability of the family as vital to national progress. They expected discipline to begin in the family, and parents were asked to provide an example of high moral standards. In one sense, they envisioned governmental regulation as an extension of family control. As the family head provided discipline and the example of virtuous conduct, so must governmental authorities. As the formation and endurance of the working-class family became increasingly premised upon the male laboring for a wage, squandering of wages on vice threatened the family's destruction and, with it, a means of disciplining the masses. When middle-class Chihuahuans spoke of regenerating the lower classes, they not only meant regeneration from dishonorable to honorable and from useless to socially productive, they also hoped to build ideally happy homes out of the rubble of families fractured by vice.

4

Prostitutes and Guardian Angels

Women, Work, and the Family

In homes along the northern border, there are many instances in
which the daughter faithfully interprets the beautiful qualities of
obedience, docility, and submission and goes to great trouble to
please and serve; she takes a real interest in all things domestic
and loves work together with education; she stays in her place
and keeps up her ideas and thoughts, her customs and qualities,
arriving at the position of the proper woman (*mujer digna*).

—M. A. Sanz, *La mujer mexicana en el santuario
del hogar* (1907)

References to family predominate in the rhetoric of middle-class
Chihuahuans. According to members of *sociedad culta,* working-class
life needed to be diverted from the streets, taverns, billiard halls, fair-
grounds, and town centers of the state to the private sphere of the family.
Their goal was to form the working-class home as an antidote to social
instability and as the best site for inculcating values of thrift, sobriety,
hygiene, punctuality, and patriotism in succeeding generations of workers. The discourse on family cannot be understood simply as a means of
social control, however. It also served as a crucial form of social self-
definition for members of *sociedad culta.* With as much enthusiasm as
they campaigned against vice, middle-class Chihuahuans advocated a new
cult of female domesticity in which they carefully prescribed women's
role: women were to serve as properly educated mothers and guardian
angels of the home. While they insisted that women's "natural" place
was in the home, by contrast the prostitute reigned as a particularly co-
gent symbol of Mexico's dangerous classes.

Attempts to form the working-class home were not limited to Chihuahua. Moralizing workers and forming them into stable families was also
a central preoccupation of French mine owners in the nineteenth century.
In French mining communities between 1860 and 1880, a "vast revolu-

tion" took place simultaneously at work, at home, and in morals as employers sought to "familialize" and "moralize" their workforce. In order to destroy the influence of the "wine shop, the bar, and other evil places," the bourgeoisie attempted to assign "precise, enclosed and obligatory places for lovemaking" in a home, in which family feeling was exalted and celibacy and concubinage eliminated. In French mining communities, as in many of those in northern Mexico, companies refused to hire bachelors and gave jobs only to "men of family."[1]

Moralizing the worker and safely restraining him within the working-class home were two aspects of the same project: the regulation of the body. In the European context, this regulationist impulse was at the center of the bourgeois agenda: "The creation of a sublimated public body without smells, without coarse laughter, without organs, separate from the Court and the Church on the one hand and the market square, alehouse, street and fairground on the other—this was the great labor of bourgeois culture."[2] For Pierre Bourdieu, the apparently superficial reformation of manners is one of the most powerful ways in which the organizing principles of a culture can be inculcated; concessions of politeness always contain political concessions.[3] Similarly, in late colonial Mexico, the Bourbons attempted to impress "a new sense of embarrassment and disgust upon the poor, to inscribe the ordering principles of the regime into their very bodies."[4]

In Europe and Mexico alike, the regulationist project was premised upon the assumption that women's primary, if not exclusive, roles would be that of wife and mother in both the working-class and bourgeois family. The new ideal of domestic life in early independent Mexico was even more circumscribed than its colonial counterpart, as many liberals no longer envisioned any role for wives in productive labor.[5] Instead of being encouraged to work, women were to be taught to serve as guardians of private life in the home—now conceptualized as the nursery of the nation—where they were to inculcate the values of patriotism and the work ethic in future generations. Much as in postrevolutionary France, a sexually differentiated standard of virtue emerged: whereas women were perceived to be most virtuous when performing private duties as mothers, sisters, and wives, men attained such standing when they fulfilled their public responsibilities as citizens.[6]

By the time of the Porfiriato, so powerful was the ideal of the domestic role of women that one contemporary analyst divided Mexican society into social groups based solely on the criterion of what he called "private life." In *La génesis del crimen in México,* published in 1901, Julio Guerrero postulated that society in the central valley of Mexico comprised (A) a large and growing group of street people, including beggars, ragpickers, and others; (B) the rank and file of the military; (C) workers without skills or trades; (D) male and female servants; (E) artisans, policemen, and lower-level public and commercial employees; and (F) those dedicated to intellectual work, including lawyers, doctors, engineers, artists, professors, merchants, military men, and high governmental officials.[7] For Guerrero, the defining characteristic of each group was not wealth or occupation, but the "moral" behavior of women, which ranged from promiscuous, in the first group, to monogamous, in the last (polyandry and polygamy characterized the sexual relations of those groups in the middle of his evolutionary scale). A moral chasm separated those in group E from the morally-suspect and generally vice-ridden members of less-evolved groups (A–D): here, men, cleaner and opposed to drunkenness (at least in theory), and women, described as "modest" and "virtuous," came together to form a definite home. In group F, women, ever faithful, had taken yet another step in the evolution of Mexican domesticity, and their superiority was revealed in emotional, and even physical, terms: in addition to being in sole possession of "inexhaustible altruism" and a "delicacy of sentiments," these women were organisms in which egotistical instincts and the crudeness associated with life close to nature had atrophied. In short, they had turned into *"señoras decentes."*[8]

According to Guerrero, the *señora decente* brought together the qualities most valued in Mexican society. Such women tirelessly interceded to see that the domestic and public authority of the head of their household (*jefe del hogar*) was not exercised with severity. They always tried to economize so that they could both build up the domestic reserve (a fund to be set aside in case of emergency) and have bread to give to the needy. Orphans, destitute old people, or women who were poor but too proud to beg never came away from the house of a *señora decente* empty handed— they always received clothes or money with a minimum of fanfare. While *señoras decentes* were the recipients of many blessings, they never expected gratitude, prizes, or praise for their charity, which they continued to provide without fail. Within the home, they devoted all of their efforts to being worthy of the position they occupied, and they refined their matronly virtues: in all of their relationships they aspired to be more good-natured; more caring with their husband; and more tender with their children. Moreover, the *señora decente* refined her intelligence with study; and as if encased as in a glass jar, in her home, surrounded with light, art, calm, and harmony, she formed the most superior being in Mexican society, in whom, under these conditions, the most exquisite qualities of the race could best evolve. For Guerrero, the *señora decente* represented Mexico's leading classes, much as one biological species represented the flora of a particular location. While there might be other plants present, she was the most perfect and abundant specimen in the homes of those who ruled Mexico.[9]

Historians of the Porfiriato have begun to assess the emphasis placed on domesticity by members of *sociedad culta* like Julio Guerrero. By analyzing the content of late nineteenth-century periodicals directed toward women, especially *La Mujer,* Carmen Ramos Escandón points to the ways in which bourgeois women reaffirmed their social status and that of their families. She also concludes that the pronatal message and stress on female domesticity advocated by the Porfirian bourgeoisie represented an attempt to ease tensions between increasingly antagonistic classes.[10] In his study of the "new woman" that Protestant missionaries were attempting to fashion during the same period, Jean-Pierre Bastian notes the connection between the perceived need to educate women and the inculcation of the capitalist work ethic. Bastian emphasizes the need to create a new type of worker for Porfirian factories, one who had disciplined her sexual instincts and committed herself to the fight against alcohol. Protestant missionaries wanted to create habits of discipline, hygiene, thrift, and family morality among working-class women.[11]

Verena Radkau combines the study of working women with an analysis of the dominant discourse on gender in Porfirian Mexico. She finds a veritable army of writers, most of whom subscribed to the notion of unlimited progress and were preoccupied with women's roles. Perceiving women of all social classes to be excellent guardians of the status quo, these writers carried the cult of domesticity with crusading zeal to all levels of Porfirian society. Radkau finds, moreover, that traditional models of womanhood appealed to incipient proletarians, both male and female, as well as to the middle class. For many working-class males, women's salaried work threatened patriarchal authority within the family as well as men's monopoly of certain skills and qualifications. For Radkau, contradictions of class were intertwined with contradictions of gender.[12] In this chapter, I analyze the discourse on domesticity as part of the effort to inculcate the capitalist work ethic and to differentiate classes in Porfirian Mexico.

Women's Education

Because family formation could be accomplished only by properly educated women, women's education became an important theme of middle-class discourse. This had also been the case in the late colonial period, when Bourbon reformers advocated practical education for women as a means of instilling values of work, thrift, and initiative in future generations. During this period, motherhood became a civic responsibility that only enlightened women could fulfill. After independence, republican officials continued to view the education of women as essential to solving the problems facing the new nation. Following Bourbon precedents, these governments expanded primary education. For Bourbons and republicans alike, educating women implied creating excellent mothers and useful members of society.[13]

During the Porfiriato, these same developmentalist motives compelled middle-class Mexicans to take action. In Chihuahua, education became a state priority. In Hidalgo District, for example, *jefe político* Rodolfo Valles proudly emphasized increased school attendance in reports to the governor. Between 1902 and 1906, the average number of students attending schools in the town of Parral grew from 526 to 1,480. School construction took place throughout the district. In 1906, Parral boasted five schools (*escuelas oficiales*); Villa Escobedo, five; Santa Bárbara, three; and San Francisco del Oro, two. Valles asserted that along with inculcating a sense of order and love of country, the mission of the educator was to make people realize that the school led directly to the workshop. At the end of a day's toil, the worker hurried back to a home sanctified by honor and hard work. Officials like Valles shared the hope that education would create suitably motivated workers, and they expected enlightened wives to greet workers as they returned home from their travails.[14]

Increased emphasis on domesticity and the exaltation of motherhood led to the establishment of industrial schools for young women (*escuelas industriales para señoritas*) in Chihuahua. According to Luz Fernández M., an alumna of one such institution, education existed to enable a woman to fulfill better her role as man's auxiliary. Women graduating from the industrial school for young women were true women: hardworking (*trabajadora*) and homebodies (*de casa*). Moreover, the school formed useful women, not know-it-alls; modest women, not pretentious harridans; women who were not offended by housework, but who knew something about science and language. Women existed to help men; and although inferior in physical nature, in dignity they were men's equal. Luz Fernández M. closed her address by stressing women's role in inculcating developmentalist values in the next generation.[15] As in no other single issue, the question of women's education linked moral reform, gender, and class.

The Porfirian educational project was to be national in scope and to include all social classes. While the present generation might not possess suitable work habits or exhibit attributes necessary for inclusion in refined society, reformers stressed that properly educated women could successfully inculcate these values in the next generation. Thus, they denounced upper-class pretensions and fears of social mixing—the obvious consequence of sending their daughters to public schools, where they encountered the progeny of the lower orders. They were no less vehement in criticizing fathers of laboring families for keeping their children out of school during peak work periods of the agricultural cycle and religious pilgrimages. Middle-class Chihuahuans also confronted the parental fear of entrusting daughters to the supervision of male teachers, and the widespread belief that women need not receive an education.[16]

Widely accepted educational theories stressing the mother's role in establishing lifelong habits of industry and morality in young children added urgency to the task of educating women. Many of these theorists viewed education given by parents to children—that is, family education—as the basis for national greatness and prosperity. They bolstered the belief that the mother of the family offered the means of creating a progressive society. Good teaching began in infancy; it was the only means of ensuring that education took firm root.

Members of *sociedad culta* cited Francis Bacon: "that which we call education is basically a habit contracted from the tenderest age."[17] They looked to other European authors for support of the thesis that children's education was nothing but the acquisition of good habits that would eventually become instinctive. Habits worked more consistently than reason; and mothers were to impress on children the values that middle-class Chihuahuans treasured: charity, virtue, modesty, and integrity. Underlying the rhetoric was the assumption that individuals acted as reasonable and rational beings who, once they were educated, would adopt obviously correct forms of behavior. Education of the masses thus became one important means toward resolving the problems confronting Porfirian society.[18]

Education was also meant to be practical. In place of excessive concern with imparting proper manners and the correct appearance in society, reformers constantly impressed on parents the necessity of teaching children dedication to work so that they might become *hombres trabajadores*.[19] In a manner reminiscent of eighteenth-century Spanish attempts to promote manufacturing, they chided upper-class society for disparaging manual labor and for barring its children from choosing such work. Newspapers offered allegorical tales of sons going against family wishes and choosing useful occupations, often artisanal, in place of legal careers, which they described as a burden to society. One newspaper contributor summarized the frustration with elite attitudes toward work: it was better to have one useful artisan than to educate five unproductive *licenciados*.[20]

Middle-class Chihuahuans also donated substantial funds to establish institutions to educate women, such as the industrial school for young women that Luz Fernández M. attended in Parral. Funding such schools became one of the foremost expressions of progressive philanthropy, indicating the importance that donors attached to women's useful education. Subjects considered useful and thus taught in these schools included typewriting, telegraphy, sewing, cutting, weaving, dressmaking, household duties, bookkeeping, typesetting, arithmetic, grammar, and English. Opened in Ciudad Chihuahua before the turn of the century, an industrial school for young women was founded in Parral in late 1906 by Parral's notable citizens, including Rodolfo Valles. It was attended by middle-class, not elite, women. In 1908, students petitioned Valles for an end to Saturday classes. These young women described themselves as poor (*todas pobres*). Attending school on Saturday left them unable to tidy their clothes, because they could not afford to hire anyone to do their household duties. The petitioners believed that an end to Saturday classes would allow punctual attendance during the rest of the week.[21]

Contributors to Chihuahua's newspapers eagerly anticipated the possibility that women's education would bring conservative consequences rather than broader horizons or increased self-sufficiency. Education Porfirian style would serve to inform women of their "proper" place in society. For most middle-class Mexicans, this meant compliance with women's duties as daughters, wives, and mothers. Enlightened Porfirians viewed excessive pride as one of the principal defects of the poorly educated woman. By contrast, the well-educated woman was modest and humble, and knew how to sacrifice her own happiness and well-being. The well-educated woman never showed off her family, her titles, or her physical or moral qualities.[22]

Other commentators drew on Catholic teachings that mandated the mother's educational duties. Writing in the pro-Catholic *El Correo,* these Chihuahuans believed that the maternal mission encompassed religious as well as moral and civic instruction.[23] Good mothers formed good families that feared and worshiped God. Many writers described the family as a representation of the Holy Trinity, likening the mother's role to a conduit or means of communication between father and child. As one contributor explained, the father was the intelligence that illuminated, and the mother the sentiment that brought it to life; but the light of the father was not able to reach the child during infancy. As childhood represented an age devoid of reason, the father's teachings could only reach the child through the sentiment of the mother.[24] While Catholic contributors criticized the contemporary educational system and characterized it as devoid of religious and moral instruction, they could agree with non-Catholic reformers about the mother's familial duties. Like nineteenth-century Italian reformers, enlightened Porfirians often used Comtean positivism and social Darwinism to reinforce rather than challenge the traditional religious prescription of the female role.[25]

Middle-class Chihuahuans predicted disastrous consequences for the family if women remained uneducated and uncultured. More than a flower without an aroma, the uneducated wife represented a "harmful plant that poisoned the holy garden of the home with its contagion."[26] Women needed to be educated, instructed, and virtuous in order to penetrate the spirit of man, to study the sentiments of his soul, to be his equal, to advise him, to care for him, to sweeten his existence—in short, to transform the nuptial home into a true paradise.[27] For M. A. Sanz, author of *La mujer mexicana en el santuario del hogar,* published in 1907, home and school went together like virtue and science, morality and duty, work and obligation, love and relative happiness. He contrasted the education of young women in the past—which, in his opinion, little prepared them for ruling in the "Santuario del Hogar"—with that of the present, which offered the prospective wife and mother skills that were suited to her domestic role.[28]

While education was geared to prepare mothers to bring up suitably enlightened families, members of *sociedad culta* also expected domestic life to reinforce values needed in the workplace. Women were to run *hogares blancos*—"pure" houses that radiated cleanliness, punctuality, and usefulness; houses in which mothers exercised skill in preparing schedules and allocating time.[29] Home and work were to adhere to the same capitalist principles. Some went so far as to demand that time and work discipline be imposed on household chores, admonishing mothers to teach their daughters to distribute the time given to domestic chores by the quarter-hour from morning till night. Middle-class Mexicans presented home and work as interrelated, and only through the transformation of both could middle-class aims be accomplished. "Capitalist" organization of the home seemed to promise orderly behavior on the job. Family and home relationships symbolized ideal worker behavior.

From the sanctuary of her home, the ideal wife also engendered patriotic sentiments. M. A. Sanz identified two ways in which this could be accomplished. First, women in the home promoted nationalism by making patriotism an important part of family education, thus inculcating such values in succeeding generations. Second, Sanz pointed to the heroic examples of Josefa Ortiz de Domínguez, a collaborator of Hidalgo; Agustina Ramírez, whose children gave their lives in defense of her country; Margarita Maza de Juárez, wife of Benito Juárez; and Sra. Monteverde de Torres, wife of the contemporary governor of Sonora. These women, along with all others who knew their place and displayed the qualities of obedience, docility, submission, and willingness to serve, formed homes that could serve as examples for those in other social groups. Although all this could be accomplished by mixing with other social classes—a desirable duty, according to Sanz—the very fact of their existence as exemplary mothers and wives served to foster civic pride.[30]

In much the same manner that work served as the antidote to vice for the working class, domestic work promised to safeguard morally all women from boredom, idleness, and laziness—the origins of vice. One member of *sociedad culta* characterized domestic work as a virtue that reestablished order and conserved health. Laziness, on the other hand, led to the rule of passion, adulation, furtiveness, hypocrisy, and egotism. According to this commentator, the woman who knew how to work in the home, to scorn worldly dissipations, and to discover happiness in her family was the providence of her husband and children.[31] Domestic work thwarted vice and was to serve as a model for working-class behavior outside the home in northern Mexico.

Middle-class Chihuahuans stressed sustenance of the soul as well as the body. One contributor to *El Correo* admonished young girls to be industrious and to learn to cook, sew, wash, iron, and do other necessary and useful domestic chores; yet he also encouraged women to embroider, arrange flowers, and learn to play musical instruments for pleasure as well as utility. He criticized women who neglected this aspect of their training, in the same manner as others criticized the working class. To describe such one-sided personal development, he drew a metaphor from the new conditions of work: young girls who only embroidered represented mere embroidery machines, while those exclusively arranging flowers were virtually machines for arranging flowers.[32] Nurturing the soul seemed a necessary condition for human existence—one that was deemed to be absent in an ever-increasing working class and threatened in the family itself.

Occasionally, reformers likened women's modest behavior to a national virtue. One writer contrasted U.S. and Mexican women: seclusion and constant supervision, even vigilance, under the mother's watchful eye produced the virtue of modesty in Mexican women. He asked, "Will the Mexican woman renounce this precious jewel that exalts her in everyone's eyes?"[33] Such a question seems to suggest a growing fear of women's changing behavior. Modesty could cover many defects, and reformers viewed the timidity that accompanied modesty as one of the most beautiful adornments of the feminine sex. According to them, beauty without education led such women to believe themselves superior to all other women, viewing them with scorn. Suitable education promised to correct this fault.[34]

Members of *sociedad culta* contrasted simplicity and modesty in the domestic sphere with the excessive luxury of women on the street. When questioned as to why women in the mining town of Santa Bárbara turned to prostitution, *jefe municipal* Agustín Páez advanced three reasons: the relaxation of social customs in the region, the misery and necessity brought about by the increasingly high cost of living, and the excessive desire for luxury on the part of some women.[35] What most enraged those discussing moral reform and domesticity was the perception that Chihuahua's prostitutes indulged their taste for luxury, exemplified by fine clothes, expensive jewelry, and makeup. Editorial campaigns favoring moral reform never failed to mention prostitutes' flaunting of luxury and their lack of respect for society and its authorities.[36] Whether or not clothes were considered luxurious also depended on the socioeconomic status of the wearer. While condemning prostitutes for their vanity, middle-class Chihuahuans denigrated working-class women who dressed like their social betters. In both cases, excessive luxury seemed a direct affront to refined society.[37]

Members of *sociedad culta* viewed luxury as an unmistakable symbol of societal decadence, corruption, and loss of virtue. Writing in *El Correo,* a woman identified only as María warned women against showing off and, above all, against indulging in the horrible passion of luxury. María described luxury as a contagious plague devouring modern societies, with women as its principal victims.[38] To many others, luxury seemed the opposite of cleanliness. One editor rejected luxury as the criterion for beauty and, instead, called for women always to have needle, thread, and an abundant supply of soap and water on hand.[39] Using a question-and-answer format for didactic purposes, El Correo pondered the characteristics deemed most and least desirable in Porfirian women. Which woman was happiest with herself? She who used only soap and water at her dressing table. Who was the most virtuous woman? The one who occupied herself solely with her domestic tasks. Which was the best? The most humble. The ugliest? She who always looked at herself in the mirror. The most natural, simple, and innocent? She who loved children. The coquette was described as the most contemptible.[40]

Also apparent in the comments of many sharing the Porfirian persuasion was the belief that luxury in dress confused social boundaries. One commentator complained that anyone who did not know the locale and saw the luxury of women's dress at fiestas, dances, and parties would conclude that these women enjoyed material comforts and at least an average income. He maintained that such was not the case and that these women sacrificed their true needs in order to dress in such a manner. Women accepted hunger in order to wrap themselves in expensive cloth, morocco leather, belts, and ribbons.[41] Some described the spirit of luxury as a characteristic inherited from one's parents. Once again, only proper education promised to free the present generation from the grasp of that vice.

Prostitutes and Other Social Symbols

The embodiment of luxury and many other social ills lamented by self-proclaimed cultured Porfirians was the figure of the prostitute. For Luis Lara y Pardo, author of La prostitución en México, published in 1908, "science" had clearly proven that prostitution was a degenerative state of social and psychological inferiority. While he regarded vagrants, beggars, criminals, and all forms of social parasites as degenerate phenomena, only prostitutes displayed the full cluster of traits so threatening to sociedad culta. Laziness, indifference, apathy, superstition, the desire to call attention to themselves, and functional perversions of the nervous system were all embodied in this figure. Once they joined a brothel, prostitutes lost their power to reason, their will, and their sense of morality. Even their language degenerated into brothel slang. They became slaves to superstition, forming the principal clientele of fortune tellers and adopting practices such as leaving two burning matches crossed on the floor in hopes of avoiding confinement in the hospital for venereal diseases.[42]

Using statistics gathered by the *inspector de sanidad* in Mexico City, Lara y Pardo argued that most prostitutes came from the working class. With their work experience as domestic servants, tortilla makers, cleaning women, and waitresses, and their family background in the artisan and working classes, prostitutes served as the dominant symbol of lower-class moral and cultural degeneracy.[43] Through his discussion of the behavior of prostitutes, Lara y Pardo revealed his beliefs about workers, in his opinion the lowest members of the social body. Women became prostitutes not because of poverty or hunger, but because of their environment; they had grown up in working-class neighborhoods, where, according to Lara y Pardo, they had witnessed a daily display of drunkenness and vice. One of the most prominent images they retained from their childhood was that of the prostitute dressed in her "uniform." Indeed, many would have counted prostitutes among their relatives and friends.

For Lara y Pardo, poverty was not responsible for creating this working-class environment. In fact, he asserted that working-class women had an easier time in making ends meet than women of other classes; he believed that those at the bottom of the social scale enjoyed greater opportunities for work and had only minimal necessities. Lara y Pardo maintained that lower-class women frequently left one of the most economically favored categories of employment, domestic work, to become prostitutes. Rather than poverty, it was social and psychological inferiority, combined with the power of example, that led to prostitution. In short, the working-class woman lived in a "repugnant" and "terrible" promiscuity that left her ready to prostitute herself simply out of habit. For these women, loss of virginity was either voluntary or trivial.[44]

In transferring debate from the subject of class conflict and the economic conditions of workers to that of the supposed moral degeneration of the working class, Lara y Pardo and middle-class Porfirians in general were acting like elites elsewhere. Discussing Parliamentary Commission reports of working conditions in British factories and mines in the first half of the nineteenth century, Jeffrey Weeks observes an obsessive concern with the sexuality of the working class and a displacement of the discussion from the area of exploitation and class conflict into a framework that Weeks considers more amenable to the British bourgeoisie—

that of morality. In both cases, the focus on morality and degeneracy made it possible to avoid a discussion of social and economic conditions while blaming the workers themselves for their problems.[45]

The preoccupation of the *gente decente* with the sexuality of the working class also confirms Judith Walkowitz's observation that the zeal for moral reform was often accompanied by a "prolonged, fascinated gaze" from the bourgeoisie. Urban investigators in London at the end of the nineteenth century felt so compelled to possess a comprehensive knowledge of the Other that they were willing to engage in cultural immersion, social masquerade, even "intrapsychic incorporation" in the effort to obtain it. In transgressing the distance between themselves and those they studied, bourgeois observers confirmed the symbolic importance of the "low-Other" in the "imaginative repertoire of the dominant culture."[46] In Porfirian Mexico, middle-class commentators shared Lara y Pardo's fascination with lower-class manners and morals. Criminological studies, for example, often included numerous "case studies" containing descriptions of the drinking and sexual habits of the delinquents' parents. Guerrero's work (discussed earlier in this chapter) offers detailed descriptions of the private lives of women from the lower classes. Finally, M. A. Sanz asks his readers to imagine the consequences for two young women from the country who find themselves to be victims of poor parental supervision and exposed to the example of vice. Readers were able to fill in the rest.[47]

As the city was the site of female independence, some observers began to contrast what they saw as the morally pure countryside with an evil, vice-ridden city. For them, it was impossible to imagine such an independent woman existing in Mexico's rural environment.[48] Many members of *sociedad culta* lamented changing social customs, a process they described as moral relaxation. To many observers in northern Mexico, working women's presence in the new workplaces and alone in the cities—separated from both paternal and conjugal homes—indicated that the world had been turned upside down. One contributor to *El Correo* exclaimed that only twenty years earlier it would have been shocking to see a young woman carrying home books from a commercial house, working as an employee or shop assistant, or directing a telegraph or telephone office.

This phenomenon was not unique to northern Mexico. In nineteenth-century Italy, society's almost hysterical fear of prostitution can be understood only against a background of economic and social change that brought visible numbers of single, unemployed, and homeless women to Italian cities. The prostitute was a woman alone, and to many middle-

and upper-class observers she embodied a cluster of traits, including idleness, illegality, immorality, and female autonomy, that were antithetical to the bourgeois ethic of the nineteenth century.[49] Likewise, in France, increased social mobility at the end of the nineteenth century led to a virtual tirade against social blurring, luxury, and the immorality of the streets. Here, the unregistered prostitute came to represent idleness, luxury, and pleasure, as opposed to the bourgeois values of work, economy, and happiness.[50] In France and Italy, as in Chihuahua, the prostitute served to symbolize class and other social conflicts.

She also provided the counterideal against which the honest woman could define herself: while prostitutes served for members of *sociedad culta* as important symbols of lower-class transience, immorality, and separateness, mothers of families represented stability, virtue, and progress. Middle-class Chihuahuans stressed women's role as mothers for two reasons. First, because mothers would nurture future generations of "cultured" workers, they represented the solution to the present social crisis. Second, motherhood became an important symbolic means of identifying proper male and female roles. Fulfillment of such roles seemed to promise a stable yet progressive society.

To accomplish this aim, members of *sociedad culta* expected to divert working-class life from the street into the home, where the working-class family offered, in theory, a means of stabilizing a society wracked by class conflict. The idealized family, inspired by the proper values, would provide an alternative to worker immorality, poor discipline, and nascent political consciousness.[51] In the struggle to control this new workforce, middle-class Chihuahuans regarded the home as the symbolic opposite of the tavern. The tavern consumed physical and moral energy, crushed good sentiments, and brutalized and eliminated life, honor, shame, and the desire to work; while the home represented joy, wholesome happiness, healthy enthusiasm, moral and physical regeneration, and progress. *El Correo* implored wageworkers to listen to their conscience in choosing between the two. Along with alcoholic libations, the tavern offered crime, shame, and repugnant passions, while home offered dignity, hope, high ideals, life, and the sweet nectar of domestic bliss.[52]

At the heart of the working-class family was the wife and mother. Indeed, many believed women to be a part of nature, able to live only in paternal or conjugal homes as daughters, wives, and mothers. They described women venturing outside the home or trespassing in man's sphere as mannish or hairy-chested.[53] Middle-class Mexicans were concerned that women would virtually become men, which illustrates that for them, deviation from traditional social roles seemed a violation of nature itself. After considering the merits of educating women, one *El Correo* contributor decided that women could only become experts at the cost of their charm, their purity, and their duties in the home. He concluded: "Each one in their own place. Women are able to be superior, but as women. In wanting to imitate men, they convert themselves into parrots or monkeys."[54] Family formation was considered to be woman's most important task in the Porfirian household. This was the duty that society and nature entrusted to women, and middle-class commentators identified the mother as more important than the nation-state in this task. One contributor to *El Correo* suggested that the Mexican mother could reasonably claim, "I am the state" (*El estado, soy yo*).[55]

Middle-class Chihuahuans, moreover, maintained that as natural dependents, and thus never entirely self-supporting, women could be paid a lower wage. Women entering the labor force to supplement family income or earn pin money, especially the wives and daughters of wageworkers, decreased wages by increasing the labor supply. Instead of utilizing supposedly natural family roles to justify paying women workers less, however, Porfirians employed the so-called law of the female labor market to justify enforced female domesticity. Woman had not come into the world to live in isolation; her place was with her husband in the conjugal home (*hogar doméstico*). It was the husband's task to sustain her and maintain the home. In place of working women, one contributor to *El Hijo del Parral* proposed better remuneration of masculine work and an increase in "family spirit" (*espíritu de familia*). Material and moral problems posed by working women be resolved when all males married and earned sufficient income.[56]

Middle-class Mexicans also regarded the working-class family as the best site for inculcating Porfirian developmentalist values. Women's central role in domestic life promised to sustain the working-class family and to provide a means of eliminating vice and of instilling the capitalist work ethic in the masses. For example, coal-mine managers in nineteenth-century French company towns, such as Decazeville, expected workers' wives to play similar roles. Such towns passed through stages, from company provision of material benefits, such as housing, to company encouragement of large families and the training of children in work discipline, and finally the introduction of shift work in mines and factories. The demands of this last stage prompted managers to stress wives' crucial duty in maintaining households in which their husbands, sons, and boarders could recuperate.[57] Although middle-class Mexicans emphasized the mother's role in inculcating the work ethic, they also regarded the home as a place of moral and physical regeneration.

According to members of *sociedad culta,* all these tasks could best be accomplished by ugly women: by contrast, beauty in women threatened proper male and female roles in the conjugal home. Writing in *El Hijo del Parral,* Dr. Manuel Flores characterized the family as woman's supreme mission on earth. How is it, he asked, that beautiful women, always triumphant in the world, found it so difficult to "assail and conquer a home"? In his opinion, beauty "intoxicated" much like alcohol, transforming a woman from submissive to dominant, from humble to snobbish, from slave to empress. The husband of a beautiful woman knew that he could not be master in his own house, boss in his home (*jefe en su hogar*), guide and conductor of his family. Not only was the beautiful woman a luxury, she was dangerous. Flores maintained that men married in order to have a woman whose only thought was of them, who loved them exclusively, but beautiful women ended up marrying their own beauty. On the other hand, ugly women (*las feas*) felt obliged to be intelligent and instructed. Of perhaps greater importance, they easily accepted their modest position, their isolation from the world, and their reclusion in the home. These women would not be distracted from maternal and wifely duties.[58]

Along with modesty and seclusion in the home, moral reformers described additional traits of the ideal mother. Not only did she embellish the home with her beauty, she was also to serve as guardian angel of her family. This entailed establishing domestic peace and contentment, sweetening the hours of suffering, and generously giving herself to husband and children. Middle-class males desired women to possess the trait of self-denial. The good mother sacrificed herself for her children. Even if she lived in opulence, surrounded by luxury, she should not abandon her children to a wet nurse unless physically unable to feed them herself. Far from losing her beauty through child-rearing, the good mother would always remain beautiful and enchanting to those who adored her. *El Correo* added that a good mother formed a Christian family that loved, feared, and worshiped God. Another writer described her as God on earth. She was the symbol of tenderness and the emblem of self-denial; a shield for sufferers, a guardian angel for children, and a redeeming arm for man.[59]

Other contributors offered advice to prospective mothers. One listed fifteen points of child care—including advice on breast-feeding, cleanliness, and general sanitation—and admonished women not to bundle or restrict their babies' movements.[60] Another proffered ten hygienic tips that combined characteristics of good motherhood with the work ethic: get up early, go to bed early, and keep busy during the day; the cleanest machines are those that last longest; adequate rest repairs and fortifies, too much rest debilitates; start to work at sunup; the clean and happy house makes an agreeable home; if living by manual labor, do not forget to embellish your intelligence and expand your thoughts.[61]

The ideal woman advocated by middle-class Chihuahuans valued simplicity, openness, and virtue. They contrasted her characteristics with those they regarded as unacceptable. Paralleling the ideal woman–bad woman division were dichotomies of simple–complicated, virtuous–degraded, open–deceptive, good–evil, and *sociedad culta–gente baja*. Desired characteristics could be acquired; through proper education, order, economy, cleanliness, integrity, valor, abnegation, and resignation would replace envy, pride, vanity, worries, superstition, gossip, jealousy, and rancor.[62]

Basic differences between men and women necessitated women's possession of these virtues. Married women could obtain lifelong happiness by acting as angels of peace, by not demanding the impossible, by providing tranquillity, and by never being seen disheveled or in dirty clothes. In the domestic sphere, prudence, tranquillity, hidden sacrifices, and self-denial were the opposite of domestic storms and annoyances. As one woman correspondent stressed, women in Mexico married for love and to spend the rest of their lives beside the men they loved. Men, on the other hand, placed ambition, social position, and comfort before love.[63]

Women, indeed, also contributed to *El Correo*, often blaming neglectful wives for problems in the home and for husbands' indulgence in vice. The advice, gleaned from personal experience, that a few women shared with their literate *compañeras* in northern Mexican homes suggests a tremendous sense of female guilt. According to these texts, a good wife was expected to transform inept and lost single men into reliable husbands and magnificent fathers. This was accomplished by anticipating and catering to all of their desires. How many husbands would not lead an orderly life, these women asked, if on returning home tired after work they found a caring reception and a table covered with simple, well-prepared food? Finally, if the husband should indulge in drink, the wife's duty was to discover the reason and take action. Such action typically meant love and patience, followed by more love and patience. If she herself were to blame for his drinking, it was up to her to change. Many characterized matrimony not as liberty, luxury, or the opportunity to be rid of domineering parents, but as a heavy burden requiring valor, virtue, and abnegation on the woman's part. While heroic actions were not necessarily required for a marriage to work, continuous effort was needed, because the happiness and honor of the family rested almost completely in the hands of the wife.[64]

The Mirror of the Middle Class

In the United States at the turn of the century, concepts of race, marriage, family, motherhood, womanhood, and manhood were essential components of what has been referred to as "civilized morality."[65] The married woman stood at the focal point of these ideals. In Chihuahua, middle-class Mexicans added virtue, education, work, and moralization to their definition of civilized morality. The mother ensconced in the conjugal home seemed to stand at the core of enlightened thought. Members of *sociedad culta* stressed the role of the mother in educating future generations of suitably motivated, sufficiently patriotic Mexican workers.

Similarly, in the United States during the Progressive era the middle-class family faced the possibility that a son or daughter might escape the confines of respectability to frequent saloons, brothels, theaters, gambling halls, boardinghouses, and city streets. The decision of members of the middle class to participate in moral reform might reflect less the wish to control others than the impulse toward self-definition, a need to avow publicly one's own class aspirations.[66]

Likewise, during the first half of the nineteenth century, the prime task of the emerging British ideology of home and family was less to influence others than to articulate the class-related feelings and experiences of the bourgeoisie itself. The domestic ideal became a "vital organising factor in the development of middle-classness, and in the creation of a differentiated class identity."[67] In Chihuahua, railing against alcohol, prostitution, gambling, and vagrancy, along with reaffirming the Catholic prescription of male and female roles, provided commentators with a means of articulating their membership in *sociedad culta*. Meanwhile, the cluster of qualities taken to characterize refined society—morality, education, virtue, family, motherhood, domesticity—furnished middle-class Chihuahuans with a means of class and self-definition.

In mid-nineteenth-century France, sexuality formed a part of the process of "class construction."[68] In France, middle-class self-definition included notions of sexual self-control that depended on opposite examples, or social "others." For these writers, the working class provided the social "other." Middle-class Mexicans also viewed the working class as the social "other"; yet they advocated a class-defined vision of national development that was meant to mobilize and control the entire society. They expected their actions to have an impact on all social classes: elite, middle, working, and vagrant. They believed that antivice legislation and school attendance would reshape the future of the country. Members of the middle class criticized elite behavior and attitudes as well as the perceived lack of patriotism and duty in the working classes. They also scolded their own number: in many tracts against vice, middle-class drinkers, vagrants, and gamblers received especially harsh criticism because they provided poor moral examples for the lower orders.

The message of home and family clearly was intended for mass consumption. In the mining town of Villa Escobedo, I. Sandoval, the *jefe municipal,* organized a mutual-aid society for mine workers (*operarios*). Membership benefits included insurance in case sickness or injury should prevent members from attending work. Sandoval campaigned extensively in all district mines, hoping miners would be encouraged to affiliate themselves with the society named, appropriately enough, "Protección del Hogar."[69] Clearly implied was the possibility that unprepared workers, should they become sick or injured, faced the loss of their home and family. References to the proletarian wife also predominated in middle-class condemnations of the high cost of living, a situation that weighed most heavily on the state's working-class families. Members of *sociedad culta* lamented the abuses carried out by small-scale merchants, one of the prime causes of the high cost of living, in their opinion: not only did it impose hardship on the lower and middle orders, but it ultimately threatened the destruction of the family.[70]

The debate over Sunday closing of commercial establishments in Chihuahua also exemplified middle-class hopes of reforming workers. In early 1903, the merchant association in Ciudad Chihuahua approved Sunday closing of clothing, vegetable, hardware, and grocery stores. Many middle-class commentators heralded the move as a great step forward in national progress because employees in the city could now enjoy rest and licit amusement. Instead of being merely work machines, workers who enjoyed Sunday rest could also be men; licit amusements promised to create cultivated men who would balance nutrition of the soul with that of the body. *El Correo* drew parallels between the legislation in Chihuahua and that of so-called cultured countries.[71] Others, however, were not so certain. Many believed that until *cantinas* followed Sunday-closing rules, nothing would change; workers would simply spend their time drinking on Sunday. In their opinion, work provided a more wholesome setting than these dens of iniquity.[72]

In Parral, a similar Sunday-closing movement met with resistance. Owners of the infamous "mixed establishments"—those selling alcohol in addition to groceries or other goods—refused to cooperate with municipal officials, citing the fact that they did most of their business on Sunday, payday for mine workers. Ignoring these complaints, local authorities implemented Sunday closing in Parral's commercial establishments in late 1906. They expected the measure to be a positive benefit to workers and to result in an overall improvement in morality.[73] While store owners who signed the accord generally followed its provisions, stores established after the agreement sometimes posed unfair competition by remaining open, as did many of those who made their living by selling alcohol. Seven employees of one maverick *cantina* owner complained directly to the governor: stressing the recuperative nature of Sunday closing and the moral and cultured example that it set, they demanded to be treated in the same manner as all other commercial employees.[74]

Conclusion

From the late colonial period through the Porfiriato, women of all social classes faced the "master discourses of domesticity."[75] Either as guardian angels or as prostitutes, women served as symbols for the *gente decente:* whereas the first category represented stability, virtue, and progress, the second embodied luxury, idleness, immorality, and criminality—all traits associated with the growing working class. While members of *sociedad culta* sought to form the working-class home as a space in which to discipline workers and inculcate developmentalist and patriotic values, women's domestication also offered an easily recognizable sign of membership in *sociedad culta.* In short, as women's domestication seemed to promise an orderly society, members of *sociedad culta* expected all women to fulfill the role of guardian angel in the home.

This same universalizing feature of middle-class ideology can be noted in France during the first half of the nineteenth century. There, the middle-class idea that workers need only adopt the values of the bourgeoisie in order to solve their problems was truly innovative. This belief would have no place in a society in which different classes were seen as "hierarchically organized groups with essentially different needs, mores, and aspirations."[76] In France, as later in Porfirian Mexico, members of *sociedad culta* struggled to reduce the cultural differences between worker and bourgeois that seemed to threaten the future of their society. In Chihuahua, enlightened Porfirians enacted morals legislation, founded schools, pressured parents to ensure their children's attendance, and advocated strengthening the mother's role in the home. At stake, they believed, was the future of their country. Only through education could a new generation become part of a *sociedad culta*. Order and progress did not merely entail economic development; they also meant moralization and "familialization" of all social groups in the image of the middle class. In this way, Mexico would become prosperous, civilized, and progressive.

Ironically, many residents sensed that progress was being imposed upon the community, prompting them to complain formally to local officials. Near the end of the Porfiriato, the *jefe político* attempted to enforce regulations requiring the installation of new sanitary plumbing in houses in Parral. Here was another municipal effort to promote hygiene and cleanliness, including threats of fines for noncompliance, which led to a flood of complaints. Petitioners, many of whom described themselves as workers (*operarios*) in local mines, emphasized their inability to pay for such improvements, given the lack of work in the district. One complainant captured the mood of many of the workers, declaring that such compulsion represented forced progress (*progreso forzado*).[77] It remains to consider how mine workers in Hidalgo District responded to moral reform, the cult of domesticity, and efforts to inculcate the capitalist work ethic.

5
Forced Progress
Workers and the Developmentalist Ideology

As investment in new technology transformed the mining industry at the turn of the present century, mine workers in Hidalgo District experienced a new regime of labor and personal discipline. Their response to it varied according to their circumstances, options, ideas, background, experiences at work, and lives in communities composed predominantly of mine workers and their families. Above all else, they constructed their view of the world and of themselves in reaction to the disparaging view of workers presented by members of *sociedad culta*. A basic division within the workforce is evident. On the one hand, many workers retained links to subsistence agriculture, thus avoiding complete dependence on wages and the market. They formed part of the *población flotante* that so infuriated middle-class Porfirians and American mine managers. On the other hand, many workers, often those completely dependent on wages, subscribed to the tenets of the developmentalist ideology articulated by those in the middle class. Rather than signifying complete acceptance of middle-class values, however, adherence to aspects of the moralization package helped express and reinforce working-class identity.

Yet working-class formation cannot be explained simply by reference to position in the process of production. Certainly, the long hours workers spent laboring in the mines and on other jobs associated with the mining industry contributed to the emergence of shared assumptions about work, wages, and justice. So did life in miner *barrios*. In urban spaces, working-class Mexicans jostled with their self-proclaimed social superiors for access to the streets and for the right to attend fairs and to express themselves in popular celebrations; they frequented *cantinas* and brothels, joined mutual-aid societies, and attended night school. More than this, however, the response of mine workers to capitalism and the Mexican state was informed by a popular perception of individual rights inherited from nineteenth-century Mexican liberalism. This folk liberalism—forged in the liberal-conservative struggles of nineteenth-century Mexico and fashioned by villagers to fend off a centralizing state—provided workers with the moral basis for legitimating their claims.

The Four Levels of "Class"

"Class" is a contested term. It has been used to refer both to location within a system of production and to the capacity to consume goods and services in the marketplace.[1] In *The Making of the English Working Class,* E. P. Thompson rejects defining class as a structure or a category. For him, class represents a historical relationship that occurs when common experiences lead some men to articulate their common interests against other men whose interests oppose theirs. In Thompson's work, the working class becomes an active participant in the making of its own history.[2] Although Thompson has been criticized for portraying the working class in romantic and heroic terms, his emphasis on the agency of the working class continues to influence strongly the research agenda in labor history. As Richard Price states, the task at hand is to "find a way of approaching labour history that will pay proper regard to its divergencies but still retain the notion that labour has been an agency in the making of its own history and in shaping the history of society."[3]

To accept "class" as a historically determined relationship is also to accept culture, traditions, values, and beliefs as part of the expression of class. Thompson uses the term *class consciousness* to define the way in which class experience is handled in cultural terms. Others have distinguished between "class-in-itself" and "class-for-itself." However, the in-itself/for-itself model implies that class formation can be inferred from class structure and that at some moment a class "in-itself" must act "for itself." To avoid this essentialist perspective and to incorporate within the study of class formation the new directions developed by social historians, Ira Katznelson has proposed disaggregating the concept of "class." He suggests that class in capitalist societies be conceptualized as four connected layers of theory and history: those of structure, ways of life, dispositions, and collective action.[4] By separating class in this manner, Katznelson also avoids a logical flaw apparent in Thompson's definition of class consciousness: that once a working class is "made" by external social conditions, it necessarily develops class dispositions and engages in class activity and politics. In Katznelson's framework, this becomes a matter for analysis rather than a given. His model is employed in this chapter to analyze working-class formation in Hidalgo District.

Katznelson defines the first level of class as the specific empirical contours of economic development. Here, class is an "experience-distant" construct concerned with identifying broad patterns of economic development at the national or regional level. The contours of economic development in Hidalgo District during the Porfiriato have been discussed, in the first two chapters. As mining increasingly became a capital-intensive proposition, managers of large industrial establishments, known as *extractories,* expanded gross output, implemented economies of scale, and embarked on a more thorough division of labor within the mines under their control. The utilization of labor-saving machinery, including compressed-air drills, aerial trams, and mechanical crushers, allowed them to replace skilled workers with those who were less skilled. Many peasant workers, forced off the land, became completely dependent on wage labor, while others combined subsistence agricultural work with seasonal work in the mines. Managers utilized force, economic incentives, and paternalism to try to create a disciplined and subordinated workforce; at the same time, state and local officials established new police forces and attempted to eliminate vice and popular celebrations. Moreover, increased dependence on foreign capital markets and on the world-market price of silver exposed mine workers to several periods of boom and bust.

At the second level of class, Katznelson treats the development of capitalist societies both at, and away from, work. Much nearer to actual experience, this level includes workplace social relations and ways in which class is lived in communities. In Hidalgo District—although a number of different and overlapping arrangements and relationships existed for accomplishing mine work—mine workers could be divided into two basic categories: a shrinking, well-paid group with skills; and a growing number of poorly paid workers, often with an agricultural background, doing dangerous and heavy work. For men in both of these categories, work could be carried out in exchange for a daily wage, payment by the task, or by means of a number of contract arrangements where *contratistas* often assumed the responsibility of forming and paying their own gangs of workers. In addition, as managers introduced new technology, tasks became simplified and arranged hierarchically.

Despite these important differences, all mine workers confronted danger on a daily basis in the mines and in the ore-processing facilities in the district. In the early twentieth century, Mexican mine workers and their counterparts throughout the continent labored in North America's most hazardous industry. In 1910, for example, a hard-rock miner in the United States was ten times more likely to be killed on the job than a worker in manufacturing. Moreover, disease, especially silicosis, killed more miners than accidents.[5] In Hidalgo District, the local newspaper lamented the fate of mine workers in a series of articles entitled "¡Pobres mineros!," in which the frequency of accidents and the high miner death toll were blamed on the apathy of mine owners and their *encargados*. *El Hijo del Parral*, in considering the behavior of mine owners to be criminal, called for governmental inspection and supervision of mines.[6]

There were many ways to die in and around mines in Hidalgo District. Premature explosions, explosions from left-over powder in old drill holes, equipment failure, inexperienced winch operators, improperly installed timber, falling rock, water, and falls all took the lives of mine workers. Although available records do not permit the calculation of the total number of accidental deaths in the district, anecdotal evidence reveals that few months went by without some fatalities. In July 1900, *El Hijo del Parral* described the carnage during a particularly destructive two-day period. On the first day, two workers were killed while descending into Las Cruces Mine. The next morning, three were buried alive in San Antonio Mine, while later that same day, a collapse in Los Remedios Mine killed four and injured six more.[7] In 1903, five workers perished when a spark ignited dynamite being transported by the mining company train to the Tecolotes Mine. Officials in Villa Escobedo listed three deaths for the month of September in 1904. The following year, three or four died each month in the Palmilla Mine alone. By 1906, the local press was lamenting the frequency of mining accidents in the district: *El Hijo* concluded that once workers went below ground, they were in imminent danger of never resurfacing.[8]

Nor did most mine owners make any provision to care for injured workers or to compensate the families of those who died on the job. One worker (*operario*) in Minas Nuevas complained to officials in Parral that those injured in the ore-processing facility of La Preseña Mine received no aid; lacking sufficient resources to tend to a coworker burned by molten lead, he requested assistance from local authorities.[9] Five years later, the situation still had not improved. In early 1905, *El Hijo del Parral* urged mine owners to provide economic assistance to workers injured on the job and to aid the families of those killed while working. According to the newspaper, meager wages made it impossible for workers to save money, and they and their families faced a desperate situation in the event of an injury.[10] As for the families of those killed at work, one commentator concluded that the "bourgeoisie" refused to give them even "the crumbs from their table."[11] Mine workers suffering from disease faced an equally bleak future. The seemingly endless number of miners who suffered from silicosis and the inhalation of mine gases (known as *maduros* in the mining towns) had no recourse but to roam the streets begging for charity.[12] Mine workers in the Apodaqueña Mine, for example, complained to José María Botello, the mine owner, that the foreman had forced them to work in stopes full of the gas released when dynamite exploded: such gases not only threatened to destroy their health, but to end their productive lives.[13]

After work, mine workers returned to settlements populated by other mine workers and their families. To be within walking distance of the work site, they settled in isolated camps throughout Hidalgo District. For example, many workers, rather than live in the town of Santa Bárbara, resided in their own neighborhood (*barrio*), known as "El Ultimo Esfuerzo," which was located near the Tecolotes and San Diego mines. Although the *barrio* was only a kilometer from the city center, local officials described it as "remote" and "isolated." Mine workers may have felt the same way: they chose to keep their children from attending school, rather than have them walk into town.[14] Often, mine workers lived in small groups clustered around outlying mines and company stores. The United Mines Company, for example, maintained a store and work group two kilometers from town. Likewise, Los Azules was six kilometers by rough road from Santa Bárbara. As Table 5.1 indicates, this settlement pattern was common in the district.[15]

Table 5.1
Miners within the Jurisdiction of Santa Bárbara yet Outside the Town, 1904

Company	Number of Workers
El Gavila	25
La Vencedora	20
Mina Adela	600
Perros Bravos	300
La Alfareña	300
San Francisco del Oro	200
San Diego	150
Grandeña	60
Guadalupe	30
La Paz	150
El Rayo	100

In the eyes of district officials, such a pattern of settlement prevented effective police vigilance of mine workers; in response, municipal authorities organized mounted patrols in an effort to enforce order and morality.[16]

Apart from mine workers and their families, few lived in these isolated communities. Even in the larger municipalities such as Villa Escobedo, workers comprised an overwhelming proportion of the population. This fact can be deduced from the reports of local officials. In early 1908, for example, municipal authorities there reported that the municipal treasury had spent little on public assistance because, as they put it, almost the entire population was composed of workers (*gente de trabajo*) earning a wage.[17] During downturns in the mining economy, workers had no choice but to leave town to search elsewhere for work. Police reports for Santa Bárbara suggest another reason why few nonworkers took up residency in mining areas. After the robbery of a Santa Bárbara company store, police maintained that they suspected three newcomers whom they had questioned the previous day. To discourage those not willing to work, the police commonly stopped new arrivals and asked them their reasons for coming to town. Those with little intention of working were simply not welcome.[18]

In Parral, many mine workers lived with their families in areas removed from the city center. As fluctuations in the mining economy made for a migratory existence, most were short-term renters living in poorly constructed adobe houses that lacked latrines and running water. Almost all described their homes as very small and isolated. Shortly after the near-collapse of the mining industry at the end of 1907, owners of urban properties reported to municipal authorities in Parral that most of their houses were now unoccupied. They stressed that mine workers—the largest group of renters—were no longer in Parral, but had been forced to leave the city to search elsewhere for work.[19] This was a pattern common across North America at the turn of the century. In Arizona, for example, the Phelps Dodge Company reported an annual labor-turnover rate of 100 percent. Such high rates of labor turnover have been interpreted in distinct, even contradictory, ways. Whereas Julian Laite views migration as a form of freedom and as a solution that miners adopted to avoid onerous working conditions, David Crew stresses that mine workers would have readily traded this questionable freedom for steady work. In addition, Crew notes that economic recession forced mainly unskilled workers to leave German mining cities.[20]

In Parral, economic downturn dislodged unskilled workers first. Many belonged to the transient, floating working class who rented rooms and occupied any available urban space. By contrast, some skilled workers, and even some lacking skills, had managed to acquire property, making it more difficult for them to leave town during a recession. In Parral, for example, the *jefe político,* in recognizing that workers owned their own homes, praised their efforts to improve these properties.[21] Lack of funds, however, prevented them from doing as much as the municipality demanded. In early 1908, the passage of municipal regulations mandating the installation of drainage systems in all houses and the threat of fines for noncompliance prompted working-class homeowners to petition state authorities for exemption from this requirement. Many petitioners, describing themselves as wageworkers (*jornaleros*), mine workers (*operarios*), and artisans, reported that they lived with their families in one or two rooms that they owned, or, in some cases, in one poorly built room, on a small lot they had managed to purchase. Petitioners stressed that because they were completely dependent on wage labor, the acquisition of property had taken a great deal of saving, sacrifice, and personal effort.[22]

Despite their ability to acquire property, these members of the more-or-less permanent working class were far from well-off. According to petitioning workers, the imposition of a five-peso fine for failing to install new drainage systems mandated by the municipality threatened them and their families with starvation. They described themselves as needy, poor, and without resources (*gente menesterosa*): the loss of even one centavo from their wage (*jornal*) would reduce their families' daily bread.[23] Along with emphasizing their poverty, petitioners pointed to their status as working people (*personas trabajadoras, operarios,* and *artesanos*). They stressed that they had no resources at their disposal other than those they earned working for a wage. For these petitioners, being a wage earner defined them in two ways: first, it revealed their dedication to work, and second, the precarious nature of their position. In the best of times, work in the mines did little more than furnish them with enough money to pay for the basic necessities. After late 1907, when fewer jobs and lower wages became the rule, life was even more difficult for wageworkers.

The high cost of living in the towns where mining predominated exacerbated the precarious economic situation of mine workers. As explained in Chapter 2, foodstuffs from surrounding regions found a ready market in the mining municipalities. While the need to import food contributed to the high cost of living, middle-class observers identified additional culprits, including speculators, monopolists, and greedy merchants. *El Correo* chastised small-scale merchants (those engaged in the business of provisioning workers) for abusing their clientele by raising food prices. While a liter of milk sold for thirty-eight centavos in Parral, it cost only fifteen in Valle de Allende, located a short distance away. Eggs were also overpriced. *El Correo* lamented that high food prices threatened to destroy both the proletariat and the middle class in Chihuahua, and the newspaper warned that the day was coming when only capitalists would be able to live.[24] Likewise, in Parral, the press held speculators and monopolists responsible for food shortages and high prices. *El Hijo,* believing that monopolists and trusts grew rich by deceiving the people, likened them to "vampires who suck the blood of the poor."[25] Another newspaper, *La Nueva Era,* concluded that the manipulation of markets led to high food prices in times of plenty as well as dearth. All expressed outrage that one individual or company should get rich by depriving the poor of their subsistence.[26]

Between 1900 and 1910, boom and bust in the mining economy caused fluctuations in the price of basic commodities and the cost of renting a room. In 1902, the *jefe político* gathered data on the relative cost of purchasing a kilo of bread, beef, mutton, and pork in predominantly mining and nonmining municipalities under his jurisdiction. The figures, presented in Table 5.2,[27] reveal the high cost of meat in the mining towns. Expensive in 1901, meat may have been beyond the reach of workers even during the boom periods before late 1907.

Table 5.2
Meat and Bread Prices in Hidalgo District Municipalities, 1901
(in centavos)

	Parral	Zaragoza	Minas Nuevas	Santa Bárbara	Balleza
One Kilo Bread	32	40	20	40	23
One Kilo Beef	24	20	30	30	24
One Kilo Mutton	30	20	35	30	30
One Kilo Pork	30	18	50	40	30

The *jefe municipal* in Santa Bárbara concluded that primary necessities were extremely expensive in all the mining towns.[28] In short, merchants charged whatever the market could bear. In times of great demand, the cost of rent went up along with the price of basic commodities. In 1910, for example, one Parral homeowner who rented to mine workers stated that he had reduced rents more than 50 percent since the end of the boom in late 1907.[29]

In contrast to workers who had managed to buy their own property, members of the floating population occupied any available location. Unfenced lots, uncultivated fields, and unwalled properties provided urban spaces where the floating population could gather and, even worse, at least according to middle-class observers, indulge unseen in vice. The *jefe político* described the temporary dwellings erected on these lots as pigsties and centers of filth, which offered a sharp contrast to the elegant and properly constructed buildings that often existed next door, and in his opinion, such sites attracted both material and human refuse.[30] More permanent residents concurred. In mid-1903, twenty-nine *vecinos* of the Viborilla *barrio* in Parral complained to municipal officials that seventy-five such shacks existed in their neighborhood. The petitioners refused to consider these inhabitants as residents of Parral because the occupants "come and go, without having a fixed and known domicile."[31] In another case, residents petitioned municipal officials to control their less permanent neighbors, who lived in a row of houses or in huts on their street. In their opinion, as the liquor sales that took place there attracted women of suspicious conduct, they found it necessary to keep their houses closed at all times to avoid scandal. They described the floating population that passed through these lodgings as the lowest class of people in town (*la gente mas baja del pueblo*), much given over to drink and consorting with prostitutes.[32]

The floating population was also perceived to be physically, as well as morally, threatening. According to *El Hijo del Parral*, the lack of proper sanitation facilities in most rental houses outside the center of the city prevented mine workers and their families from practicing "individual and domestic hygiene." Such "primitive" conditions forced renters—described as members of the disinherited classes—to cook, eat, and sleep next to their night soil. Public health, then, suffered when they disposed of their fecal material at the foot of the hill or on the riverbanks. Like many middle-class Chihuahuans, the newspaper associated the working class with dirt and envisioned working-class neighborhoods as the breeding ground of infectious and contagious disease. These sites promised potentially fatal consequences for all Chihuahuans, as epidemics, once started, would soon spread from the humble dwellings of workers to the mansions of the upper classes. While the newspaper blamed the rich for failing to keep up their rental properties, it remained convinced that, along with submissiveness and dedication to work, Mexico's people needed to be taught cleanliness.[33]

Middle-class fears of contagion were not groundless. Workers and their families suffered the consequences of high food prices, overcrowding, and inadequate sanitation facilities. Almost everyone connected with mining camps commented on the constant presence of epidemic disease. In Candelaria, Chihuahua, for example, Morris Parker recalled that many of the mine workers were covered with scabs and smallpox sores.[34] Ralph McA. Ingersoll, an employee in a mining camp in Sonora, described a continuous procession of funerals during the summer months where he worked. He recounted: "Living in their own filth, horribly overcrowded, the people were easy victims to disease, which would sweep through the camps like wild-fire."[35] In Hidalgo District, smallpox broke out in Villa Escobedo, in early 1905, and in Santa Bárbara, in 1909. In the latter case, officials reported that the disease spread in such an alarming manner that it caused panic among the inhabitants.[36]

Far from being inactive bystanders, district officials took measures to reduce the threat to public health. Between 1900 and 1910, the *jefe político* presided over an active vaccination campaign, his main weapon in the fight against smallpox. In Villa Escobedo, for example, 590 children were vaccinated in 1905. By the end of 1908, despite the emigration of workers from that municipality, 75 children received the vaccine. In Santa Bárbara, 1,160 inhabitants were vaccinated in 1909 (because of the smallpox epidemic). Even before that date, however, authorities had been active: over 300 children there had received the vaccine in 1905.[37] The year before, Governor Luis Terrazas had reminded Rodolfo Valles, the *jefe político,* of his public-health responsibilities; clearly, governmental officials at the state level expected district officials to contain or, better yet, prevent epidemics.[38] In addition to administering vaccinations, district police monitored incoming train passengers to prevent those with contagious diseases from disembarking. Moreover, during the 1909 epidemic in Santa Bárbara, municipal police disinfected houses that had been inhabited by smallpox victims. They also prevented anyone with the disease from leaving town and enforced a series of municipal regulations concerning sanitation and purification of the water supply. Inhabitants faced a twenty-five-peso fine for failing to have their children vaccinated.[39]

Lack of an adequate supply of fresh water contributed to the poor health of the residents of Hidalgo District. In Los Azules, even though local officials considered the piping of spring water to the center of town to be of vital importance for the health of residents, the project was not completed until 1908.⁴⁰ Elsewhere in the district, those living in Villa Escobedo obtained water from the drainage operations of mining companies. When the companies stopped operating after 1907, the municipality had no source of fresh water. In Parral, inhabitants complained that companies dumped sludge from their ore-treatment plants into the river, making the water unsuitable for use by those living downstream. During the final year of the Porfiriato, extensive use of the cyanide-treatment process created more dangerous waste. State officials requested that the Rayo Mining and Developing Company keep its waste as far away as possible from running water. Still, problems in obtaining access to fresh water earned Parral a reputation as an unhealthy place to live.⁴¹

Mine workers in Hidalgo District shared many aspects of a way of life both at and away from work. All confronted danger on the job, yet acknowledged the necessity of earning a wage: failure to work meant extreme hardship. Moreover, mine workers and their families lived in communities, either *barrios* near the mines or on the outskirts of larger urban centers like Parral, which were distinguished by their specifically mining makeup. Mine workers did not constitute a homogeneous group, however. Some became property owners and members of the more or less permanent working class that authorities and middle-class observers had hoped to create. This phenomenon can be confirmed from company sources. One ASARCo manager, for example, reported that after twenty-five years of operating a smelter in Aguascalientes, a generation of trained, and regular, workers provided labor. Likewise, in Cananea, company officials observed that Mexican skilled workers, especially mechanics, foremen, and others occupying responsible positions, worked as steadily as those from the United States.⁴² In Chihuahua, workers adopting similar habits can be distinguished from those more transitory, mostly unskilled workers who rented rooms and camped out in unoccupied lots in Parral's city center. Because workers in this second group were not completely dependent on wage labor in the mines, they were the first to leave during an economic downturn.

Working-Class Women

Women in Chihuahua also experienced working-class formation. Despite the advantages that accrue from disaggregating the concept of class, Katznelson's model is not without fault. He himself laments that neither he nor the contributors to his volume attend to the fact that class was experienced in gendered terms. In the hands of other historians, recognition of the gendered nature of class formation has already yielded impressive results. For example, in nineteenth-century England, working men and women, although influenced by the gender ideals of the middle class, developed their own notions of masculinity and femininity.[43] Whereas the ideal of those in the middle class was to exclude women from matters concerning money and household management, members of the working class emphasized the frugality of their women, whose task it was to make men's wages stretch as far as possible. Similarities in outlook also existed: working-class men, along with their counterparts in the middle class, while legitimizing themselves as workers, envisioned and valued women primarily as wives and mothers.

Wives, lovers, children, and other kin accompanied those who came to search for work in Hidalgo District. In Santa Bárbara in 1910 (a year of recovery for the mining industry there), census results reveal that 6,526 males and 5,751 females lived within the thirteen districts (*cuarteles*) that comprised the municipality.[44] Although the exact number of males and females within the jurisdiction of Villa Escobedo at the same time is not known, municipal officials there reported that a total of 5,060 inhabitants formed 961 families, occupying 743 homes.[45] Throughout Hidalgo District, a total of 29,005 males and 28,145 females were enumerated— a surprisingly high number of women, given the importance of mining in the district and the transient nature of the mining labor force.[46] Anecdotal evidence supports the conclusion that females migrated: the large number of families from Zacatecas, as well as their propensity to stick together, prompted local residents to refer to one neighborhood in Santa Bárbara as the *colonia* Zacatecas.[47]

In addition to providing unpaid domestic labor, women in Hidalgo District engaged in a variety of occupations and endeavors. They owned *cantinas*, ran brothels, worked as domestic servants, and sold fruit, vegetables, clothing, prepared meals, and other goods in the market and on the street. Women also peddled goods door to door and ran small neighborhood stores and pharmacies (*boticas*), where they often combined the sale of liquor with that of other foodstuffs and products.[48] Some of these enterprises were fairly substantial; in Villa Escobedo, for example, women owned five of the nineteen *cantinas* operating in 1906.[49] Others were so marginal that a small downturn in the mining economy put them out of business. Women also worked for wages: in the Colonia Galvan in Valle de Zaragoza, an area in Hidalgo District dedicated primarily to agricultural pursuits and livestock raising, Federico Sisniega employed forty women and thirty men in his thread and textile factory known as Bella Vista. All workers, male and female alike, earned the same wage—one peso per day.[50]

Many of these activities represented an extension into the public sphere of what were considered to be the private or domestic duties of women. The preparation and sale of food was a common occupation; in the early hours of the morning, for example, Rosa Polanco served *menudo* to workers before they went off to the mines, while in the afternoon, María Enriques served them meals in a small market in Villa Escobedo.[51] Also common was the job of providing accommodations: women rented out rooms on a temporary basis to mine workers and others who came to the mining towns. Yet another woman earned eight pesos for being a midwife (*partera*) to a mine worker's common-law wife.[52]

In their dealings with district authorities, many women, like their male counterparts, emphasized that they needed to work in order to live. Two women, faced with the prospect of a fine for failing to adhere to municipal drainage regulations on their property, pleaded with the *jefe político* for an exemption, basing their plea on the fact that wages from their "miserable" job, on which they depended completely to live, enabled them to buy little more than food of poor quality.[53] In another instance, in Santa Bárbara, a mother and daughter, accused of being clandestine prostitutes, denied the charge, claiming instead that they earned their meager living by sewing clothes for individual customers. The elder woman, describing herself as a "poor mother" and demanding justice, stressed that the only way she could earn a living was through work. In her next sentence, however, she seemed tacitly to admit her guilt. "Is it a crime," she asked rhetorically, "for a mother to make sacrifices, if necessary, in order to feed her children?"[54]

Although not necessarily a crime, such sacrifices, if they meant working in public, could call into question the moral character of the woman. In 1909, for example, the fact that she left her own home to work in that of another brought suspicion on Lusana López. Accused by the police of being a clandestine prostitute, she demanded to be left in peace until something could be proven against her.[55] In another case, the *jefe municipal* in Balleza noted that a certain widow, who operated a small stand selling fruit and sweet drinks next to the plaza, was a "woman of the bad life," destined for the bull ring, the place where female prisoners were kept.[56] While, in this instance, the person offering the opinion was clearly one of the *gente decente*, these attitudes often held among workers as well. For example, in Villa Escobedo, a mother and stepfather, an *operario* in the mines, despite not being certain from day to day of earning enough money to buy food for the entire family, refused to allow their fifteen-year-old daughter to serve as a domestic servant, even in an honorable home (*casa de honradez*).[57]

Although women often worked for wages or sold goods outside the home, male workers still expected their wives and partners to prepare food and keep house; in return, they promised to provide sustenance by bringing home the paycheck. Sometimes this "understanding" was made explicit: when B. T.—the fifteen-year-old would-be domestic servant mentioned in the preceding paragraph—was asked by judicial authorities if she had been seduced by M. F., her abductor (*raptor*), she replied no; given the insecurity of her existence, she had agreed to go with M. F. because he had promised to maintain her as long as she remained at his side.[58] Such arrangements outside the institution of marriage, of either the religious or legal variety, were fairly common. In one family in Parral, for example, two sisters lived in common-law relationships (known as *amasiato*) with mine workers—one a *jornalero*, and the other an *operario*. When one of the men broke off the relationship, he took the woman to her mother's home, stating: "Here, have your daughter, I don't want to continue living with her, thanks very much."[59] After exchanging numerous threats and few possessions, the relationship was over. Common, too, were illegitimate children (*hijos naturales*); of the 507 births in Santa Bárbara in 1909, 140 were illegitimate, as were 37 of the 193 births in Villa Escobedo in the following year.[60]

While common-law relationships often lasted for years, considerable violence could accompany the changing of partners. Six days after leaving one *amasio* to be with another, Luisa E., while out fetching water, was shot and killed near the company store of the Perros Bravos Mine. As her mother had overheard B. B., her former *amasio,* threatening to kill her if she refused to return to him, he figured as the prime suspect in the murder.[61] In another instance, Margarita A. entered a *cantina* in Parral and, without uttering a single word, took a knife and wounded a *barretero* at the bar. Although he stated that he had no quarrel with A., he did admit that he had recently left her after eight months of living together as man and wife.[62]

Physical abuse also occurred when males believed that their partners had not fulfilled their domestic responsibilities. When María Isabel M., a newlywed in Villa Escobedo, refused to grind corn to make tortillas at eleven o'clock at night, promising instead to do so in the morning, her husband, a day laborer (*jornalero*) in the mines, assaulted her. Despite the fact that she could barely move her arms because of the beating, he ordered her to make tortillas and serve breakfast the next morning. While judicial authorities did not consider this to be acceptable behavior (the marriage ended and he received forty days in jail), the husband justified his behavior by arguing that disciplining his wife was his right, given that she had failed to carry out housework (*trabajo doméstico*) that he had ordered her to do.[63]

Preparation of the mid-shift meal for mine workers, known as the "*lonche,*" was also considered to be one of the domestic duties of women. More than merely providing sustenance to workers, carrying this meal to work signified that female family members or *amasiatas* existed to prepare it. Its absence was noted by coworkers; as one mine worker testified at the inquest held to investigate the death of another, the deceased did not bring a *lonche* to the mine because he had no one at home to make it for him.[64] Preparing the *lonche* could also provide the setting for domestic violence: while putting coffee in a bottle, Felicitas A. was attacked by her husband, a mine worker, who became irate because he had not been informed the day before about the lack of meat and other provisions in the house.[65]

A list of a wife's material possessions confirms her domestic orientation. After her marriage to C. R. ended because of his violence, María Isabel M. demanded that the following items be returned to her from the house of her former husband: a *metate,* a bowl, a plate, two crystal glasses, a salt container, two aprons, two white linen dresses, eight petticoats, three coats, a hand-operated sewing machine, a dresser, and a picture of the Holy Child.[66] Variation from the norm of woman in the home carrying out domestic duties and man at work earning a wage was thought to be important enough to state explicitly when testifying before judicial authorities. When describing her relationship of five years with her common-law husband, Florentina A. noted that not only had she been faithful, but that it was she who had maintained him, not the other way around.[67]

An analysis of how class was lived in communities reveals that women, as well as men, experienced working-class formation. Women chose or were forced by their circumstances to labor for a wage and to provide goods and services that often represented an extension of what was considered to be domestic labor. Although the distinction between women's duties in the home and men's responsibilities in working for a wage was maintained by many in the working class, the ideal of the middle-class marriage was not. Consensual unions (*amasiato*) were fairly common, and often implied a bargain in which women agreed to provide domestic service in exchange for their daily bread, earned by means of a male's paycheck. As with their male counterparts, women laboring for a wage or selling goods generally stressed the precariousness of their economic positions. Moreover, both sexes depended on the jobs generated by the mining economy for their survival.

Dispositions

The third level of the Katznelson model, that of dispositions, attends to the ways in which people construct meanings to make sense of their experiences and the ways they share these meanings with others. Such dispositions may or may not be class based; that is a matter that must be demonstrated rather than assumed. In Hidalgo District, both skilled and unskilled workers shared with their rural cousins many features of what can be called popular culture. Drinking, gambling, and prostitution flourished in the mining centers. Rather than representing the breakdown of traditional popular values, these habits reflected the continued expression and vigor of such values. At the same time, in *cantinas,* billiard halls, and brothels, members of the new working class imposed their own schedule and rules of behavior. Wage earners confronted municipal authorities and middle-class society over access to streets and public places, and they asserted individual worth measured by honor and physical prowess rather than by family origin and wealth.[68]

Although males in all social classes acted in defense of their honor, contemporary observers insisted that lower-class males exhibited an exaggerated sense of personal honor.[69] Even though the *presidente municipal* in San Francisco del Oro found it difficult to restrain himself when his honor had been tarnished by drunks who failed to recognize his authority, he managed to do so.[70] Among the lower classes, however, it seemed as though a glance or an ambiguous word was sufficient to provoke a knife fight, for only through physical violence could a male salvage his honor after an injury or offense. Officials in isolated rural settlements throughout Hidalgo District concluded that no matter how insignificant the affair, many residents worked out their differences with bullets (*á balazos*). According to officials, in the rural areas honor served as a shield for almost any action, for rural residents considered stealing to be the only real crime. For many, there were no greater guarantees, either in the street or in court, than their rifles. In one episode in Santa Rosa, two families inhabiting a hacienda declared a feud to the death. Even though officials described the families as honorable, a veritable war erupted when one of the Sánchez clan galloped his horse over the Olivas's family dog. Local officials petitioned for help.[71]

In the mining camps, workers settled affronts to their honor by fighting. Although exact figures are unavailable, the crime of fighting (*riña*) appears frequently in judicial records. Officials in Santa Bárbara lamented the knifing death of a mine worker and the incarceration of another because they considered both to be hardworking. Likewise, in railroad construction camps, workers seemed to be brawling constantly. J. G. Peristiany notes that honor and shame are the preoccupation of individuals in "small-scale, exclusive societies where face-to-face personal, as opposed to anonymous, relations are of paramount importance."[72] The continuing importance attached to personal honor testifies, in part, to the rural origins of the wage-labor force.

So does the prevalence of popular or folk beliefs speak to such origins. *El Correo* anguished over popular health-care practices that included belief in witches and curses and the use of home remedies that it described as poisonous.[73] In Parral, *La Nueva Era* reported that witches (*brujas*) stuck pins in dolls and cast spells by using potions concocted with toads, rats, and various substances, including *pellote*.[74] These reports were not simply an airing of the prejudices of the *gente decente*. On one *rancho* within the jurisdiction of Santa Bárbara, for example, several women carried a young, and apparently sick, female relative to the doorstep of a widow to accuse her, and possibly her son, of causing the young woman's illness by casting a spell. The mother of the sick woman swore that her husband would take revenge on the widow's son, while yet another female relative vowed to rent a room opposite the widow's so that she could cast her own spell and, thus, make the widow suffer as she had caused the young woman to do.[75] In another instance, female teachers armed with mining candles confronted superstition head-on. Disregarding the popular belief that women underground brought bad luck, state officials gave the teachers a tour of the interior of a mine, where they observed Mexican drillers at work.[76] In a manner similar to those reformers in eighteenth-century France, members of *sociedad culta* in Chihuahua railed against folk beliefs in an attempt to regulate the frontier of superstitions.[77]

Rural and urban residents also shared beliefs concerning the proper role of government. All resented arbitrary local officials. In petitions tailored not to offend state leaders, petitioners lamented that despite honorable, clean, and just state government, local officials dreamt of absolute power and tried to become *caciques*.[78] Near the end of the Porfiriato, when the *jefe político* in Parral attempted to enforce regulations requiring the installation of new sanitary plumbing in Parral's houses, his actions resulted in a flood of petitions. Petitioners, in describing themselves as mine workers, emphasized their inability to pay for such improvements, given the lack of work. Crescencio Sáenz captured the mood of many workers who had managed to acquire small properties when he protested that such compulsion represented forced progress (*progreso forzado*). Sáenz lectured authorities on the true laws of political economy. He envisioned a more humanitarian and moral definition of progress that placed the greatest possible sum of goods with the greatest possible number of individuals. Under this kinder, gentler version of progress, the economy would operate in a consensual manner to develop resources without exhausting them. According to Sáenz, the *jefe político* in Hidalgo District was corrupting true progress with his arbitrary and tyrannical local rule, in which he treated inhabitants with the arrogance of a sultan.[79]

Such views constituted popular or folk liberalism.[80] Throughout Mexico, the popular classes drew their own lessons and heroes from the past. They revered Benito Juárez, honored the Constitution of 1857, and celebrated victory against the French and the conservatives in the 1860s; these figures both inspired and justified resistance against abusive governmental authorities. That the popular classes premised their critique of society on the same events that Mexican elites glorified and idealized in ritual to legitimate the social order confirms James Scott's conclusion that the dominant discourse often provides the symbolic tools from which resistance can be fashioned.[81] Like plebeians in eighteenth-century England, the popular classes in northern Mexico borrowed the dominant themes of elite political rhetoric and turned them back against their own rulers.[82] Residents of Hidalgo District, like other industrial workers in Mexico, protested the abuse of rights that they firmly believed the revered Constitution of 1857 guaranteed to all Mexican citizens.[83]

Moral Economy

While mine workers shared certain beliefs with rural and other residents of Hidalgo District, a working-class culture based on life in the mines and in mining communities is also apparent. Workers, especially those who earned their living exclusively from laboring in the mines, subscribed to a set of values that informed and legitimized their actions—values that managers and state officials characterized as nothing other than thievery and the violation of private property. Faced with the law, workers cited custom to defend what they considered to be their inherent rights. When faced with authorities whom they deemed had acted against norms sanctioned by the mining community, they took action. In short, mine workers contested official versions of reality and advanced their claims to a livelihood by positing an ideal, or moral economy, the unwritten rules of which, they felt, all in the community, including those in power, were obliged to share.

More than twenty years ago, E. P. Thompson employed the term *moral economy* to characterize the strongly held notions of rural residents in eighteenth-century England that defined legitimate and illegitimate practices in marketing, milling, and baking. He argued that the violation of these beliefs, held as traditional rights and customs and supported by community consensus, rather than food shortage itself, motivated and legitimized collective action in times of dearth. Since then, moral economies have been discovered underlying collective action in societies as varied as Burma and Bolivia, Madras and Morelos.[84] While Thompson agrees that no other term seems to describe the way in which peasant and early industrial communities regulated many "economic" relations according to nonmonetary norms, he prescribes caution and the need to redefine the term depending on the historical context at hand. Although the moral outrage associated with food shortages in the English case was absent in northern Mexico, the term *moral economy* must be retained, for it alone conveys the sense of workers that earning enough to live on was their due. In northern Mexico, mine workers advocated a moral economy in the market in labor rather than in subsistence goods, as in Thompson's case.

According to mine workers, their most basic inherent "right" was that of earning a living. Depending on the circumstances, they drew upon this assumption to legitimize numerous actions, including entering into mines not being worked by companies or individuals to remove ore; pocketing pieces of ore rich in silver or gold from mines where they worked; augmenting what they considered inadequate remuneration by theft; reselling supplies, especially powder, that had been provided by the company; and striking in support of increased wages. Although managers and officials tried vigorously to prosecute workers engaging in such behavior, hoping that making an example of those caught would deter others, these practices were so widespread and sanctioned by the mining community that they could not be stopped. As one *contratista* stated when accused of theft, if the resale of blasting powder was going to be considered stealing, then, without a doubt, the jail would be full because everybody was a thief.[85]

Many would also have to be considered guilty of trespassing, for mine workers regarded unworked mines as legitimate places to prospect and to remove ore. The fact that the Los Remedios Mine, near Santa Bárbara, had not been worked or patrolled by a watchman for four years persuaded four *barreteros* that they were justified in extracting metal from it, even though it had been denounced by the Compañía La Montezuma.[86] Common enough during the Porfiriato, the practice of taking ore from unworked mines escalated to unprecedented levels during the Mexican Revolution as mines closed, throwing men out of work and leaving them without a way to secure a livelihood, and the means of repressing such behavior evaporated. While thefts had taken place in the Palmilla Mine before the outbreak of the revolution, James Long, of the Alvarado Mining and Milling Company, complained to the *jefe político* that well-organized gangs of men were robbing the mine on a regular basis in 1911. Although watchmen reported armed gangs at work on 10, 15, and 28 October that year, local authorities could do little to stop them.[87] Two years later, ASARCo managers in Santa Bárbara reported that up to four hundred workers entered company mines each day to "steal" ore; according to managers, these workers, whom they described as *peones*, believed they could enter mines and take all the ore they wished. So well organized and sanctioned was this behavior that many workers who had labored for the company in Santa Eulalia formed ore-stealing gangs that operated with the connivance of state and local officials. In 1914, ASARCo, the Chihuahua Mining Company, the Buena Tierra, and the San Toy Mining Company formed a protective association to try to stop the theft and the subsequent sale of ore. Its lack of success can be judged from the fact that former workers continued to gouge out the richest ore, load it onto burros, and then haul it to Santa Eulalia and Ciudad Chihuahua to be melted down in adobe furnaces for eventual resale in El Paso.[88] The increased incidence of "theft" during the Mexican Revolution represented not a new form of resistance, but given the inability of the state or companies to mount a response, an opportunity for workers to exercise more fully an older form of resistance that had long been sanctioned by popular custom.

In early 1913, the capture of one such gang in Santa Bárbara resulted in testimony that exposed the workings of this informal economy as well as the attitudes of mine workers. In this case, *contratistas* labored by night (not in itself unusual in a mining district with a tradition of regular night shifts) in an old mine known as the Espíritu Santa, an ASARCo property. After removing the ore, they loaded it onto burros and delivered it to a local merchant. When confronted by armed ASARCo managers, the mine workers denied any wrongdoing, claiming that because the mine had not been worked for a long time and, thus, in their opinion, had been abandoned, anyone could work there. Pomposo Rico, the merchant for whom they were working and a man of some resources and standing in the community (the mine workers referred to him as "don"), also denied breaking the law. He explained that he had rental agreements with local mine owners to work the El Carmen, Las Margaritas, La Indita, and La Eureka mines, giving 15 percent of the amount mined to the owner while he kept the rest. To carry out these operations, he had employed the workers who had been caught as *barreteros,* paying them about two pesos a day to do the work. Once the easily accessible ore in these properties had run out, he had hired these same workers as *contratistas,* providing them with the necessary supplies to locate and mine any ore they discovered on their own. In other words, it was not his fault if ore had been illegally obtained, but that of the *contratistas.*[89]

The knowledge possessed by workers and their multiple identities as wage laborers, independent prospectors (*gambusinos*), and *contratistas* both nurtured workers' attitudes and made it impossible for authorities to control their behavior. When thefts of rich ore occurred, managers often suspected their own *contratistas,* not simply because their daily presence in the mine gave them plenty of opportunities to steal, but rather because they had the ability to differentiate between grades of ore. As D. H. Bradley stated when describing the *contratistas* at work in his mine in San Francisco del Oro, the only people who had knowledge of the existence of metal and the richness of it were his *contratistas* because, as miners by trade, they knew the quality of the rock.[90] Although he was not so sure about the capacity of the rest of his workforce to be so discerning, other documents reveal that many workers, who described themselves as *barreteros* or simply *operarios,* worked as *gambusinos* on their own time or between stints of waged labor, indicating their ability to do just that. Such specialized knowledge made workers potentially dangerous.

The case of a sixteen-year-old *operario* accused of theft reveals both his sharp eye and the continuing practice of independent prospecting. Charged with stealing ore from the Shephard Mine in Batopilas, Ygnacio Moreno protested his innocence, maintaining that he had obtained the ore in question by working as a *gambusino* in the nearby *arroyo* del Camuchin. Although he had worked for four years in the Shephard Mine (that is, since the age of twelve), he, along with many others, took off weeks, even entire months, at a time to prospect on their own. As ore discovered in this way was taken to Batopilas on a daily or weekly basis to be melted down—often by workers who regularly worked for Shephard—it was impossible to distinguish between ore that had been obtained by *gambusino* methods and ore stolen from the mine.[91] Further complicating the situation for authorities in Batopilas was that work there continued to be carried out under the *partido* system well into the twentieth century. Because mine workers received a share of the ore rather than, or in addition to, a wage, not only did they regularly have ore from the mine in their possession, but their remuneration depended upon their ability to distinguish between grades of ore.[92]

Although the *partido* system was not used in Hidalgo District, mine workers there were, at different times and among a great many other things, wage laborers, *contratistas,* and *gambusinos.* They infuriated managers by stealing ore, like the three workers who hid rich ore in sacks throughout the San Juanico Mine where they worked, intending to retrieve them later.[93] For workers, a thick layer of custom blanketed this behavior with legitimacy. As a young *barretero* working in the Palmilla Mine admitted to judicial authorities when caught red-handed in 1920, of course he had taken the ore in question. Yet, as far as he was concerned, his actions did not constitute theft. Rather, because it was impossible to live on the salaries paid by the mining companies, he believed it to be "fair" (*lícito*) to take some ore that the company was not likely to miss anyway. After all, he argued, this was a long-established custom among mine workers (*mineros*).[94] Other workers advanced the same justification to defend the sale of supplies, especially powder, that they had originally obtained from the mining companies in order to carry out their work. Managers admitted as much. It is well known, stated S. E. Reed, manager of ASARCo, that workers took powder that was left over, after setting off the *barrenos,* from the interior of the mine to sell in small quantities to local merchants. When confronted by authorities, local merchants denied breaking the law and cited the force of custom in their defense: How could this be considered a crime when they had always bought powder from workers? As in the case of "don" Pomposo Rico, the sale of powder and other mining supplies linked workers to legitimate businessmen in the local community; in this case, to those in the secondhand-goods business.[95]

In many ways, the theft of ore and mining equipment in northern Mexico had much in common with poaching, as favored by European peasants in the eighteenth and nineteenth centuries. In both cases, not only did subordinate groups make off with goods that enabled them to subsist; they also felt that their acts were a legitimate means of enforcing natural or inherent rights. The theft of tools, for example, supported two strategies for eking out a living: workers stole supplies to obtain cash from local merchants, on the one hand, and, on the other, to get the equipment necessary for undertaking mining on their own. While one mine worker in Santa Bárbara pawned the level, two hammers, bar, and brace he had taken from the San Nicolas Mine for cash, others valued these commodities as tools of the trade.[96] Access to mining tools was so important that one worker saw fit to attack another almost two years after he had refused to lend him a hammer.[97] Almost always, mining managers blamed past or present workers when thefts occurred, because workers possessed the knowledge, opportunity, or motivation (or all three) to carry out the crime. Often, they identified a particular grievance, especially the loss of a job, as the factor precipitating the robbery. Their comments reveal that theft formed part of the struggle over the appropriation of the product of work.[98] Theft is essential to an analysis of class relations once it comes to follow a consistent pattern and takes on the dimensions of a struggle in which property rights are being contested. The theft of ore and mining supplies by mine workers in northern Mexico meets both these criteria.[99]

Additional informal patterns of worker behavior emerged in northern Mexican mines. Rather than comply wholeheartedly with the dictates of managers and *pobladores,* workers reserved for themselves the power to make certain decisions on the job. In doing so, they often treaded a fine line between economic necessity and self-preservation. Workers occasionally refused to labor under conditions that they considered unsafe or in a manner that violated customary arrangements, despite the fact that most of those laboring for a wage needed to work regularly to feed themselves and their families. Such was the case when Pedro Corral, a twenty-year-old *carrero,* showed up for work at the Tecolotes Mine in 1899. Although he usually pushed the ore car with his uncle, Feliciano Corral, sickness had prevented him from working that day. When the company refused to provide a work partner, or *compañero,* Corral decided to return home rather than work alone, for he feared the car would overturn. That Corral decided to forego work was not unusual: *barreteros* often avoided working in stopes where rocks seemed poised to fall or old drill holes indicated the potential for explosion. They also left mines with poor working conditions like dampness for drier ones.[100]

Workers, especially those underground, chose overwhelmingly to leave when confronted with dangerous or unsatisfactory working conditions.

While managers lamented the existence of the *población flotante* and often blamed worker absenteeism on the supposedly inherent inability of those of the "Mexican race" to apply themselves consistently to work, for workers mobility represented one of their few available options. Both a strategy against complete dependence on wages and a spontaneous, collective response on the part of those who already were, mobility formed part of a traditional way of life in mining communities dating to the colonial period. By choosing to look elsewhere for work, workers could apply pressure on managers—who, after all, were intent on securing a stable, dependable labor force—to ameliorate the worst of the poor working conditions and even, occasionally, to improve wages. Moreover, even when workers remained with the same company, they often refused to accept permanently the work categories assigned to them by managers. Rather than labor exclusively as a *perforista*, for example, workers took jobs above ground when they became available.[101]

These strategies and the beliefs that prompted and legitimized them, while subscribed to by many in the mining community, found perhaps their most complete expression in the work gangs, or *cuadrillas,* formed by mine workers. The *cuadrilla,* assembled to complete specific tasks or responsible for the entire mining operation, brought together skilled and unskilled workers under the direction of a *contratista.* For those with skills, working as a member of a crew offered some control over the process of production and the chance to develop into a craftsman; for apprentices, assistants, and unskilled workers, it could be a place to pick up some skills and learn the secrets of the trade. Sariego Rodríguez and Santana Paucar conclude that the productive autonomy of the *cuadrilla,* with each gang responsible for its own actions and often working in relative isolation, created a strong sense of internal cohesion among *cuadrilla* members.[102] Too much emphasis, however, should not be given to the solidarity among *cuadrilla* members. *Contratistas* frequently formed *cuadrillas* from those who happened to show up at the mouth of the mine each morning. Unskilled workers often began their workday by walking from mine to mine, hoping to pick up any job. In many cases, the *cuadrilla* lasted only until the particular task had been accomplished.[103]

Within more permanent *cuadrillas,* ties of family or regional origin could reinforce the sense of unity created on the job. Workers in the *caudrilla* formed by Eleno Medina to work in the San Diego Mine in Santa Bárbara, for example, all came from Zacatecas, as did many of their wives.[104] In other groups, brothers, cousins, and in-laws worked side by side.[105] Unfortunately, the statements of workers in accident reports offer a mere glimpse into the social composition of work groups.

Members of *cuadrillas,* regardless of the extra-work ties that bound them, often socialized with fellow *cuadrilla* members once the work was done. In part, this was natural given the mobile, transitory nature of the workforce and the consequent absence of friends and family. The shared work experience, close contact on the job, and the need to depend on coworkers also promoted this pattern of sociability. Members of a gang at work digging a tunnel in the Tecolotes Mine in Santa Bárbara, for example, were together twenty-four hours a day as they grabbed a few hours sleep in the mine between 3:30 in the morning, when they quit work, and 6:00 A.M., when they woke up.[106] Workers often stopped to call on coworkers or to share a bowl of *menudo* with them before setting off for work. They attended the same dances and local fiestas and got drunk together.[107]

Cohesion among *caudrilla* members was so apparent that it could bring suspicion to the entire *caudrilla,* rather than to the individuals composing it, when criminal activity or a challenge to the status quo took place. Such was the case with Eleno Medina's *caudrilla* after a blast of dynamite damaged the roof of the house where the *jefe municipal* lived. According to an unreliable witness, Medina admitted to selling powder, and all of the material needed to set off explosions in drill holes, to others rather than back to the company. In this instance, however, one member of his *cuadrilla* had supposedly smuggled a charge out of the workplace and had been heard conspiring with coworkers to blow up the *jefe municipal.* Although Medina, members of the *cuadrilla,* and their wives stated that the group had been working and knew nothing of the affair, another witness claimed to have heard three of Medina's men debate whether or not the bomb was made well enough to go off. Although the investigation was inconclusive, the case seemed to confirm the worst fears of managers and officials—that the logical consequence of adherence to the moral economy was an overturning of the social order.[108]

Collective Action

The experience of the new conditions of industrial work led skilled workers, especially, to a common consciousness of being dependent on earning a daily wage. Wage laborers (*jornaleros*), in petitioning for relief from drainage regulations, stated that the only resources they had at their disposal came from work. For them and their families to subsist, they were "subject to a daily wage, earned with most sacred work."[109] Forty-four petitioning *operarios* made the same point when they revealed that they had no resources other than those they earned by working. One worker from Santa Bárbara explained, "The day I don't work is the day my family doesn't eat."[110] Not surprisingly, skilled workers coalesced either to defend their earnings or to demand increased wages. In 1906, striking carpenters (skilled workers) in the Tecolotes Mine made one demand—a salary increase. Moreover, shortly after the fall of the Porfirian regime, an *operario* from the same mine attempted to win election in the district by promising mine workers that his first act as an elected official would be to call a strike to demand increased salaries and fewer hours of work for miners.[111]

Above all else, workers constructed their view of the world and of themselves in response to the disparaging view of them presented by members of refined society. Those completely dependent on earning a wage perceived and resented being characterized as having no standing in the community. Like their counterparts throughout Mexico, Hidalgo District workers resented the lack of respect accorded to them by the rest of society.[112] Rather than reject the moralizing discourse of the middle class, they strove to be accepted as equal members of decent society.

Other Mexican skilled workers also hungered for respect. Stung by accusations in the press and from Porfirio Díaz that they did not know how to apply themselves to work, skilled members of the Union de Mecánicos Mexicanos insisted that they had been trained since apprenticeship in the American system. Over the years, they had acquired the custom of working like foreigners to the point that they believed that the work of Americans and Mexicans should be regarded as equal in efficiency and quantity. In 1908, in the face of stiff criticism, Silvino E. Rodríguez, general president of the union, defended the mechanics' goal of obtaining a holiday paying tribute to work. Mexico City's press pointed to the many holidays (both official and unofficial) already enjoyed by workers, and to the great damage inflicted on industry by worker absenteeism. Rodríguez's response testifies to the degree to which skilled workers accepted the dominant ideology. He maintained that his union had been one of the first to reduce and to limit the "innumerable days of fiestas" that had caused the economic failure of so many industries and so much hardship for the working class, and he added that he hoped to reduce the total number of holidays to eight per year. Moreover, he dreamed of the education, moralization, and elevation of the working class—all concepts esteemed by those in *sociedad culta*.[113]

Forming and joining mutual-aid societies provided workers, especially artisans (*artesanos*) and employees (*empleados*), with an important means of proclaiming their membership in *sociedad culta*. In fact, the mutual-aid societies organized in Chihuahua during the Porfiriato were composed almost entirely of men in these two categories. Between 1890 and 1910, painters, bakers, tailors, shoemakers, printers, mechanics, blacksmiths, carpenters, employees, and others formed societies, often with the encouragement of the Catholic church as well as of those in power.[114] In 1904, for example, the Sociedad Juárez de Obreros organized a series of conferences for workers covering such topics as political economy, morality, hygiene, and civic instruction.[115] Later that same year, the society joined other associations, including the Cámara de Comercio, the Círculo Mercantil Mutualista, the Sociedad de Mecánicos Mexicanos, the Sociedad de Carpinteros Mexicanos, and the Unión de Garroteros Mexicanos, to protest the publication of a book by Francisco Bulnes in which he criticized Benito Juárez.[116] These activities reveal the cultural values that artisans and employees shared with the *gente decente*.

Attendance at night schools, many of them established by mutual-aid societies, provided another opportunity for workers to portray themselves as *gente decente*. The Sociedad Cooperativa de Obreros, established in Parral before the turn of the century, operated a night school attended, on average, by thirty-five workers.[117] So did the Sociedad Mutualista de Trabajadores Unidos de Hidalgo. Formed in Parral in the late 1870s, this mutual-aid society, in which mine workers comprised the largest single category of membership, stressed the importance of education. In cooperation with the Biblioteca Franklin de Hidalgo del Parral, it helped found schools in the district.[118] In Santa Bárbara, the *jefe municipal* granted the Sociedad Mutualista de Obreros "Vicente Guerrero" permission to establish a night school in 1906, with classes to be held in the public school building.[119]

Those in power, far from perceiving mutual-aid societies as a threat to the status quo, viewed them as noble institutions. In Ciudad Chihuahua, Federico Sisniego, principal shareholder in the "La Paz" factory, insisted that factory workers—most of whom were women—use money usually spent on raffling off a bonus to form a mutual-aid society.[120] Nearby, in Santa Eulalia, Francisco Aguirre y Varela organized a mutual-aid society that offered mine workers, in exchange for a monthly payment of two pesos, medical care and food if they were injured, and a decent burial, as well as a small sum for the family, if they were killed on the job.[121] In Villa Escobedo, the *jefe municipal* established a mutual-aid society, known as

Protección del Hogar, and encouraged all mine *operarios* to join. Membership entitled workers to assistance in paying their medical expenses as well as financial help if illness prevented them from working.[122]

In other areas of the state, like Jiménez, the Catholic church sponsored classes for workers. In this instance, education was meant to serve as an antidote to worker violence; as *El Correo* concluded, not only would night schools open new horizons of morality and progress to the working class, they would also substitute education and instruction for dynamite, armed strikes, and violent confrontations.[123] The newspaper featured a regular column for workers, and many contributors saw themselves as engaged in a struggle against socialism for the allegiance of the working class. Others, however, were not convinced of the redemptive power of education. Although they acknowledged the need for workers to be enlightened, doubting Catholics considered education, which they described as the "ignorant Jacobin solution," to be part of the problem rather than a possible solution. In their opinion, workers were in much greater need of religion.[124]

For many artisans and employees, the exclusive association of specialists, whether organized under the auspices of church, state, or independently, was judged the best course to follow because it seemed to offer, when combined with instruction, moral and intellectual redemption. Intellectual development was the stated goal of the Unión de Carpinteros Mexicanos, the Sociedad Mutualista de Empleados, and the Sociedad Cooperativa de Obreros, among others, and it was to be accomplished through education and moral improvement.[125] Middle-class observers grudgingly acknowledged the impact of mutual-aid societies. Describing in extremely paternalistic terms the activities of the Sociedad Cooperativa de Obreros that attempted to promote the instruction and advancement of the working class, *La Nueva Era* conceded that it was imparting, albeit on a "rudimentary basis," knowledge to intelligences that lay "in the most complete ignorance."[126]

Along with schools, the establishment of libraries denoted individuals and societies as respectable. In Parral in 1907, the Sociedad Mutualista de Empleados announced plans to found a library, as did the Liga Anti-Alcohólica "Ocampo" the following year. In place of educating the minds of workers, however, members of this latter organization, with their motto of "For the country and for the home," anticipated that their library would support the "honorable and studious youth" of the middle class.[127] Cultural activities also separated "respectable" from "rough." A description of a reception hosted by the Sociedad Cooperativa de Obreros in

1900 reveals the aspirations of its members to be regarded as part of the first category. The evening's activities included a recitation of poetry by Professor Juan Holguín, a mandolin performance by don Jesús Gutiérrez and Professor Aurelio Páez, and a vocal solo by María Barbachano. Colonel Ahumada, the governor, served as the society's honorary president.[128]

Workers who did join mutual-aid societies also found that they could take action through such societies on issues of importance to them. Officials of the Unión de Carpinteros Mexicanos, for example, complained of the treatment they received at the hands of foreign bosses. Disgruntled carpenters resented the foreign boss not so much because of his nationality, but because he discriminated against them in the workplace. Not only did he pay foreign workers twice as much; he offered to hire Mexicans only as helpers for the American workers, rather than as skilled carpenters.[129] In Cananea, Sonora, the high proportion of American skilled employees and the higher wages paid to Americans prompted Mexican skilled workers to protest and to organize unions. Unmet demands for better pay, promotion, and "Mexicanization" led workers there to strike in 1906.[130]

Before 1910, managers of foreign mining companies in Mexico responded to some of the demands of Mexican skilled workers. After the 1906 strike in Cananea, managers there implemented a policy of replacing foreign with Mexican skilled workers "in all ordinary cases as rapidly as possible . . . and to promote [them] to the more responsible positions as rapidly as they could be trained for such positions."[131] In this way, American workers there were gradually reduced from 40 percent of the workforce in 1906 to 16 percent in 1910, and finally, 13 percent in 1912. By 1916, Mexican nationals occupied the positions of sub-foreman, assayer, civil engineer, department manager, store manager, and bookkeeper in Cananea. After 1906, the Mexican Mining Journal considered the replacement of Americans by Mexicans to be general policy throughout the mining industry in northern Mexico.[132]

Conclusion

The different levels of the Katznelson model—structure, ways of life, dispositions, and collective action—do not imply the existence of a series of stages along which a working class "progresses" or "develops." Rather, the model offers a means of organizing disparate subject matter, usually lumped together in a discussion of class and class consciousness, to facilitate analysis. In Hidalgo District, mine workers and their families shared many aspects of a way of life. Most lived in neighborhoods with others much like themselves, either in *barrios* near the mines or on the outskirts of larger urban areas. For both men and women, failure to work meant extreme hardship. Male-female relationships, either of *amasiato* or marriage, were often premised upon a tacit agreement that a woman would exchange domestic labor for sustenance by means of a man's paycheck. Men claimed the right to "discipline" women, usually through corporal punishment, if they felt that they had failed to live up to their side of the bargain.

At work, mine workers confronted danger on the job and came to experience the necessity of earning a wage. The shared work experience, close contact on the job, the need to depend on coworkers, and their pattern of socializing meant that these beliefs were often most fully expressed in *cuadrillas,* the work units formed by skilled and unskilled workers under a *contratista.* Workers also posited an ideal, or moral, economy, premised on the assumption that they had an "inherent" right to earn a living. All in the mining community—from day laborer to skilled carpenter to *contratista* to merchant in the town—justified their actions on the basis of this widely held belief. Yet mine workers did not form a homogeneous group. Both on the job and at home, some—most often those with skills—received better wages, acquired property, and began forming mutual-aid societies.

Neither did dispositions necessarily follow from one's place in the process of production. Skilled and unskilled workers shared many aspects of what can be called a rebellious popular culture that included indulgence in vice, especially drinking, gambling and prostitution, and the importance of masculine honor. Such beliefs attest to the rural origin of much of the labor force. Moreover, workers borrowed the dominant themes of elite discourse and turned them back against their own rulers. All shared a set of beliefs—about the proper role of government and their rights under the Constitution of 1857—that constituted folk liberalism. These assumptions, when applied in the setting of the workplace, had the potential to overturn the status quo.

Moreover, skilled workers, in particular, were drawn to the moralizing discourse of the middle class. To emphasize their adherence to morality, progress, and enlightenment (characteristics denied to them by the *gente decente*), they formed mutual-aid societies and attended night schools. These workers constructed their view of the world and of themselves in reaction to the disparaging view of workers presented by the *gente decente.*

Although they asserted their membership in *sociedad culta,* skilled work-ers also developed a distinctive concept of their own worth, based largely on their dependence on wages and pride in their role in the process of production. Through mutual-aid societies, they began to struggle over the wage bargain, demanding the same pay as foreign workers and re-spect for their skills. These were the workers who, along with employees (*empleados*) and others, responded to Madero's message by forming anti-reelectionist clubs in 1910. Their insistence that the revolution applied to the workplace as well as to politics helped shape the early years of the Mexican Revolution.

6

The Great Awakening

Mine Workers, Companies, and the
Mexican Revolution

The development of strikes in Mexican industrial circles was first
hailed as the natural harbinger of a great national
awakening, from the fact that it seemed to indicate the coming
into being of a desire on the part of the toiling masses to
better their condition through the demanding of a wage in
keeping with the amount of toil exacted.

—*El Paso Morning Times*, 1911

I personally don't care who runs the government, or how much
they fight, so long as they fight among themselves.

—American mine owner, Parral, 1912

Despite the destruction of railroads, the difficulty in obtaining fuel
and supplies, and the damage inflicted by the ragings of war, mining companies in Hidalgo District continued to operate, even if sporadically,
between 1910 and 1920. This was possible because, for the most part,
revolutionaries did not identify American-owned mining companies as
their targets. Nor did mine workers. Little evidence exists of a general-
ized anti-Americanism nurtured by economic dependency. Although
Madero's success in toppling the Díaz regime inspired workers to act in
defense of their own interests, between 1910 and 1920 workers became
even more dependent on large, foreign companies for the provision of
basic necessities. They had few choices, as dependence on earning a wage
gave workers a vested interest in the continuation of mining. For their
part, large companies like ASARCo found the revolution to be a good
business opportunity, at least up to late 1916. They acquired new mining
properties and cultivated closer ties with workers by providing food and
other necessities. Companies with access to extensive resources emerged
in an even stronger position after 1920 than they had enjoyed under Díaz.

Anti-reelectionist Movement

During the summer of 1910, anti-reelectionist supporters in Parral, anticipating the upcoming presidential election, jostled with followers of Porfirio Díaz for access to symbolic space, among other things. On 30 July, the official celebration of the anniversary of the death of Miguel Hidalgo y Costilla, the symbol of Mexican Independence, took place in the Plaza de la Independencia in front of a monument to this figure . The following day, José Guadalupe Rocha, while attempting to place a wreath of flowers before this same icon, was roughed up and arrested by Pedro López, the *comandante* of police, and two of his officers. According to the official version of events, the police were merely carrying out the orders of Manuel Gómez Chávez, the interim *jefe político,* to prevent anyone from holding a celebration within view of the statue, thus portraying themselves as Hidalgo's heirs in the struggle for freedom. Moreover, the *comandante* testified, as Rocha was at the head of a group of hundreds of workers—all anti-reelectionists—and inciting them to riot, he posed a threat to public order. A number of people had witnessed the arrest, and as each recounted the day's events, the number of workers in the group following Rocha grew and grew: whereas a policeman, one of the first to testify, estimated the size of the contingent to be three hundred men, the last person to offer testimony claimed to have seen Rocha at the head of two thousand men, mostly workers (*obreros*) and all coreligionists in the anti-reelectionist movement.[1]

Rocha told a somewhat different story. According to his version, he had been at the Plaza Porfirio Díaz when a group of workers (*obreros*) and some members of the anti-reelectionist party had sought permission from district authorities to hold a meeting and to place flowers before the statue of Hidalgo. Having heard that they had received permission to do so, Rocha drove to the Plaza de la Independencia to witness the event. He denied leading the procession or having any connection with the group.[2]

Regardless of which version of the events one chooses to believe, two points are salient: first, the presence of a large number of "workers" in the ranks of the anti-reelectionists, and second, the overwhelming preoccupation of district officials with the threat posed by the popular classes. As for the first point, the term *worker* needs to be clarified. One witness to the events in the Plaza de la Independencia declared that a better term to describe those taking part in the ceremony honoring Hidalgo was "artisan" (*artesano*). A closer look at the anti-reelectionist movement in Parral confirms this observation. While the Club Antireeleccionista in that city (boasting one of the largest memberships in the entire republic, according to *El Correo*)[3] had been founded and supported by miners and merchants like Guillermo Baca, its ranks included men who described themselves as employees (*empleados*) and skilled workers or artisans. José Guadalupe Rocha, for example, was an *empleado particular,* as were a number of others taking part in club meetings; Leopoldo Civiza, Miguel Hernández Escamilla, and Alberto Hernández, a miner, shoemaker, and blacksmith, respectively, also attended regularly as did a watchmaker and teacher (*profesor*). The composition of the anti-reelectionist movement provides additional evidence that the most important social divide in this society was not the one between "workers" and employers, but the one separating those who considered themselves *gente decente,* including *empleados* and artisans, from the "uncultured" masses, which included *operarios* and unskilled workers.[4]

Many of the *gente decente* joined the *Club Antireeleccionista* to work within the law for the recovery of their political rights. When Francisco Madero visited Parral in January 1910, four thousand people, all maintaining a "correct attitude" (according to *El Correo*), gathered to hear him speak.[5] Merchants in town declared a public holiday to accommodate local celebrations. By June of that year, the Club Antireeleccionista had organized special commissions to invigilate each voting booth (*casilla*) with the aim of avoiding "all disorder" in the upcoming presidential election, to be held on 26 June.[6] Club spokesmen explained, in public meetings, the meaning of the election and the manner in which those in attendance could go about exercising their civic duties, always stressing that party members should campaign for their candidates in the most orderly manner so as not to give the political authorities even the slightest motive for complaint.[7] Even Pedro López, the *comandante,* who had been welcome at club meetings, had to admit that he had never heard any club member attempt to incite the people against the authorities.[8]

He had heard rumors, however. Although the elections transpired without disorder, López had been informed that Guillermo Baca and Manuel Becerra, both connected to the Club Antireeleccionista, had bought arms and ammunition and were distributing them to the people. This charge was partly based on fact. Manuel Becerra, a merchant who had made his home available for anti-reelectionist meetings, had indeed purchased a large quantity of ammunition that summer. Rather than being given away, however, it was to be sold in his stores; his son, appearing before the *jefe político,* could account for all of the cases of ammunition making up the recent purchase. Rather than the beginning of armed insurrection, the charge reveals the preconceptions of district officials, who characterized the popular classes as incapable of acting on their own: such groups, they assumed, depended on the *gente decente* for both arms and ideas.[9]

The Madero Revolution

Although many artisans and members of the urban middle class participated in anti-reelectionist politics in Parral, armed support for the revolt came from the countryside. After an abortive attack on Parral led by Guillermo Baca in the name of the Madero revolution, on 21 November 1910, the revolutionaries enjoyed greater success in the rural municipalities of Hidalgo District, as well as in other mountain districts in Durango and western Chihuahua. While Madero, in the Plan of San Luis Potosí, had denounced the Díaz dictatorship, called the populace to arms to recover their constitutional rights, and set the date for the revolution to begin—on 20 November 1910—it was rural, popular, and agrarian leaders and their followers who responded, acting to right local wrongs. Middle-class civilian political leaders, who had been at the forefront of anti-reelectionist politics in 1909 and 1910, now found themselves superseded by popular leaders of local status with military skills. With Madero nominally in charge, the revolution became a series of popular uprisings, based on local grievances and centering on the municipality, political discontent with local government, agrarian issues, and private grudges that spread throughout the country.[10]

In Hidalgo District, on the night of 21 November, seventy-five "anti-reelectionists" took the town of San Isidro de las Cuevas. While municipal officials there languished in jail, the revolutionaries seized arms, horses, and saddles, and shouted *vivas* to Madero. Antonio Rodríguez, a municipal official in the town, reported that the rebel group was comprised of residents of San Isidro de las Cuevas and men from *ranchos* surrounding the municipality.[11] The same situation prevailed in Valle de Olivas. By December 1910, municipal officials in that town described the inhabitants of the nearby communities of San Javier and San Ignacio as sympathizers of Madero. Many from San Ignacio had already joined the revolutionaries.[12] State officials also noted that rebels were spreading "seditious propaganda" among the Indians living within the municipal jurisdiction of Balleza.[13]

By contrast, the mining municipalities in Hidalgo District remained quiet. In late 1910 and early 1911, Agustín Páez, *jefe municipal* in Santa

Bárbara, reported that there had been no threats to public order. The same situation prevailed in Los Azules. In March 1911, Páez requested that a detachment of soldiers be left there to protect the El Rayo Mining and Development Company from what he characterized as bandit attacks; he feared that the company, which was still operating and giving employment to most of the men in the camp, would be forced to suspend operations once the soldiers were withdrawn.[14] Mining in San Francisco del Oro also continued during the Madero revolt. In early 1911, R. Sapien, the ex-*presidente municipal,* reported that there had been no demonstrations against Porfirio Díaz. Perhaps indulging in a little wishful thinking, he maintained that not one individual from either San Francisco del Oro or the surrounding *ranchos* had joined the revolutionaries.[15]

Nor did workers in Villa Escobedo act to overturn the established order. In his year-end report for 1910, Manuel Martínez, the *jefe municipal,* expressed outrage that revolutionaries had attacked Parral. He lamented the existence of "enemies of order" and congratulated the *jefe político* for his energetic response to those who had tried to "topple to the ground the magnificent monument to Progress, Civilization, and Peace that had been erected under the wise guidance of the current illustrious President of the Republic."[16] Given the response of workers in the mining communities, it is difficult to characterize the Madero revolution in Hidalgo District as a *"revolution miniere."* Rather, workers dependent on wages and the purchase of goods in a market economy acted in this instance, as they did for the rest of the decade, to preserve jobs and maintain their standard of living.[17]

This is not to suggest that mine workers in Hidalgo District were not sympathetic to Madero's cause. Despite the fact that there had been no demonstrations against Díaz in San Francisco del Oro, local officials believed that many supporters of Madero lived in town. In Villa Escobedo, authorities feared that workers there were organizing a seditious movement in early 1911. In a confidential report to the *jefe político,* the *jefe municipal* stated that he had named trustworthy people—well connected with the mine workers and mechanics (*los barreteros y mecánicos*)—to uncover the details of the plot.[18]

District officials regarded workers' shouts of *viva* to Madero as yet another example of their moral laxity and indulgence in vice. In late January 1911, for example, the *jefe municipal* in Santa Bárbara sent one worker—who was constantly drunk, in violation of the gun-control ordinance, and propagating anti-reelectionist ideas—under guard to the *jefe político* in Parral.[19] Martínez reported two scandals in Villa Escobedo—

and both allegedly caused by drunken workers—in which Madero had been cheered.[20]

Madero's success in ending Porfirian rule in May 1911 and the encouragement offered to workers by Madero's close associate, Abraham González, first as interim and then elected governor of Chihuahua, ushered in a period of optimism for the laboring classes in the state. During the summer of that year, workers vigorously pressed their demands in a wave of strikes. In Ciudad Chihuahua, employees of the electric street railroad, smelter workers, factory operatives, and seamstresses all walked off their jobs in support of demands for increased wages and shorter working hours. Seamstresses in the clothing factories of "La Paz," "La Novedad," "El Progreso Industrial," and "La Concordia"—describing themselves as hardworking and honorable, yet condemned to premature decrepitude and sickness by unhealthy working conditions—demanded wage increases ranging from 15 to 25 percent. In place of the existing piecework system, they proposed a guaranteed daily salary of 1.25 pesos, even if faulty material prevented them from reaching their daily quota.[21]

Striking workers also demanded respect from the rest of society. For example, workers on the street railroad, in a petition sent to their employer, lamented that their meager salaries made it impossible for them to dress properly. For conductors, motorists, and inspectors, the humble, often threadbare, clothing they were forced to wear was a source of great shame and dishonor.[22] In addition to increased salaries, workers in the ASARCo smelter at Avalos complained that the appointed *comisario,* paid by the company, acted like a police chief in administering fines, carrying out corporal punishment, and even sentencing workers to jail; they demanded that the *comisario* be an elected rather than appointed position. They also requested that the current doctor on the staff, an American, be replaced by one who spoke Spanish. In their opinion, the inability of the present doctor to understand the language prevented them from receiving proper medical treatment.[23]

.In Santa Eulalia, the mining district just outside the state capital, 250 mine workers petitioned Abraham González to intervene on their behalf. They insisted that, along with increased salaries and a workday of eight hours instead of ten, they be paid daily and in cash. While mine workers admitted that merchants in Santa Eulalia did not operate company stores, merchants did advance loans to workers, enabling them to purchase the basic necessities of life between bimonthly pay periods. Then they charged from 20 to 25 percent for this service. Workers reasoned that daily payments, in cash, would free them from the grasp of merchants as well as enable them to buy their daily needs.[24] A few days later, workers in Santa Eulalia struck in support of these demands. While mining companies agreed to replace bimonthly with weekly pay periods (to take place on Saturday), merchants continued to infuriate workers. Instead of reducing the amount they charged for loans, many simply refused to advance mine workers any money at all. So there would be no mistake as to where the blame should lie, they hung posters in their shops stating that, by order of the governor, they could no longer advance money to workers. *El Correo* characterized their behavior as detrimental to the working class.[25]

As in Santa Eulalia, workers in Mineral de Ocampo also found themselves subject to the predatory behavior of merchants. Not only were they forced to purchase goods in stores operating under concession from the mining companies; they were also paid in scrip in place of cash. To add to their problems, merchants refused to make change, demanding instead that workers accept goods equal to the amount of company scrip. Likewise, in Naica, an abusive medical scheme and a system of fines and punishment prompted workers to strike.[26]

In Hidalgo District, residents empowered by the end of Porfirian rule called for the dismissal of corrupt local officials. In April 1911, petitioners in Parral demanded the removal of Porfirian municipal officials, including the police commander, the district secretary, and venal tax officials, whom they described as "*caciques.*" Petitioners portrayed themselves as victims of corrupt officials who had extorted forced loans, charged excessive taxes, and employed a system of secret police to hound those unable to pay.[27] Such a police force did in fact operate in the district: when, for example, José Guadalupe Rocha was arrested in connection with the incident in the Plaza de la Independencia, he urged that the testimony of one of the witnesses be discounted on account of "bad moral antecedents" and his status as a member of the secret police.[28] Grievances against local officials like these, often imposed from outside the district, had led many residents of Hidalgo District, as elsewhere in the state, to participate in Madero's revolt. In one of the major acts of his administration, Governor González, to help restore municipal autonomy, succeeded in passing a law abolishing the office of the *jefe político* in late October 1911.[29]

Workers in Hidalgo District also celebrated the change in rulers. Many believed that Madero's successful revolution heralded the beginning of a new era that would transform them from "unworthy and underprivileged" to equal and important members of society.[30] For those belonging to mutual-aid societies, the summer of 1911 was a time to organize "not

to exterminate capital but to demand that it be fair."[31] To workers, moreover, the new state authorities, especially Governor González, personi-
fied justice and the rule of liberal principles: as they shared these ideals,
they anticipated an improvement in their material conditions. As one mine
manager noted, workers had begun to feel their oats, a statement with
which the *El Paso Morning Times* could only agree:

> The development of strikes in Mexican industrial circles was
> first hailed as the natural harbinger of a great national awakening,
> from the fact that it seemed to indicate the coming into being of a
> desire on the part of the toiling masses to better their condition
> through the demanding of a wage in keeping with the amount of toil
> exacted.[32]

Unfortunately, in the opinion of the newspaper, workers' demands for
"natural" and "inalienable" rights had begun to trespass on the rights
and privileges of others by August 1911.

Irrespective of the attitude of the border press, workers applied Madero's
political rhetoric to their work situation. In short, they expected the banner of "Effective suffrage, no re-election" to fly over the workplace as
well as the *ayuntamiento*. In their opinion, mine foremen and railway
bosses were as much "*caciques*" as municipal officials. In August 1911,
unskilled laborers working for the Mexican National Railway
(Ferrocarriles Nacionales de México) in Hidalgo District petitioned Governor González for assistance: they lamented that many *caciques*, the worst
of whom were Mexican railroad construction bosses, still oppressed the
poor proletariat (*pobre proletario*) of Chihuahua. The immediate reason
for petitioning the governor was the company's reduction of the workforce;
managers, in refusing to keep workers who were unaccompanied by their
families, had let single men go. Petitioners were outraged: "It is as if only
those with a family have a right to live in our Mexico."[33]

They also took the opportunity to air long-term grievances. Railroad
workers explained that the onset of economic depression in late 1907
had led the railroad to reduce wages to ninety centavos for a full day's
work (from sunup to sundown, as workers described it). Although this
had been instituted as a temporary measure, as of August 1911 wages
still had not been raised to the old level. Petitioning workers, describing
ninety centavos as insufficient remuneration for even seven hours of their
work, demanded a peso and a half per nine-hour workday. Along with
these demands, they wanted job security; after all, they reminded state
officials, guaranteeing secure jobs and just pay were among the first promises made by the leaders of the revolution.[34]

By late summer 1911, many workers in Chihuahua, including those petitioning the governor, clearly had become disillusioned with the pace of change in the workplace. In fact, as no change had yet occurred, petitioners were forced to conclude that "all the efforts we made to help the holy cause [the revolution] have been useless."[35] Swearing that they would rather die than continue living under the same Porfirian system, they envisioned a society organized in accordance with the principles established by their beloved Benito Juárez. Tired of the "yolk of oppression," petitioners wanted to be "free and subject only to the sacred laws of the 1857 Constitution."[36] Rather than establishing a more just social system, as workers had hoped, revolution under Madero meant continued subservience, low pay, and arbitrary treatment from abusive bosses at work. More than disillusioned, workers felt betrayed. "We are ignorant of everything," they stated. "The single thing we are not ignorant about is the end that the triumphant Revolution promised to defend."[37]

Railway laborers were not alone in demanding changes in the workplace. For example, workers in the Apodaqueña Mine, near Parral, took the opportunity to address issues of importance to them. They informed José María Botello, the mine owner, that changes he had instituted in the work process endangered their lives. Such change, they explained, would only be accepted if accompanied by increased wages. In short, Botello's actions violated their notions of justice and of a fair day's pay for a fair day's work.[38] Elsewhere, in Santa Bárbara, workers also took advantage of the opportunity presented to them by Madero's success. In this mining town, Dionicio Castañeda—described only as a "mine worker"—initiated a process that would culminate in the election of a workers' slate to the municipal presidency in 1922. In November 1911, he pledged, if elected, to authorize a strike for increased salaries and shorter working hours.[39]

Likewise, in San Francisco del Oro, officials of the San Francisco del Oro Mining Company faced a new municipal president, Rafael Aguilera, who demanded that the company change its methods of paying workers. Should the company not accede to this request, Aguilera threatened to organize a strike.[40] In Villa Escobedo, mine workers complained of irregular pay and the abusive conduct of the mine administrator. In the name of *patria*, effective suffrage, and no reelection, they demanded regularly scheduled paydays and the removal of the administrator. Although workers preferred to be paid daily, they indicated that they were willing to accept a weekly payment if it took place on Saturday instead of Sunday.[41] Santos Esparza, the new *jefe municipal* there, sided with workers and threatened to force the Alvarado Mining and Milling Company to comply with their wishes. When Bazile Davidson, the company superintendent, announced his intention to seek protection under the law, he was informed: "There is no law in Mexico except us" and "We are the law." Davidson, in response, gave the successful revolutionaries a taste of their own medicine. Since *caciquismo* no longer existed in Mexico, he replied, no governmental official could force him to do anything.[42] More than rhetoric separated the two men. Each held fundamentally different perceptions as to the character of the Mexican working class: while Davidson viewed workers as a "bunch of drunks" intent on working as little as possible, Santos Esparza saw men with legitimate grievances. Company officials finally agreed to pay workers once a week, but on Sunday, not on Saturday, so that workers would not be tempted to drink and spend all their money on Saturday night, to the detriment of themselves and their families.[43]

Many of those adhering to Madero's cause would have sided with Davidson. Upon being granted their requests, workers often behaved in ways that shocked Maderista leaders. For example, to offset complaints about the cost of goods at the work site of the new Boquilla dam (designed to deliver power to Parral), Governor González and company officials agreed to place a train at the disposal of workers so that they could travel to Camargo every Sunday to buy provisions. The result of this act, supposedly meant to benefit workers, appalled Jesús M. Yáñez, first captain of the liberating forces. Instead of buying provisions and other necessities for their families, workers purchased mescal and tequila. In horror, Yáñez described the scene one Sunday evening, when the train from Camargo pulled into camp, and almost half of the thirteen hundred workers disembarked drunk, a good fifty of whom were beyond even that point (*guantoniados ó apredriados*). In his opinion, the weekly train was a source of disorder that needed to be eliminated, rather than a benefit to workers. Moreover, Yáñez described those men inciting workers to strike as "evil" and "unemployed," and to preserve order, he advocated that they be thrown out of camp.[44]

As the new political authorities subscribed to the same developmentalist ideology propounded, yet not fully implemented, by the Porfirians, moral reform dominated the political agenda. Governor Abraham González set the tone by initiating campaigns against drinking and vagrancy; he also sponsored detailed legislation regulating gambling.[45] In Parral, General José de la Luz Soto, the military commander, instructed district officials to stamp out drunkenness. In response to this directive, R. R. Escarcega, the municipal authority in Guadalupe y Calvo, dispatched troops to impose what he described as "constitutionalist conditions" in outlying mining settlements.[46] These troops acted very much like their Porfirian counterparts. In one mining camp, they arrested mescal dealers, locked up drunks, and attempted to end scandals; the officer in charge proudly reported that, at least here, there would be no more drunken and disorderly behavior caused by the illegal sale of intoxicating beverages.[47] In Santa Bárbara, military authorities prohibited all types of card games and games of chance, even those usually associated with the town's traditional festival in September. In August 1911, municipal officials were instructed to eliminate vagrancy in all areas under their jurisdiction.[48]

New municipal officials, who had been among those demanding effective moral reform during the Porfiriato, seized their opportunity to act under Madero. For example, Juan Chávez, *jefe municipal provisional* in San Antonio del Tule, imposed strict new regulations on the sale of alcohol and the carrying of firearms. As well as mandating stiff fines for *cantina* owners who served alcohol during restricted hours and the incarceration of anyone caught drunk outside their house after 10 P.M., the new rules dealt especially severely with those committing scandals; firing a shot while intoxicated would now result in a stiff fine, as would singing in the public plaza and riding through the streets while inebriated.[49] Even though they were determined to stamp out vice, officials quickly discovered the difficulties involved in enforcing such policies. No one could have been more resolute in his opposition to *cantinas* than Julián Baca, *síndico* in Villa Escobedo. According to Baca, the germ of immorality was "incubated" in *cantinas* and, from there, spread to even the humblest homes, where it infected mothers, wives, and daughters. Despite the strength of his convictions, Baca could do little; he confessed that the shortage of police agents rendered local officials like himself powerless in the struggle against vice.[50]

By late 1911 and early 1912, municipal officials, increasingly unable to rely on the police or armed forces to preserve order, formed their own forces. In Santa Bárbara, for example, local authorities, in fearing that the few troops and police would not be able to repel "bandit" attacks, organized a defensive committee (*junta defensiva*). Although the force was described as having no "political" character, its mission was to protect commerce, which was described as being of interest to all inhabitants.[51] In Villa Escobedo, mine owners demanded protection from what they described as frequent disorders. While Santos Esparza maintained that he had maintained "perfect order" despite the insignificant number of troops at his disposal, merchants disagreed, and in March 1912, they formed a defensive committee similar to that in Santa Bárbara.[52]

Revolt of Pascual Orozco

In January 1912, Pascual Orozco, excluded from politics after attempting to run for governor in opposition to Abraham González and dissatisfied with the way he had been treated by Madero, resigned his command of the *rurales*. He was not the only one disgruntled with the new regime. By late 1911, many of those in western Chihuahua who had supported Madero, members of rural society who were frustrated with the slow pace of change and the apparent ingratitude of Madero, now declared against him. As revolt spread, Orozco waited until, in March of 1912, he too sided with the popular groups rebelling in the state. Of the leaders who had originally joined Madero in revolt, only a few, including Pancho Villa and the Herraras of Parral, remained loyal to the Madero government.[53] Even before Orozco chose sides, American mine operators in the state capital observed that "the entire state of Chihuahua is under revolt." Although they reported that the feeling was "not particularly anti-American," the U.S. consul recommended that American families gather together in central locations in the city and under the protection of the American flag.[54]

Although the mines themselves were not the targets of revolutionary ire, the revolt against Madero made it difficult for mining companies in western Chihuahua to obtain supplies and ship bullion. For example, L. S. Cook, a mine owner with a self-declared "million-dollar" investment in Parral, reported that the only inconvenience his company was suffering was on account of the railroads. Not only were cyanide mills unable to get supplies of cyanide of potassium, but the storage areas of concentrating plants were overflowing with concentrates that they were unable to ship. Banks, Cook reported, had a similar problem: they were fully stocked with bullion, yet no money was available. Another difficulty reported by managers was that skilled American workers, including the operators of diamond drills, were leaving Mexico.[55]

Parral, held at first by forces loyal to Madero (including Pancho Villa), was taken by Orozquista forces in early April 1912, when the town was violently sacked. Prominent citizens like Arnulfo and Fidel Martínez, the manager of the slaughterhouse "Rastros de Torreon y Parral" and the owner of the Hacienda of Vallecillo, respectively, were dragged into the street where, after striking them with his rifle, José Inés Salazar had them killed.[56] As a result of these and other acts, business was badly crippled and most of the mines suspended operations. Late in 1912, a local merchant reported that the foreign mining companies around Parral remained closed.[57]

Not all companies, however, quit the district at this time. In the immediate vicinity of Parral, the Alvarado Mining and Milling Company, managed by James I. Long, not only kept operating, but gradually increased production.[58] In Villa Escobedo, the Minas Veta Grande y Anexas also continued to do business, with company officials disbursing a bimonthly payroll of fifteen hundred dollars (Mexican) in late 1912.[59] The San Francisco del Oro Company, the El Rayo Mining Company, and the American Smelting and Refining Company, all located near Santa Bárbara, also kept on mining and concentrating ore. Elsewhere in the state, foreign mining companies continued operations despite the destruction of railroads and the uncertainties caused by war. ASARCo officials, stressing that they had been well treated by both federals and rebels, kept the company's smelter near Ciudad Chihuahua running between late 1910 and mid-1912. As long as the smelter remained in operation, three thousand mine workers labored to provide it with ore.[60] Despite the revolutionary disturbances, at the annual meeting of ASARCo, Edward Brush, vice president of the company, proclaimed 1912 a banner year, for earnings from the company's mining properties in Mexico were the largest in its history.[61] The border press drew similar conclusions. In April 1912, the El Paso Morning Times reported that none of the important mines and concentrating plants in Parral had suspended operations; later that year, it pointed to "substantial investment" taking place in the mining industry around Parral, Cusihuiriáchic, and Santa Eulalia.[62]

Although General Victoriano Huerta, commander of the forces that Madero had ordered north, defeated the rebels in May 1912, many of Orozco's supporters in western Chihuahua engaged in guerrilla warfare for the rest of that year. Officials of the Parral and Durango Railroad, for example, reported that small bands were "raiding and looting indescriminately [sic], Mexicans and foreigners alike."[63] Likewise, managers of the Mexico North Western Railway reported that José Inés Salazar and his men were tearing up track and destroying bridges. In July, Salazar forced the Mormons, who had established several colonias near the railroad line, to leave Mexico for the United States. When Huerta toppled Madero from power in February 1913, Orozco, Salazar, and others came to terms with the new government in exchange for positions and money.

Villa responded immediately in the opposite fashion. Having only recently escaped from jail in Mexico City, he entered Chihuahua from El Paso in March of that year to take the field against Huerta and Orozco.

Chihuahua under Villista Rule

As Villa did not gain control of the greater part of Chihuahua until the summer of 1913, fighting continued to disrupt mining that year. In March, ASARCo continued operations despite the pitched battles taking place in the streets of Parral between federal troops and Maderistas under the command of Manuel Chao. R. F. Manahan, the assistant general manager of ASARCo in Santa Bárbara, reported Minas Tecolotes y Anexas running full force that month. When Chao demanded that the company give him five thousand pesos to pay his troops, W. P. Schumacher, the superintendent, balked, informing Chao that as a foreign company, "we have nothing to do with the present struggle."[64] Although Chao stated that the money could be regarded as an advance on ASARCo's taxes, company officials still refused to pay. It was only when Chao mentioned that his men were in a surly mood and that they might get beyond his control that Schumacher acted, giving Chao 2,750 pesos.[65]

By April 1913, managers were complaining that more companies were now being hurt than at any time since the beginning of revolutionary troubles more than two and a half years earlier. In Hidalgo District, they reported tense conditions in May, as rebel activities and the lack of supplies jeopardized the jobs of three to four thousand miners. That summer, when ASARCo and most other foreign-owned mining companies suspended operations (ASARCo activities in Santa Bárbara were shut down on July 22, and by that date every mine, mill, and smelter owned by the company in Mexico was closed),[66] managers experienced their first taste of worker anti-Americanism. Because mine workers blamed the Americans for putting them out of work, managers reported that it was unsafe for them to walk the streets due to the danger of assault from the more than three thousand unemployed mine workers.[67]

This scenario was common in the mining camps of northern Mexico: after they had been forced to suspend mining operations, managers often became the targets of workers' wrath. In Cananea, Sonora, for example, when the state of war in March 1913 compelled the Cananea Consolidated Copper Company to suspend work and release three-quarters of its Mexican workforce of four thousand men, workers ran the company's general manager, James Douglas, out of town. He was fortunate to escape with his life; had he refused to leave, a group estimated to number between two and three thousand men was ready to mount him on a burro and drive him out.[68] Likewise, at Sierra Mojada, in the state of Coahuila, a federal officer explained to Gates, superintendent of ASARCo operations there, that if he stopped work in the mines and threw laborers out of their jobs he would not give "a snap of his fingers for Gates' life."[69]

When they did continue to operate, the large foreign mining companies represented a source of funds for the revolutionaries. After Chao had obtained money from ASARCo, he turned to the Alvarado Mining and Milling Company, the largest plant remaining open in the summer of 1913. Demanding money to pay his troops, Chao made apparent the threat of violence that lay at the base of the relationship between foreign companies and revolutionaries:

> . . . as soon as I see that I cannot secure enough money to pay them in full then these men of mine will mutiny and I will have no control of them and they are liable to cause a lot of trouble for every one who has any money at all. This loan which I now ask for I wish you to make to me personally, to me Manuel Chao, and not to me as a revolutionary leader. This money I will secure with the signature of any of my friends in Parral or with the real estate of my father-in-law. I do not demand this money from any of you, but I simply come to ask for it as a last resort for if I do not get it I shall have to let my soldiers loose and tell them to get it wherever they can and then they might go to the Alvarado Mill and from there take a bar of silver. They are liable to cause injury to property and to person too.[70]

When Chao further maintained that the Alvarado Mining and Milling Company owed ten thousand pesos in export taxes on their bullion and the El Rayo Company fifteen thousand pesos, managers in Parral concluded that the rebels would "stay at Parral and try their best to live off the Americans since the natives who were left in the town have nothing more to let loose of [that is, no more money or seizable assets] as the Maderistas have completely ruined many people there."[71]

In order to continue operations under these circumstances, companies had to overcome a number of obstacles. For example, managers of the Alvarado Mining and Milling Company, one of the few companies to stay open throughout 1913, solved the problems occasioned by damage to the railroads by using wagons both to import food and export bullion. During the last six months of 1913, managers sent two shipments, each carrying over 400,000 dollars in silver bars, to the United States on bullion trains composed of sixteen wagons, each pulled by sixteen mules.

Another problem was the lack of currency. In May 1913, ASARCo officials in Santa Bárbara reached an agreement with their workmen and local merchants to issue "countersigns" in lieu of currency. To work within the confines of the Mexican Commercial Code, which prohibited issuing promissory notes at sight and in favor of the bearer, these documents bore only a number and two signatures without stipulating any kind of contract or promise to pay, or obligation of any description whatsoever. All parties agreed that these notes would not be used for circulation outside Santa Bárbara and that the company would not redeem the notes if they were presented by anyone other than the merchants or workmen of Santa Bárbara. The system was so successful (these documents formed almost the only circulating medium in town) that the revolutionary authorities demanded that the company pay a considerable sum as a stamp tax.[72]

Managers of the Alvarado Mining and Milling Company employed a different strategy to make up for the lack of cash and yet, at the same time, ensure a supply of ore for the cyanide plant belonging to the company. They opened their mines to anyone who cared to work in them. In place of receiving a daily wage, men working on their own, known as *gambusinos,* were paid according to the grade and amount of ore they delivered to the mill (the company charged ten dollars per ton to treat the ore). Such an arrangement was to the company's advantage; the high-grade ore, for which the company's Palmilla Mine had become famous, had run out earlier in the year. One observer calculated that the ore the *gambusinos* were now digging out was so "lean" that they could barely get enough to earn a peso and a half per day. As the mill also accepted ore from other properties, it provided many mine workers with a means of obtaining a livelihood and an alternative to participation in the revolution.[73]

Far from employing workers during difficult times for philanthropic reasons, managers had a vested interest in continuing mining: they found that keeping the mines in operation was an effective means of protecting ore and safeguarding the long-term condition of their mines. As discussed in Chapter 5, workers believed that they were within their rights to take ore from mines not being actively operated. In 1913, for example, managers in Santa Bárbara reported *peones* entering mines and making off with all the ore they wished. Nearby, in Guacenví, Durango, revolutionary authorities threatened to allow townspeople to enter all idle mines.

Not wishing to see their mines worked in a "haphazard" fashion and possibly destroyed, managers of the Guanaceví Mining Company acceded to rebel demands and employed a limited number of men in each mine.[74]

Keeping workers on the company payroll also reduced the likelihood that they would join the revolution. During the summer of 1913, although no trains had been running to Santa Bárbara for months, ASARCo furnished supplies to workers and kept the mine and mill there in operation in order to give them employment. Despite these efforts, managers reported that their offices had been raided and money and other movable items taken.[75] In nearby Asarco, Durango, the superintendent of the Velardeña plant drew the same conclusion: "Every workman who is able to dig up a gun and horse is joining the forces of the rebels, due to the fact that there is nothing else for them to do."[76]

By the end of 1913, with the fall of Ciudad Juárez and Salazar's defeat, Villa controlled the entire state of Chihuahua. For military and economic reasons, one of his first tasks was to convince foreign mining companies to renew their operations. ASARCo—following its usual policy, which was the policy of other foreign companies, of carrying on business once one faction controlled the territory in which they operated—made plans to open their smelter in Chihuahua. By April 1914, observers in El Paso concluded that business activity in Ciudad Chihuahua was "remarkable" and had not been equaled in years. As for Villa, he was heralded as "not only one of the bravest men involved in the Mexican troubles, but . . . one of the cleanest and fairest so far as American interests are concerned."[77]

Actual conditions, however, were not so rosy. Early in 1914, a freight train en route from the Chihuahua plant of ASARCo to El Paso, carrying a large amount of bullion, was wrecked and burned. A large portion of the bullion, scattered over the ground, was stolen and two freight cars, left intact, ended up (according to ASARCo officials at any rate) in the possession of General Máximo García. Although the company had an "understanding" with Villa that the bullion would be returned, it was still in García's grasp at the end of the year.[78] In fact, the trajectory of this bullion reveals both the extent of smuggling operations and the company's determination to retrieve it. Early in 1915, in an attempt by revolutionaries to disguise its origins, the bullion was sent to the Torreón smelter, where it was remelted and then recast in the moulds of the Compañía Metalúrgica de Torreón, whose mark was then roughly eradicated. After a few months of being shipped to various locations in Mexico, tracked carefully all the while by a detective in the pay of ASARCo, it ended up in Ciudad Juárez, where the company again failed in its efforts to claim it.

In Ciudad Juárez, the bullion was melted down yet again and recast in the moulds of the Santa Rosalia smelter, and as of early 1916 it remained in the border city.[79] ASARCo was not the only company to suffer the loss of bullion; both the Batopilas and Yoquivo companies negotiated with Villa for the return of their bullion in late 1913 and early 1914.[80]

The American occupation of Vera Cruz in April 1914 also put a damper on the revival of business. Managers of the Mexico North Western Railway, having already suffered the loss of fifty-two passengers and employees when Máximo Castillo alledgedly caused a wreck in the Cumbre tunnel on their line in February 1914, concluded that the occupation of Vera Cruz marked the first time since the beginning of the Mexican Revolution that the situation had grown so serious "as to close down all of the industries in our territory and the bringing from the country of all Americans."[81] The president of the Parral and Durango Railroad concurred. He reported that there had been "practically no business" on his line after Americans had left Mexico in response to instructions they had received from Washington.[82]

Worse still, from the companies' perspective, in June 1914 ASARCo officials in Chihuahua discovered that each day up to four hundred men entered mines pertaining to the company to extract the richest ore, a practice known as "highgrading." Workers formerly employed by the company in Santa Eulalia had organized an extensive ore-stealing ring, with the connivance of local and state authorities. In the summer of 1914, they were busy gouging out the richest ore, loading it onto burros, and melting it down in homemade adobe furnaces in Santa Eulalia and Ciudad Chihuahua, for subsequent sale in El Paso. Despite taking up the matter with Villa and the best efforts of the companies, including, in addition to ASARCo, the Chihuahua Mining Company, the Buena Tierra, and the San Toy Mining Company, this practice could not be stopped.[83] Likewise, in Batopilas, Chihuahua, mining men reported that as of 1914, hundreds of thousands of pesos worth of ore had been stolen by "ore thieves."[84]

Although ASARCo undertook the construction, repair, and unwatering of a mine in Santa Bárbara in late 1914, the company did not resume active mining in Hidalgo District. In fact, for the last six months of 1914 and the first few months of the following year, officials of ASARCo concluded that it was not in the interests of the company to attempt to operate, to any considerable extent, any of their mines and plants in Mexico.[85] Those mining companies in Chihuahua that did continue to operate reported difficulties in retaining their workforce. Managers of the Mines Company of America, for example, were forced to close down their op-

erations in Parral because their workers "quit and joined Villa's army."
At Cusihuiriáchic, the superintendent stated that while they had not lost
a single day on account of the revolution, they would now have to close
down because their men had joined Villa. In this case, recruiting officers
were reportedly offering mine workers two pesos a day and a bounty of
two hundred pesos to join Villa's forces.[86]

William K. Meyers maintains that the low world-market price of silver
convinced ASARCo and other mining companies not to reopen their properties once Villa controlled Chihuahua. He observes that Mexico's mining production reached its low point in 1914–15, a period that coincided
with the low point for the price of metal: "Despite Villa's efforts to woo
back mining interests . . . the mines remained closed as long as mineral
prices remained low."[87]

Certainly, executives of the large American mining companies paid
close attention to the world-market price of metals. Yet, rather than complain about market conditions, company officials pointed to the high price
of metals during the first six months of 1915. ASARCo, for example, ran
its Chihuahua plant to a "considerable extent" in May, June, and July of
that year and, by June, had resumed smelting in Monterrey and Velardeña.
To provide ore for these smelters, the company resumed operation of
most of its mines in northern Mexico by the summer of 1915. Shipping
this ore was expensive, for not only did the company pay freight charges,
it had to provide its own locomotives and railroad crews. According to
Edward Brush, vice president of ASARCo, this was money well spent:
"the high price of metals seemed to warrant the extra expense."[88]

Even in 1914, when mining production declined, the low price of metals was not the sole culprit. Officials of the mining companies took into
account factors of equal or greater importance in determining the bottom
line in company ledgers. Rather than assuring a future supply of ore,
ceasing to work mines when the price of metal was low led to substantial
losses. Once mines closed, hundreds of workers, believing it to be their
right to work in mines not being operated, and often egged on by the
revolutionary authorities—who at various points threatened to confiscate properties not being actively worked—removed the highest grade
ore. To protect their investment, then, officials of mining companies were
interesting in resuming work.[89]

More than the loss of ore, "highgrading" often damaged the mine
itself. As the *Engineering and Mining Journal* explained, "it takes much
capital and years of exploration and development to put mines in a producing condition, and profitable production will not continue if such in-

vestment of funds is not carefully and systematically kept up."[90] Usually, companies invested a considerable amount of money over a long period of time before a mine reached the point where it could begin to produce ore. It was in the interests of the mining companies, then, to continue mining to protect their properties and investment. How can their failure to do so be explained?

First, mining companies needed assurances before reopening. It did not make economic sense, for example, to invest tens of thousands of dollars to unwater a mine or carry out other work unless a lengthy period of sustained operation could be guaranteed. Any interruption of drainage operations meant that the mine would fill with water, requiring a repetition of this costly process before mining could be resumed. This was the case with the Tecolotes property of ASARCo in Santa Bárbara, where managers explained: "on account of the mine being flooded an expensive and protracted period of pumping will be required which cannot be undertaken until reasonably normal conditions have been reestablished and the continuance of same can reasonably be assured."[91] In short, company officials envisioned mining production and smelting operations over the long term. Those managing the Mexican side of the company were even told by executives in New York to disregard present market conditions when making decisions about their properties. Rather than the low price of metal, difficulties in transporting goods and ore, along with the impossibility of carrying out sustained operations, given the instability accompanying the revolution, led to the decline in production.

Mining in Chihuahua again suffered in late 1915, when Villa's forces retreated north after being defeated by Obregón. Despite the report submitted by the American consul in Chihuahua, stating that managers of foreign mining companies believed they had nothing to fear from Villa's forces, which were reported to be retreating in an "orderly manner,"[92] executives of ASARCo in New York characterized Villa as being in "a very dangerous frame of mind" and in a "constant rage." They anticipated that American governmental action, such as recognition of Carranza, which came in October 1915, would result in "deflecting the rage of the northern leader against Americans and American interests."[93] ASARCo and other mining companies heeded the warning issued by the State Department on 11 September 1915, ordering all American citizens to leave Mexico. By 21 September of that year, officials of ASARCo had withdrawn their employees, some fifty-eight, from the country, as had officers of the Batopilas Mining Company and the Mines Company of America.[94]

At about the same time, the Mine and Smelter Operators' Association, formed in early 1915 to represent mining companies operating in Mexico, was trying to stack the deck in its favor. Having been informed by Villa that he desired to meet with managers of mining companies operating in Mexico on 9 August, and fearing a shakedown, Mr. Beaty and Mr. Hollis, executives of the association, went to Washington, where, through Paul Fuller, a lawyer retained by the association, they brought about the immediate departure of General Scott, who succeeded in "straightening out" the difficulties with Villa. The cost for this service, some five thousand dollars, and the bill in connection with the thousand tons of coal delivered to the Constitutionalist Railways by the association, were shared by members of the association, with each company paying in proportion to its July payroll.[95]

Access to coal, however, made it possible for the revolutionaries to operate the ASARCo smelter near Ciudad Chihuahua on their own. In October 1915, General Avila, governor of Chihuahua, asked C. F. Galan, the agent of ASARCo in Ciudad Chihuahua, to resume operation of the smelter and mines pertaining to the company so that workers would be able to buy the necessities of life. He also informed officials that if they refused to smelt ore belonging to the government, he would confiscate the plant and smelt ore with his own men.[96] After ASARCo declined the offer, the governor made good his threat, and by the end of the month his forces were using fuel and ore belonging to ASARCo to make bullion in the smelter. Company losses from these smelting operations (described as "crude" by company officials), totaling about twenty thousand dollars (U.S.), threatened to mount when Villistas talked of firing up the smelter once again in November 1915. To prevent this from happening, ASARCo officials put pressure on the State and Treasury departments to block shipments of coal to Villa. Managers of the company felt that because they had cooperated with the State Department and withdrawn their employees in September, the State Department should cooperate with them in preventing the loss of half a million dollars' worth of ore at the company's smelter in Chihuahua.[97]

The governor needed men with skills in order to operate the smelter. And as skilled workmen, employees of ASARCo, cooperated with him by helping to smelt ore belonging to the company, the local manager felt that he personally had been betrayed. This had not been the first case of workers "turning" on the company. The revolution both emboldened workers and deprived them of other means of obtaining a living. For example, as early as February 1912, in the Velardeña plant of ASARCo in Durango, when bands of rebels emptied the company safe, managers

reported about thirty of their own *peones* hanging around the door looking for something to start so that they could sack the office.[98] While managers were still in control in 1912, by early 1916 there was little they
could do, and even though Villistas started looting the plant in Asarco in
January 1916, the townspeople came in and completed the job. Later
that year, upon Villa's return to Santa Bárbara, residents pillaged and
looted houses belonging to managers.[99] Rather than acknowledge that
relations between managers and workers had been strained by difficult
economic circumstances, officials of ASARCo pointed to the "inability of
the Mexican to refrain from pillage and loot when once it is started,
however great his feelings of gratitude might previously have been (because of charity or considerations previously extended) towards the very
people whose property and belongings he proceeds to assist in looting."[100]
Because they felt that this behavior was caused by a trait supposedly "inherent" in all Mexicans, they concluded that nothing could be done about
it.

Although Villa had been temporarily satiated with a thousand tons of
coal in the late summer of 1915, American companies (and Americans in
general) came to be included as targets of his wrath as his military and
political fortunes declined.[101] Especially after U.S. de facto recognition of
the Carranza regime, in October 1915, and the arrival of the punitive
expedition led by General Pershing in March 1916, this feeling was shared
by many in western Chihuahua. As the Mexican national in charge of the
property of the Cusi Mining Company stated: "the same [Carrancista]
soldiers who a short time ago appeared friendly to us are now looking at
us with a marked sign of hard feeling, the reason being probably because
we work for Americans, as there can be absolutely no other reason."[102]
Moreover, officers of these troops were inciting the locals, especially the
lower classes, against Americans to such an extent that he feared the
company would have to discontinue operations.

The most dramatic manifestation of anti-Americanism took place in
early January 1916. After receiving assurances from Carranza authorities
in Chihuahua and along the border that it would be safe to send American employees into Chihuahua, the Cusi Mining Company dispatched
seventeen American employees, by rail, to its property at Cusihuiriáchic.
Near Santa Ysabel, a group of Villistas led by Pablo López attacked the
train and murdered and mutilated the American mining men.[103] Cusi was
not the only company to have sent Americans into Chihuahua, for other
members of the Mine and Smelter Owners' Association, including
ASARCo, had done likewise. To justify their actions in view of the kill-

ings, the association claimed that Ignacio Enríquez, the governor of Chihuahua appointed by Carranza, and General Treviño, the general in charge of all the Carranza forces in the north, had not only publicly announced that it was safe for foreigners to return, but had invited them to do so in order to provide employment for the many destitute workmen and their families.[104] After the massacre, American employees once again were withdrawn from the country.

Unable to carry on mining operations with Americans, foreign mining companies found nationals of other countries to watch over their properties. The Cusi Mining Company continued mining ore in 1916 (although it could not be sent to the smelter) by employing Mexican nationals as foreman, doctor, master mechanic, and timekeeper. The company also established an elaborate pay system whereby workers were paid by means of checks drawn against a bank in El Paso, which were sent to the foreman each month.[105] At the Tecolotes plant of ASARCo in Santa Bárbara, two Germans were responsible for limited operations in 1916, mostly the shipping of ore from the mine to the plant. Although they failed to persuade Villa and Nicolas Fernández, the Villista general who had taken Santa Bárbara in November 1916, that Tecolotes was a German company, their lives were spared because of their nationality. The two men reported that Villa had said in an interview that while most Germans were good people, he regarded them as "the scum and scrap of your country."[106] After berating them for working for Americans, he dismissed the two with the charge that they seek honest work. This was in marked contrast to the way Villa treated Americans. Dr. Thomas Flanagan, fearing for his life, hid out in Parral for thirty-seven days. His friend, Howard Gray, at the Preseña Mine, was not so fortunate: he was stripped and driven down the road by means of bayonet thrusts for three miles, until he died. Eighteen Chinese citizens were also executed.[107]

As economic conditions worsened in 1916, working for a foreign mining company often meant the difference between survival and starvation. At the Tecolotes plant, for example, ASARCo carried out surface work on a small scale in order to provide townspeople with a means of obtaining a living. The company, instead of paying its men in the much devalued (almost worthless) paper currency, exchanged provisions for work.[108] This seems to have been the policy of ASARCo throughout Mexico. For example, at its mining unit in Matehuala, in the state of San Luis Potosí, Mexican managers carried out development work to give employment to two hundred of the company's longtime workmen, offering corn in exchange for work. So precious was this source of food that it turned townspeople against one another; when the municipal president threatened to allow starving townspeople to help themselves to the corn, local representatives of the company warned that they had two hundred men prepared to defend it.[109] Likewise, in the state of Durango, ASARCo shipped corn from Torreón to its plant at Asarco.[110] Nor was ASARCo unique in this regard. The Cusi Mining Company became known for its system (referred to as the "Cusi scale") of providing workers with cheap merchandise at the company store, instead of paper money.[111]

This policy made sense to mining managers for a number of reasons. First, to keep working, even if ore could not be shipped out, was much less costly than abandoning mining properties, only to have them taken over by former workers and others in search of high-grade ore, resulting in loss of the best ore and damage to the mine.[112] Second, employing men and providing provisions served managers well when revolutionaries seized the area where the company operated. When Villistas took Santa Bárbara in 1916, for example, they called a meeting of all workers at the Tecolotes Mine and asked them if they were satisfied with the way they had been treated by the company. After the workmen answered in the affirmative, there was little Fernández, the Villista general, could do other than lecture them on the evils of working for Americans and invite them to join his army. In this instance, few took advantage of his offer. While this did not prevent the company from being sacked and pillaged on this and other occasions, and often by its very workers, there was generally little damage to plants and mines.[113] Finally, company officials realized that they were involved in a struggle to "capture the sympathies of the people."[114] At the very least, this meant not providing the inhabitants with any reason to lodge a complaint against the company with the civil or military authorities.

Moreover, ASARCo regarded the Mexican Revolution as a great business opportunity. As early as 1910, the company had found its Mexican operations poised at a crossroad. Company officials were most concerned with the shortage of mining properties under their control. W. M. Drury, general manager of ASARCo's Mining Department in Mexico, issued a stern warning to the board of directors in New York City, informing them that the lack of mining properties jeopardized ASARCo's smelting operations: "You must remember that most of our mines at Sierra Mojada are practically played out, that we haven't anything to speak of at Parral; Asientos will be a milling proposition in a couple of years; Angangueo is operating at a loss, simply for sulphides; Matehuala is low grade; and Bonanza small."[115] He expected his letter to spur the executive committee to allocate funds quickly for the purchase of mining properties in Mexico. ASARCo's aggressive practice of buying mines during the Mexican Revolution was an attempt to make its position secure and thus to allay these fears.

Moreover, a company with resources sufficient not only to weather the revolutionary storm, but to make investments that might take years to pay off, had an overwhelming advantage over individual mine owners and even many of the larger operators. In 1914, for example, company representatives in Mexico used Judge Gandara, an attorney in Ciudad Chihuahua, to sound out (on the sly) members of the Terrazas, Lujan, Kraft, and Stephano families about the sale of their mines. In the following two years, the company acquired valuable properties in Hidalgo District, including those of the Montezuma Lead Co., the San Diego Mine, and the Veta Colorado Mining and Smelter Company of Parral. In short, company executives were eager to acquire "valuable mines in Mexico under favorable terms because of the present turmoil."[116]

ASARCo's policy, at least before late 1916, is best illustrated in its struggle with the Compañía Minera de Peñoles, S.A., perhaps the only other mining company to take advantage of the business opportunities presented by the revolution, to carve up Mexico between them. As explained in Chapter 1, direct ownership of mines was not necessary for ASARCo to make a profit as long as the output of the mine could be secured by the smelter. As a mixture of types of ore was important for the smelting process and money was made by those who controlled the smelting of the ore, both ASARCo and Peñoles acquired mines to protect their smelting interests. This led to a showdown in 1916 over the Naica Mine in Chihuahua, as C. L. Baker, general manager of ASARCo in Mexico, explained to the head office in New York:

> It will be worth a very large sum of money to this Company [ASARCo] to prevent the establishment of a smelter at Chihuahua, and I do not consider that it will be possible for the Peñoles Company to operate a smelter there without owning or controlling the Naica mine.[117]

In other words, Baker advocated that ASARCo acquire this mine in order to eliminate Peñoles from the area controlled by its own smelter in Chihuahua. He contrasted the hesitant attitude of ASARCo executives in acquiring mining properties with the aggressive policy of Peñoles, even under economic circumstances that he considered to be prohibitive.[118]

Spurred by this competition with Peñoles, officials based in New York

City demanded to know why it had not been possible for the company's Mexican department, run by W. M. Drury, to secure good mining properties.[119] Stung by accusations of lack of effort in purchasing and leasing profitable mines in Mexico, Drury responded: "I beg to advise that to the best of my knowledge, with the single exception of the Peñoles Company, we are the only company that has acquired by purchase or lease any Mexican mines during this Mexican revolutionary period." Drury went on to list the mines purchased by the company, with mines in Hidalgo District figuring prominently on his list. Between the outbreak of the Mexican Revolution and early 1916, ASARCo had acquired the properties of the Montezuma Lead Company and the San Diego Mine, both in Santa Bárbara, and the Veta Colorado Mining and Smelter Company of Parral. Drury concluded:

> We have most decidedly taken the cream of such bargains as have been obtainable and we have our eye on others; but unless they can be obtained at bargain prices it does not seem advisable to put a lot of money into a mining proposition where there is little likelihood of our being able to work the mines for a considerable period of time.[120]

With Villa's capture of Parral, Santa Bárbara, and Ciudad Chihuahua in late 1916, officials at ASARCo changed their policy with regard to the acquisition of mines in Mexico. Despite the serious business threat presented by Peñoles and the enthusiasm of local management for expansion, executives in New York had had enough dealings with one man, namely, Pancho Villa. In late December 1916, members of the finance committee of ASARCo in New York decided that the company, at this time, would not invest "a nickel in Mexico."[121] While it is unclear from company records what additional factors contributed to this change of policy, Villa certainly headed the list. As company representatives stated in early 1917, "General resumption of operations in Santa Bárbara and Western Chihuahua impossible until Villa is eliminated."[122]

Although Carrancista troops did arrive in Hidalgo District in 1917, the treatment they afforded the large American companies was reported to be little better than what they had received at the hands of the Villistas. As the president of the Parral and Durango Railroad stated, "We have been alternatively at the mercy of the De Facto Government and of the Villistas, but can obtain no protection from either."[123] Carrancista authorities insisted that the line accept paper money of the Carranza issue from its customers, yet pay taxes and dues to the government in gold or silver coin. Moreover, military authorities refused to pay or give receipts for fuel and other materials taken, and demanded that the company pay its employees in silver to operate trains for their convenience. The situation had changed little by the end of the year; in October, Gill informed the State Department that the conditions imposed by Carranza's military authorities for the alleged protection of their interests were "worse than useless."[124] Others had similar experiences. Officials of the Cusi Mining Company, for example, reported that the area of their operations was the scene of almost constant skirmishes between Villistas and Carrancistas in 1917.[125]

ASARCo was not exempt from this kind of treatment at the hands of Carrancista officials. Believing Santa Bárbara to be a "nest of pro-Villa sentiment," military officials of the de facto government made little effort to keep a garrison there.[126] Moreover, when Carlos J. Galan, ASARCo's agent in Chihuahua, was late in paying a forced loan of five thousand pesos levied on the company by General Arnulfo González, the governor of Chihuahua, he was thrown in jail and left there overnight.[127] C. L. Baker, general manager of ASARCo in Mexico, complained directly to Carranza, reminding the president that he had twice assured representatives of ASARCo that the company would receive the assistance and protection of the government. Baker emphasized that ASARCo had already spent more than two million pesos with the aim of resuming operations at the smelters in Monterrey, Matehuala, and Chihuahua; as of July 1917, the company had also started making preparations to spend large amounts of money in Durango and Chihuahua to reconstruct plants and put them in condition for successful operations.[128]

Nor were ASARCo officials pleased with Carranza's tax policy, his decree to confiscate mining properties, or the Constitution of 1917. The first of these measures, mandating the confiscation of mining properties that had not been worked for more than two months, met with protest from American companies, as did his tax policies.[129] With regard to the Constitution, W. M. Drury, manager of ASARCo in Mexico, concluded that the labor situation throughout Mexico would be bad for a long time to come, owing partly to its scarcity and partly to new legislation. His proposal to surmount the latter was a modicum of simplicity: "Difficulties must be overcome by exercising tact and patience."[130] While this may have been possible in Chihuahua, it was not in Sonora. Drury concluded that because the attitude of political authorities was more "hostile and threatening" to American interests in Sonora than those of any other state, ASARCo should refrain from acquiring, or even investigating, mining properties there.[131]

As for Hidalgo District, the only people active in the mining business at this time were former workers who, viewing unworked mines as fair game, dug out high-grade ore for resale to merchants in Parral and elsewhere. These workers forged the first link in an intricate chain formed to dispose of the ore, which led from the mining regions of Hidalgo District to the smelter in Torreón. The involvement of former workers in highgrading ore was documented when representatives of an American-owned mining company in Chihuahua inspected a car of ore and found twenty-seven tickets, each containing a name and the quantity of ore represented by each name. As many of the names also appeared on records of the company's payroll, its representatives concluded that the car had been assembled by buying sacks of ore from former employees of the company, who were familiar with the mine and had stolen the ore.[132] Treasury agents concluded that it was more profitable for mine laborers to operate under what they called the "free and unrestrained use of American property" than to work under "legitimate" conditions.[133]

Despite their experiences at the hands of Carrancista representatives, officials of ASARCo, in hopes of resuming business, were willing to give Carranza the benefit of the doubt; they supported his representative, General Ignacio C. Enríquez, as provisional governor of Chihuahua. In the fall of 1918, representatives of the Mines and Smelters Operators' Association approached Enríquez, and hoping to avoid a forced loan, they offered to help him financially if he would employ his troops to rid the state of "bandits." Beginning in August, mining companies operating in the state began making payments of seventy-five hundred (U.S.) dollars per month to Enríquez, with the total payment to amount to forty-five thousand (U.S.) dollars. German, French and other American businessmen also advanced money to him.[134] Despite such assistance, Carrancista forces were unable to create conditions that would enable the resumption of business in Hidalgo District in 1918. Nor were they able to protect mining companies from Pancho Villa. In October of that year, Villa seized two American mining men near the Tecolotes unit of ASARCo, in Santa Bárbara, and held them for a ransom of fifteen thousand (U.S.) dollars each. Successful in this endeavor, he then informed managers of the mining companies that unless they paid him money for "protection," he would not be responsible for the loss of American lives and property in Mexico.[135] As if to back up his threat, early in 1919 Villa raided Santa Eulalia, the largest mining camp in the state and located only fifteen miles from the state capital; there, he destroyed the mines of ASARCo. Moreover, Villa publicly promised to destroy the ASARCo smelter, some three miles from Ciudad Chihuahua, on the first of March 1919.[136]

Officials of ASARCo, frantic to assist the authorities in defeating Villa, petitioned the U.S. State Department to raise the embargo on arms going to Chihuahua. While managers praised the current Carrancista officials in Chihuahua, both civil and military, they felt that the lack of arms and ammunition, especially severe in the "Home Forces," under the control of the governor of Chihuahua and responsible for the defense of towns, made them of little use in protecting their property against Villa.[137] In Hidalgo District, groups calling themselves Villistas took advantage of the lack of military protection to extort money from mining companies that had been attempting to start up operations once again, threatening to damage their milling plants. The *Jefe de las Armas* in Parral reported that the areas in which the companies were located were without garrisons.[138] Nor would they be forthcoming soon. General Castro, commander of the Federal troops in Chihuahua, confidentially informed mining-company officials that as the Mexican army would not be ready to take the field against Villa before the first of May, the Home Forces would have to suffice until then.[139] Yet again, in the summer of 1919, ASARCo withdrew American employees from its properties at Velardeña, Asarco, Parral, and Sierra Mojada.[140]

The following year, with the fall of Carranza and the triumph of the Sonorans in the Agua Prieta revolt, Villa took advantage of the situation to surrender to the new government and retire to Canutillo. By the fall of 1920, some two thousand men had returned to work in the mines and facilities of the Tecolotes unit of ASARCo in Santa Bárbara. The composition of this workforce testified to the ten years of armed struggle that had taken place in western Chihuahua. As one astute official of the Mexican Department of Labor observed, the majority of its ranks was formed by "bandits who had come down from the mountains" and "revolutionaries of all colors."[141] Most possessed arms and ammunition. Many combined wage labor with stints in bands of armed men, especially when jobs were not available. The attempt to resume the mining business in western Chihuahua in 1919, for example, had convinced many of these worker revolutionaries or worker bandits to set aside their arms temporarily, perhaps only until a more propitious moment, and take up picks and shovels in the pay of the American mining companies.[142] The behavior of these men, comprising the *población flotante*, confirms what contemporaries, both American and Mexican, believed all along—that the provision of jobs was the best way to fight popular participation in the revolution.

This is not to say that workers meekly accepted whatever the foreign companies cared to dish out. A new edge was apparent in their attitude and behavior. After forming the Unión Libre de Trabajadores in Santa

Bárbara in late September 1920, mine workers at the Tecolotes unit of ASARCo declared a strike. Their demands reveal that the old fault line in the work force endured. While skilled workers, the mechanics and timbermen, requested a 40 percent increase in salary in order to combat the rising cost of living, unskilled workers demanded a minimum salary of three pesos per day. As the strike wore on, forcing workers and their families into desperate circumstances by mid-October, and although officials feared the worst, both groups of workers, skilled and unskilled, continued to negotiate in a "peaceful and honorable" manner. When Blas Aguirre, the *presidente municipal,* suggested to J. Beraza, the representative of the Secretaría de Industria, Comercio, y Trabajo, that the conflict might be resolved if those at the lowest end of the pay scale received an increase in their wage from 1.50 pesos per day to 1.75, Beraza managed to get both company and workers to agree to this compromise.[143]

Although skilled workers were none too happy with the accord, the conciliatory words of Beraza and the celebrations in honor of the workers' victory persuaded them to return to work. Triumphant workers, led by a band of drummers and trumpeters provided by the local garrison, paraded through the principal streets of Santa Bárbara, shouting *vivas* to the Secretaría de Industria, Comercio, y Trabajo (at least according to Beraza). The following night, at a dance held for the workers, Beraza took the opportunity to encourage workers to rededicate themselves to their jobs and to hope that with an increase in the price of silver, their economic situation would improve. After another dance, this one sponsored by merchants and dedicated to the Secretaría, workers returned to their jobs.[144]

One additional aspect of this event merits further comment. Early in the strike, the president of the mine-workers' union wrote to General Francisco Villa, asking for his help and moral support in the workers' struggle. The letter is revealing in two aspects. First, even at this early date, it attests to Villa's importance as a popular symbol of resistance against oppression. In the letter, the union leader addressed him as one who has always been the "defender of the rights and needs of the Mexican people [*Pueblo Mexicano*]"; he implored him to act on behalf of the "oppressed classes [*las clases oprimidas*]," in general, and "working people [*el Pueblo trabajador*]," in particular. Second, as outlined in the letter, the demands of workers—for the restoration of their rights and the ability, which should belong to every man, to obtain legally and honestly the resources necessary for life and the proper sustenance of their homes—echoed the sentiments of those Porfirian workers who, a decade earlier, had asserted for themselves membership in *sociedad culta*.[145]

Conclusion

Mine workers certainly helped form the ranks of those revolutionary groups spawned in western Chihuahua between 1910 and 1920. This fact in itself, however, reveals little. As indicated in Chapters 1 and 2, mine workers were also *campesinos,* small property owners, *rancheros,* wage laborers on the railroad, and migrants to jobs in the United States. Their participation as wage laborers in the mining economy gave them no special proclivity for revolt; in fact, the opposite was true. Increasingly dependent on wages for purchasing the necessities of life, workers shared an interest in the continued operations of the foreign mining companies. Managers were more likely to experience hostile behavior and threats to company property when they discontinued mining, throwing workers out of their jobs—as was the case in the summer of 1913, before Villa gained control of the entire state of Chihuahua. Managers, revolutionaries, and governmental authorities in both Mexico and the United States all believed that jobs sopped up revolutionary sentiment rather than creating it.

Nor can the revolutionary movements be characterized as anti-American, although bouts of this did break out in 1912, with the American arms embargo against Salazar; in 1914, after the invasion of Vera Cruz; and in 1916, with American recognition of Carranza (October 1915) and the arrival of the Pershing expedition in pursuit of Villa. These outbreaks, however, were based on specific events and did not represent a popular, hostile anti-Americanism nurtured by economic dependency. Although American companies, with substantial resources on hand, offered attractive targets to all groups strapped for matériel and at war, mining equipment and production facilities were seldom touched. And as economic conditions worsened after 1913, and especially after mid-decade, links to a foreign mining company often meant the difference between starvation and survival, and the only alternative to enlistment in any number of armed bands in an effort to get by.

This is not to say that the revolution had no meaning for workers. Madero's successful revolt especially seemed to herald the beginning of a new era, a great awakening in which workers would take their rightful place as equal and respected members of society. Because they believed that Madero's political rhetoric would apply to the workplace, they anticipated changes in their material circumstances: arbitrary or unfair bosses would be removed, wages would be increased and work hours shortened, and jobs would become more secure and less demeaning. In short, capitalism would be reformed to take into account their contribution to progress. As social relations in the workplace were slow to change, how-ever, many concluded that the primary goals of the revolution had been betrayed.

For their part, respectable Maderistas lost no time in addressing the most serious problems, in their opinion, that plagued Mexican society: alcohol, gambling, and vagrancy. Authorities were shocked by workers' behavior—after all, what good was a weekly train from the work camp to the city if workers used the opportunity to buy alcohol rather than provisions? For those in power, giving new freedoms to workers seemed only to promote disorder and scandalous behavior. They flinched before the enormity of their task—of creating peaceful and working people—that they now seemed unable to carry out. Without sufficient police forces (and perhaps even with them) they saw themselves as impotent in the struggle against vice.

As for the foreign mining companies, at least two, ASARCo and Peñoles, found that the revolution provided substantial business opportunities. Before late 1916, ASARCo acquired properties in Hidalgo District and elsewhere in the state, while Peñoles embarked on a buying spree that hardly seemed economically rational to many in ASARCo and in the U.S. State Department. Although mining companies were hardly spoiled by the treatment they received at the hands of Carranza, he certainly was regarded as better than the alternative, Villa. The failure to eliminate him led to further disturbances in the mining industry until he came to terms with the new government in 1920. It remains to evaluate what changed and what remained the same after a decade of revolution.

7

"Honorable" Workers and "Evil" Reactionaries

Mining in the Early 1920s

Up to very recently the State of Chihuahua has been
singularly free of violent socialism and the exposition of bolshevik
doctrines. Yet only as recently as Aug. 1, two weeks before the
date of effectiveness of the new [labor] law, for the first time, in
two of the largest cities of the state, the red and black flag was
unfurled at the head of large manifestations. The sign is ominous.

—*Engineering and Mining Journal*, 1922

In March 1924, Harry B. Ott, the American vice consul in Chihuahua,
visited Parral and the outlying municipalities in Hidalgo District to determine how American lives and property were faring. He encountered a
region with a dynamic mining economy sustained by American investments that he estimated to total some thirty-five million dollars. For Ott,
it was Villa Escobedo that symbolized the changes that had taken place in
the district since the end of the violent phase of the Mexican Revolution
in 1920. Where once there had been a "crumbled mass of abandoned
adobe huts" and a "barren hillside," there now stood mills and shops,
electric ore-hauling lines, a "modern up-to-date" hospital providing free
medical care, and "American style" bungalows, home to fifty Americans
who supervised some fifteen hundred Mexican workers. The transformation wrought by American capital was considerable: "The town of Villa
Escobedo now presents a very busy sight and slowly the crumbled ruins
of yesterday are being reconstructed and stores and dwellings again line
the narrow streets."[1]

Much of this development—in Villa Escobedo, in particular, and
Hidalgo District, in general—was the work of the American Smelting
and Refining Company. As indicated in the previous chapter, at least up
to late 1916 this company aggressively sought to buy mines from owners

lacking sufficient resources to withstand the economic losses occasioned by the revolution. Once again, in the early 1920s, the depressed state of metal prices made it the time to get bargains in Mexican mines, although, initially, even ASARCo officials were cautious:

> during the past 10 years of revolution and banditry in Mexico there have occurred hopeful signs at various intervals during which foreign interests have re-entered the country with the idea of rehabilitating old properties and in developing new ones, only to be forced out again because of a recurrence of impossible political and economic conditions.[2]

Nevertheless, by 1923 the company had acquired yet more mining properties in the Parral district, including the Veta Grande mines and plants in Villa Escobedo marveled at by Ott, many of which, company officials concluded, would require a "large expenditure of time, effort and money to equip and develop."[3] With these acquisitions, ASARCo dominated mining in Hidalgo District in the 1920s, operating three distinct units in the district.

It would be wrong, however, simply to characterize the revolution as a great business opportunity for ASARCo. Changes that had begun during the Porfiriato now became more apparent. Gone was the deference to foreign investors, along with the preferential treatment that they were accustomed to receiving from those in power. At the time of Ott's visit, in 1924, Americans and other foreigners expressed a "practically unanimous feeling of insecurity," caused by the continued activities of bandits and rebels and by the lack of activity on the part of the Municipal Guard, the force that was supposed to offer them safety and protection.[4] Manuel Chao—that nemesis of American managers in Hidalgo District from almost the beginning of the revolution—still rode at the head of men known as "Villistas," who, in taking advantage of the de la Huerta revolt in 1923, had taken to the field once again, threatening to kidnap Americans and destroy their property. When over four hundred Villistas gathered in Tisonazo, a small village in Durango, to celebrate (as many did every year) the day of a local saint, no effort was made to capture them. Nor were kidnapping and banditry unusual events in the district; governmental forces seemed incapable of maintaining "law and order" in all but the major centers of population.[5]

Nor could workers be kept under control. Although the right to take pieces of the richest ore had long been claimed as part of the moral economy of mine workers, this practice, as well as the theft of equipment and tools, assumed breathtaking proportions in the early 1920s. Managers complained of the "wholesale robbery" of American companies undertaken by organized rings that encompassed merchants, workers in various mining camps, and the chief of police in Parral. Dealers in stolen goods, once they had received an order for supplies, put the word out to the mining camps, where workers would make off with the desired goods. Managers asserted that up to fifty drums of carbide, nails by the ton, and drill steel in five-ton lots could be obtained in this manner. In Santa Bárbara, where stealing was allegedly at its worst, mining companies kept large safes in all departments in order to lock up tools at the end of every working day. Given the circumstances in which they operated in the early 1920s, the companies were virtually powerless to do much about the behavior of their workers. Although they described Mexican watchmen as "practically useless," managers felt that they could not employ foreigners in that capacity for fear that they might have to kill Mexican citizens while on duty.[6] Such an action was deemed unacceptable given the new attitude of workers and governmental officials.

The early 1920s, then, was a period of hammering out a new relationship between foreign companies, workers, and the state. It began on a discordant note: state and national officials complained of the bad faith shown by foreign mining companies in refusing to comply with Mexican law. During the strike of 1920 in Santa Bárbara, for example, officials of the Secretaría de Industria, Comercio y Trabajo lamented that ASARCo was taking advantage of the lack of enabling legislation to ignore the constitutional precept mandating a minimum wage.[7] Then, in 1922, when federal authorities quashed the proposed sale of land in Chihuahua belonging to Luis Terrazas to A. J. McQuatters, an American, because of the public outcry against selling to a foreigner, Governor Enríquez abruptly changed the course of his administration, instructing state legislators to defer action on agrarian laws and, instead, to promulgate a new labor code.[8] ASARCo officials were none too happy with the move, which they described as a "complete change of front," and Drury promised company executives in New York that every effort would be made to defer legal enactment of any new law. Because he was not hopeful of succeeding, ASARCo dropped its proposed purchase of a new mine, the Esmeralda, pending the outcome of state legislation.[9]

What troubled ASARCo officials was what they saw as the state's attempt to intercede between the company and its employees. This was particularly apparent to company officials when it came to the mechanism for adjudicating labor disputes, for which the new law made provision for settlement by means of forced arbitration.[10] It was also evident because the new labor code called for the formation of committees (known as Committees on Minimum Salary and Profit Sharing), to be composed of an equal number of representatives from labor and capital and chaired by one alderman chosen by the municipal council, to fix the minimum wage for each municipality. Employers violating its rulings were to answer to the State Board of Conciliation and Arbitration.[11] In Hidalgo District, however, this committee had still not been convened as of April 1923, despite the various summons that had been issued by municipal authorities to representatives of the mining companies and unions.[12]

In the workplace, workers continued to die and get injured. But in contrast to Porfirian legislation, the new law established, among other things, a schedule of payments for those injured at work and mandated the payment of an indemnity to the family of any worker killed on the job. These payments could be quite substantial: when a worker was killed in the Mina San Patricio in 1923, the indemnity was set at eighteen hundred pesos, plus sixty pesos for the funeral.[13] The *Engineering and Mining Journal* was appalled at the prospect of "wasteful extravagance" that the payment of these sums portended. In the *Journal*'s opinion, such compensation payments would simply be "money thrown away" because the working classes of the state were totally ignorant of the uses of money (other than in very small amounts), concluding: "Only a people trained to saving can be entrusted to use properly a sum of money exceeding their customary current requirements, and the absence of the saving habit in the Mexican working classes is notorious."[14]

With the passage of the new code, government officials, known as mine inspectors, attempted to hold the mining companies to its provisions. This was a difficult task because the mining companies, particularly the American ones, were always, as one inspector put it, searching for *huecos* (loopholes) in the law.[15] While the labor law of 1922 troubled officials of ASARCo and caused them to forego the purchase of the Esmeralda Mine, it did not deter them for long: between May 1922 and May 1923, the company purchased additional properties in Hidalgo District.[16]

That the position of workers had been altered by the revolution was also evident at the level of local politics. In Santa Bárbara, the municipal election of 1922 was a bitterly contested affair, pitting the "Tricolor" party, a branch of the Chihuahuan Agrarian and Cooperatist Party (Partido Agrarista y Cooperatista Chihuahuense), against the "Verdes."[17] The campaign rhetoric expressed in political posters and broadsides, especially in those of the Tricolor party, which claimed to represent the interests of workers, revealed a great deal of continuity with the past as well as a new stridency in asserting the interests of labor against capital. With regard to the former, the Tricolor party was closely identified with and supported by the Club Morelos, described as a "respectable" institution whose members supported traditional liberal causes including public education (which, they believed, formed the basis for all "progress of the people") and campaigns to promote public health. The party also took great pains to assert that its candidates were both workers and honorable, promising that "honorable workers" (obreros honrados) would carry out all municipal acts with the "most strict honor" (la mas estricta honradez). The opposite pole to honorable remained the same as it had been during the Porfiriato, because victory for the opposition would result in a miserly daily wage of seventy-five centavos (so it was argued); this meant that each home would be converted into a house of prostitution (cada hogar se convierte en casa de prostitución).[18]

At the same time, in the campaign literature of the Tricolor party, candidates enunciated relatively new sets of binary opposites in order to differentiate a worker "us" from a capital "them." Whereas its candidates were "working class" (clase trabajadora), from the same social sphere as workers (la misma esfera social), part of the "people" (pueblo) who knew the needs of the laboring class (la clase laborante), its opponents were characterized as representing the interests of the foreign mining companies and local merchants who did not want to pay their fair share of taxes (viles reaccionarios instrumentos de los "Gringos"). Not only had one of the opposition candidates worked as general paymaster for American mining companies in San Francisco del Oro, the Tricolor party charged, but all those in opposition were "eternal enemies" of the present government and of the Mexican people.[19] As if to cement its working-class constituency, the Tricolor party promised to implement in full the new state labor laws, which it characterized as effective protection from the "attacks" of both national and foreign capitalism, especially the latter. Adherents further distinguished between the candidates of their party, who had never before run for office, and those of the opposition, who made a living out of getting elected; in other words, at least for those supporting the Tricolor party, politics was to be more plebeian and less the provenance of the professional.[20]

While the Tricolor party addressed bread-and-butter issues, promising, according to the opposition, a minimum daily wage of four pesos (much like the first worker who campaigned for municipal election in

1911), the Verde party presented itself as the legitimate heir of the revolution of 1910. For members of this party, the revolution represented the end of despotic rule and the triumph of political freedom. In place of rule by means of the spilling of blood, they offered a reign of order supported by justice which, through the development of the "principles of social evolution," would assure that the people would live in peace and worship work. By contrast, they cast those of the Tricolor party as the representatives of destruction, who would inaugurate a reign of anarchy. Although both parties courted the working class, after much acrimony, Eduardo Modesto Flores, the candidate of the Tricolor party, became the municipal president of Santa Bárbara.[21]

Much the same situation prevailed in Villa Escobedo, where partisans of the Tricolor party competed with those of the Verde for the working-class vote. Here, however, the Verde was more successful in presenting itself as the party of "working people" (el pueblo obrero), putting forward Julian Baca, a member of the Unión de Obreros Benito Juárez, as its candidate for presidente municipal. As Baca and José Moriel, treasurer of the same union, were much harassed by Gonzalo Montoya, the incumbent, unions in Parral and Santa Bárbara, as well as in Villa Escobedo, joined to deliver to state officials an energetic protest against Montoya.[22] Although united at the district level, workers were divided within the municipality itself. Opposing those of the Verde were members of the Tricolor party, who adhered to the same platform as their coreligionists in Santa Bárbara, with one notable exception: in addition to supporting public education and the full implementation of the 1922 labor law, they promised to combat gambling and other "immoral acts." In this way, members of the Tricolor party were staking a claim for their inclusion, and by association, that of all the workers they represented, within sociedad culta.[23]

Politics as practiced in Villa Escobedo and Santa Bárbara also revealed the new importance of labor organizations. While Julian Baca, a member of the Unión de Obreros Benito Juárez, stood for election in Villa Escobedo, in Santa Bárbara, Eduardo Modesto Flores seemed to support the activities of the Sindicato Confederado "Ricardo Flores Magón." When Nemesio Tejeda, a resident of Santa Bárbara, attempted to bring charges against officers of this union for hanging the following incendiary message from the windows of their headquarters, it was he, instead, who was charged by Modesto Flores. Tejeda's message read:

> Working People, Attention, Hate to the Tyrant Nemesio
> Tejeda, damned rogue; who wickedly despises the disinherited

worker element of this town. Cursed is this miserable "whale."
Receive, you cowardly shark, *el escupitajo eterno* of unionized
workers.[24]

Incarcerated as well as insulted, Tejeda spent five days in the local jail
before he could go to Parral to swear out a formal complaint against the
union as well as the *presidente municipal*.

Through their organizations and associations, many workers continued to present themselves as decent and civilized. In Parral, for example,
organized labor lobbied the city council to declare the first of May as
Labor Day (*día de trabajo*). Members of the mine-workers' union
(Sindicato de Trabajadores Mineros "Benito Juárez") extended a general
invitation to all workers and unions in Parral to participate in such an
event (in a dignified manner, of course), which they envisioned would
include a parade through the principal streets of the city interspersed with
speeches and culminating in a general assembly that evening. After all—
they reasoned with city councillors—as workers of all the civilized countries in the world recognized and commemorated this date, why shouldn't
they?[25]

Adherence to the developmentalist ideology as well as the perception
of the need for moral reform, so characteristic of the Porfiriato, continued to dominate the political agenda in Hidalgo District. In the summer
of 1920, for example, the city council of Parral refused to cede permission for the establishment of games not sanctioned by the law during the
annual celebrations there for fear of the harm that gambling would wreak
on working-class homes. Agapito Gómez, the merchant who had been
awarded the revised (and much less lucrative) concession for these games,
demanded to know why he had been singled out for such treatment; in
the past, he pointed out, gambling on cards had been permitted. As he
promised to contribute a thousand pesos to municipal coffers should he
receive a concession that included such games, he pointed out that this
sum—especially given the precarious economic situation of the municipal treasury—could be used to bankroll municipal improvements. Moreover, Gómez took issue with the charge that his concession would damage
the interests of workers; given the meagerness of their resources, he argued, workers did not even attend; rather, as in Ciudad Juárez, most of
the gamblers wagering on the outcome of games of chance in Parral were
foreigners.[26]

It did not seem that way to local residents, however. At the end of
August, more than 150 *vecinos* signed a letter of protest to the city council, condemning the "immoral acts" being carried out in the Plazuela of

Morelos in Parral under the guise of games permitted by the law. For
these residents, the games represented but one aspect of the almost daily
parade of vice and crime in this center of scandal and immorality (*escándalo
e inmoralidad*). In the name of order, security, and public morality, they
asked that the Plazuela Morelos be made safe for honorable families
(*familias honorables*).[27] At this same time, in another neighborhood in
Parral, self-described "peaceful" residents equated morality and public
health: not only was the unfenced property of one of their neighbors a
focus of infection and a danger to public health, but as people of doubtful
conduct sought refuge there, it bred crime as well.[28]

As in the past, municipalities within Hidalgo District also continued
to regulate prostitution and the sale and consumption of alcohol. With
regard to the latter, state law mandated (along with other requirements)
that places selling alcohol close at two in the afternoon on Sundays and
national holidays.[29] As for the former, records of the Inspección de Sanidad
reveal that five brothels, housing about forty-four prostitutes, operated
legally in Parral in the early 1920s. Inhabitants of these houses continued
to be inspected by the municipal medical officer on a regular basis.[30]

According to brothel keepers and *vecinos* dedicated to "work and order," however, the municipal effort in regulation was woefully inadequate
given the magnitude of the problem of clandestine prostitution. Although
those operating brothels ostensibly pointed to the threat to public health
that resulted from the failure to carry out medical inspections of clandestine prostitutes, their real concern was that the existence of unregulated
brothels made it relatively easy for the few women who actually had been
registered to escape from their control.[31] The "orderly and hardworking"
residents of Parral worried that their city was being transformed into
another border town. Fifteen *vecinos* of one neighborhood, for example,
contrasted their life of "work and order" with that of their new neighbor
known only as "Rosa": hers was a life of "disorder" given over to "buying the honor of women" and tricking gullible young women, some not
much older than children, into working as prostitutes. Like their Porfirian
antecedents, these honorable residents worried about the power of imita-
tion: not only might their own daughters be attracted to this kind of life,
but other women of the same class would follow, until, house by house,
Parral would be transformed from a peaceful and moral community to
one like Ciudad Juárez.[32]

Conclusion

This study has shown that the middle class, the *gente decente,* and the working class made themselves in relation to each other, and that manners and morals were central to this process of class formation. To do so has meant incorporating in a single study subjects usually treated separately. What brings together the disparate themes of moral reform, the cult of domesticity, the moral economy of mine workers, vice, new mining technology, and ASARCo's policy during the Mexican Revolution is the fact that all formed part of the struggle over the culture of capitalism, the need to create, or to resist becoming, subordinate and suitably motivated workers and patriotic citizens. Such a task has also meant breaking the usual temporal boundaries of Mexican historiography. Because the imposition of the McKinley Tariff and the arrival of the railroad at the end of the nineteenth century, combined with the changes in mining technology, initiated the mining boom in Hidalgo District, it made sense to begin at that point in time. Likewise, the continued predominance of the large mining companies and the adherence of Madero, and of others who would rule after 1920, to moral reform and developmentalism, along with the endurance of the moral economy and workers' sustained claims upon respectability, made the early 1920s, rather than 1910, a logical end point.

Yet this periodization can be justified only if new insights are gained in the process. There are three such insights here. First, the detailed study of a specific industry—mining in this case—reveals the danger of lumping all workers together as though a single working class existed and acted on behalf of the proletariat. Skilled workers, many of whom were completely dependent on wage labor, distinguished themselves from peasant workers, who clung tenaciously to their rural roots, by their modes of organization and protest; through the formation of mutual-aid societies and night schools; and by their manner of dress and deportment. They asserted for themselves a place within *sociedad culta,* and thereby revealed a boundary between social groups premised on manners and morals, rather than on the solidarity of class. Moreover, the relationship of workers to the state, along with the slights to their dignity which they perceived to have been dealt out by self-proclaimed social superiors, had as much to do with the emergence of workers' consciousness of their shared fate as did their position in the process of production.

A second insight concerns the impact of the revolution on the formation of the working class. Although this subject has been treated elsewhere in great detail,[1] the study of mine workers before, during, and after the revolution offers an additional conclusion worth considering. This book shows that rather than serving as a catalyst for creating new demands, the revolution provided an opportunity for the full expression of what might be called the "hidden transcript," grievances that had remained unspoken, or at least unheard, before 1910.[2] The existence of a moral economy that justified their right to take what was necessary in order to earn a living, and the inability of the companies or the state to prevent either the theft of ore or its resale to merchants during the revolution, combined with a desperate economic situation, convinced workers to enter mines on an unprecedented scale. Under these circumstances, they no longer mumbled their rights, but brashly asserted them. It is in this sense that the revolution was a great awakening.

Changes that followed in the wake of the revolution also enabled mine workers and their families to act on beliefs that were previously only rarely articulated. In Katznelson's terminology, in the early 1920s workers not only held class dispositions, but acted on the basis of these dispositions to form new labor organizations and political parties.[3] Parties campaigning in the name of "working people" contrasted their candidates, whom they described as "honorable workers," with "full-time" politicians, or in other words, men who really did not do any work; workers' parties won local elections and pressured state and national governments to enact meaningful reforms. In Chihuahua, the state government, in hurrying to keep pace with its new constituents, passed a tough labor code. From the vantage point of the early 1920s, although the ownership of mines and processing plants was being concentrated into fewer hands, it was not clear that mining companies would eventually gain the upper hand. The extent of the theft of ore, tools, and supplies; the inability of companies to do anything about it; the victory of workers' parties in local elections; the new state labor law of 1922; and the appearance of support from the national government all seemed to indicate a different scenario.

Finally, this study has shown that as workers came to be employed as permanent wage laborers in mining *extractories,* they organized to fight over the value of their time rather than advocating the overturning of the system of production. Even before the end of the Porfiriato, skilled mine workers had demanded the same pay as their foreign counterparts and organized a strike with the sole aim of obtaining an increase in salary. With the overthrow of Porfirio Díaz, a mine worker attempted to win local elections by campaigning on a platform of increased salaries and fewer hours of work. At the end of the revolutionary decade, although the gap between the skilled and the unskilled endured, all advocated increased remuneration in recognition of their contribution to production. For many workers, revolution under Madero had meant "one man, one job" and "no bad bosses." By the early 1920s, workers demanded a minimum wage sufficient for them to be able to represent themselves as respectable; only with higher wages, argued one political party, could working-class homes be kept from turning into brothels.

The conclusions reached in this book also address a larger historiographical debate concerning the role of labor in Latin America. In *Labor in Latin America: Comparative Essays on Chile, Argentina, Venezuela, and Colombia,* Charles Bergquist proposes a new and, to his mind, central category of analysis for students of early twentieth-century Latin American labor history, that of workers in export production. He observes a relationship between the capital requirements of export production and the potential for labor organization. Where capital requirements were high, three consequences usually followed: (1) foreign capital was favored; (2) capitalist relations of production dominated; and (3) concentrated, rather than dispersed, units of production were more likely to occur. On the basis of this model, Bergquist conjectures that one should expect to find a "relatively developed sense of class and cultural autonomy" within the labor movement in Mexico, especially among those in export production, with a "relatively great propensity for multiclass alliances of the reformist, nationalist, and anti-imperialist kind."[4]

As demonstrated here, such was not the case, at least not for mine workers. Although capital requirements in the mining industry were high and foreign companies dominated production, workers stubbornly clung to their rural roots. When workers did become dependent on wage labor, their identities as citizens as well as their aspirations to be treated with respect were as important to their sense of identity as their position in the process of production. Before the revolution, skilled workers joined anti-reelectionist political parties as a means of advocating change; during the revolutionary decade, they most often eschewed armed revolt in favor of organizing for economic demands.

Bergquist, however, does alert us to the importance of the comparative perspective. Historians who have analyzed the process of working-class formation in other geographical and temporal settings focus on three key issues: (1) the continuities and changes apparent in the grievances of workers, (2) the manner in which workers articulate their demands, and (3) their actions. In short, who resists, against what, and how?[5] Some interesting similarities between France and northern Mexico become apparent once these questions have been asked. Mine workers in both countries absented themselves during peak periods in the agricultural cycle, and quit the mines when they reached their targeted earnings or when other opportunities beckoned. As mine workers refused to give up their links to the soil, it took generations to change peasants into miners.

The case of nineteenth-century America reveals the important role of the state and political parties in working-class formation. Here, political parties, especially at the municipal level, helped to integrate new citizens.[6] In northern Mexico, the state was important for two different reasons. First, residents seized the rhetoric of nineteenth-century liberal rulers—especially the trumpeting of constitutional and individual rights—and used it as a measure by which to judge the Porfirian regime, which they found sorely lacking. Second, the rise to power of the *jefe político* and appointed municipal officials was regarded by many as abusive and invasive, and their actions reveal why. It was the *jefe político* who controlled new police forces funded with mining-company money; who had the power to jail, at times, even conscript, those who failed to obey; who stood at the end of a local system of repression that reached into every mine and village; and who often failed to live up to the high standards of morality and decorum deemed appropriate for members of *sociedad culta* while, all the while, disparaging workers for their supposed indulgence in vagrancy and vice. Moreover, the appointment of municipal officials violated a proud legacy of municipal autonomy. While the state in Mexico shaped the lives of workers, the reverse was also true, for workers helped in shaping the state. Unions and workers' parties formed in the 1920s pushed state and national officials to reform working conditions and to implement a system of indemnification for workers killed or injured on the job.

This study has probed the complex relationship that exists between material circumstances and beliefs. In Porfirian and revolutionary Mexico, manners and morals, as much as material conditions, separated people and provided them with a means of defining social boundaries. Members of *sociedad culta,* rather than discussing class in economic terms, employed manners and morality to symbolize class and other forms of social conflict. It would be a mistake, however, to analyze the discourse of morality in and of itself; failure to understand the economic, political, and social context from which it emerged renders it descriptive and reduces its importance.

This is not to argue that beliefs correspond to one's class. Rather, in northern Mexico wageworkers and others borrowed the dominant liberal rhetoric, redefined it, and used it for their own ends. Similarly, while workers shared many aspects of a popular culture, skilled workers subscribed to many tenets of the developmentalist ideology as well as to notions of a fair wage for a fair day's work. They demanded respect from and equality with those in *sociedad culta,* and saw moral behavior and membership in mutual-aid societies, attendance in night schools, and participation in anti-reelectionist politics as the means toward obtaining the recognition they deserved. After the violence of the revolutionary decade, they found more room to express their demands through unions and participation in politics, often in terms that contrasted a labor "us" from a capital "them." Still, they stressed their honor and morality and demanded the respect due to peaceful and working people.

Appendix

Wages, Hidalgo District, c. 1910*

Class of Labor	Wage per day (pesos)
Drillers, Single-handed	1.75-2.00
Drillers, Double-handed	Contract (1.50-2.50)
Drill Runner	3.00
Drill Chuck Tender	2.00
Drillers (Air)	2.50
Shift boss—Native	5.25
Shovelers and Rock Breakers	1.25
Ore Sorters	1.25
Car Men	1.50
Peones	1.25
Nippers	1.00
Timbermen	3.00
Timbermen helpers	1.50
Pump Men	2.50
Pump Men helpers	1.50
Hoist Men	2.50
Hoist Men Surface	2.50
Pipe Men	2.00
Blacksmiths	2.50-3.00
Blacksmiths' helpers	1.50
Boiler-Firemen	2.50

*Compiled from the records of the Engineers' Association of Parral District, Hyslop Collection, University of Texas at El Paso.

Notes

Introduction

1. Jurado's story is from "Averiguación instruida con motivo de la lesión que sufrió Catarino Jurado, Parral, 9 de noviembre 1910, Parral, Chihuahua, Archivo Municipal (hereafter cited as AM), caja 1910L.

2. On the English case, see E. P. Thompson, "Time, Work-Discipline, and Industrial Capitalism," *Past and Present* 38 (1967), and Sidney Pollard, *The Genesis of Modern Management: A Study of the Industrial Revolution in Great Britain* (Cambridge: Harvard University Press, 1965). On the U.S. case, see Herbert G. Gutman, *Work, Culture, and Society in Industrializing America: Essays in American Working-Class and Social History* (New York: Vintage Books, 1977). On France, see Michelle Perrot, "On the Formation of the French Working Class," in *Working-Class Formation: Nineteenth-Century Patterns in Western Europe and the United States,* ed. Ira Katznelson and Aristide R. Zolberg (Princeton, N.J.: Princeton University Press, 1986).

3. James C. Scott, *Domination and the Arts of Resistance: Hidden Transcripts* (New Haven: Yale University Press, 1990), p. 158.

4. This is beginning to change. On manners and morals during the colonial period, see Juan Pedro Viquiera Albán, *¿Relajados o reprimidos? Diversiones públicas y vida social en la ciudad de México durante el Siglo de las Luces* (México, D.F.: Fondo de Cultura Económica, 1987).

5. For a discussion of essentialism, see Sean Wilentz, "Against Exceptionalism: Class Consciousness and the American Labor Movement, 1790–1920," *International Labor and Working Class History* 26 (Fall 1984): 1–24. A recent volume on labor in Argentina eschews essentialism and focuses instead on the daily lives and lived experiences of workers between 1870 and 1930. See the essays in Jeremy Adelman, *Essays in Argentine Labour History, 1870–1930* (London: Macmillan Press, 1992).

6. For a discussion of gender in the sense that it is used here, see Joan W. Scott, "Gender: A Useful Category of Historical Analysis," in her

Gender and the Politics of History (New York: Columbia University Press, 1986): 28–50.

7. For a good recent study of women and class formation, see Josiah McC. Heyman, *Life and Labor on the Border: Working People of Northeastern Sonora, Mexico, 1886–1986* (Tucson: University of Arizona Press, 1991).

8. For works on class formation in other regions that take these and other factors into account, see the essays in Katznelson and Zolberg, *Working-Class Formation.*

9. Charles Bergquist, "Latin American Labour History in Comparative Perspective: Notes on the Insidiousness of Cultural Imperialism," *Labour/LeTravail* 25 (1990); see also his book *Labor in Latin America: Comparative Essays on Chile, Argentina, Venezuela, and Colombia* (Stanford, Calif.: Stanford University Press, 1986), pp. 382–83. See the excellent critique by Jeremy Adelman, "Against Essentialism: Latin American Labour History in Comparative Perspective. A Critique of Bergquist," *Labour/LeTravail* 27 (Spring 1991).

10. Emilia Viotti da Costa, "Experience versus Structures: New Tendencies in the History of Labor and the Working Class in Latin America— What Do We Gain? What Do We Lose?," *International Labor and Working-Class History* 36 (Fall 1989).

11. Bergquist makes this argument for the central importance of workers in export production in Latin American history, in *Labor in Latin America*, especially in the first chapter.

Chapter 1

1. For a further discussion of this point in a comparative context, see Thomas Greaves and William Culver, eds., *Miners and Mining in the Americas* (Manchester: Manchester University Press, 1985).

2. Alan Derickson, *Workers' Health, Workers' Democracy: The Western Miners' Struggle, 1891–1925* (Ithaca: Cornell University Press, 1988), pp. 6 and 9. For a different point of view, see Ronald C. Brown, *Hard-Rock Miners: The Intermountain West, 1860–1920* (College Station: Texas A. & M. Press, 1979). Brown states: "Miners did not, perhaps, suffer from modernization as much as other workers, because mining had always been a somewhat industrial occupation. Miners were spared some of the ongoing transitions, further divisions of labor, and extensive mechanization that characterized industries like shoemaking. In fact, improved technology was slow in altering the actual mechanics of mining . . ." (p. 166).

3. Marshall C. Eakin, *British Enterprise in Brazil: The St. John d'el Rey Mining Company and the Morro Velho Gold Mine, 1830–1960* (Durham: Duke University Press, 1989), pp. 118 and 141.

4. Florencia E. Mallon, "Labor Migration, Class Formation, and Class Consciousness among Peruvian Miners: The Central Highlands, 1900–1930," in *Proletarians and Protest: The Roots of Class Formation in an Industrializing World,* ed. Michael Hanagan and Charles Stephenson (New York: Greenwood Press, Contributions in Labor Studies, No. 17, 1986), p. 203. On the linkages between peasants and the mining economy in the central highlands of Peru, see Norman Long and Bryan Roberts, eds., *Miners, Peasants and Entrepreneurs: Regional Development in the Central Highlands of Peru* (Cambridge: Cambridge University Press, 1984), especially pp. 56–59.

5. James E. Fell, Jr., defines smelting as a complex high-heat process in which copper, lead, or other base metals in an ore serve as a vehicle to collect and hold the precious metal. In describing the development of the smelting industry in the United States in the second half of the nineteenth century, Fell pays particular attention to the need to adapt technology to the nature of the ore encountered; see his *Ores to Metals: The Rocky Mountain Smelting Industry* (Lincoln: University of Nebraska Press, 1979), pp. 19, 176–77, 218–19, and 273–76.

6. On the McKinley Tariff of 1890 and the subsequent rise of the smelting industry in Mexico, see Marvin D. Bernstein, *The Mexican Mining Industry, 1890–1950: A Study of the Interaction of Politics, Economics, and Technology* (Albany: State University of New York, 1965), pp. 37–41; see also "Notes on the Mining and Metallurgical Industries of Mexico," *Engineering and Mining Journal* (hereafter cited as *EMJ*), 26 Oct. 1901, p. 531.

7. "Hidalgo del Parral, Chihuahua, Mexico," *EMJ,* 12 Oct. 1901; Bernstein, *Mexican Mining Industry,* p. 40.

8. "Development in Mexico during 1902," *EMJ,* 3 Jan. 1903, p. 35. See also "Big Mining Deal," *Chihuahua Enterprise* (hereafter cited as *CE*), 9 Dec. 1899, 1: 1, Ciudad Chihuahua, Centro de Investigaciones del Estado de Chihuahua (hereafter cited as CIDECH), Tomo 4.

9. James Hyslop to Crawford Cook, 6 Oct. 1904, in James E. Hyslop Collection, Acc. No. 890, University of Texas at El Paso (hereafter cited as UTEP), Special Collections, Box 3. On smelters seeking silicious ore outside of Hidalgo District, see "Special Correspondence," *Mexican Mining Journal* (hereafter cited as *MMJ*) 11: 4 (Oct. 1910), p. 33. Mark Wasserman discusses ASARCo and the impact of high smelter charges on mining in Hidalgo District, in his *Capitalists, Caciques, and Revolution: The Native Elite and Foreign Enterprise in Chihuahua, Mexico, 1854–1911* (Chapel Hill: University of North Carolina Press, 1984), p. 77.

10. For a history of ASARCo, see Isaac F. Marcosson, *Metal Magic: The Story of the American Smelting and Refining Company* (New York: Farrar, Straus and Company, 1949); and Fell, *Ores to Metals,* pp. 221–24.

11. "The Smelting Trust and the Miners," *EMJ,* 6 Nov. 1902, p. 438.

12. Bernstein, *Mexican Mining Industry,* pp. 50–54; Marcosson, *Metal Magic,* pp. 57–69.

13. A. S. Dwight, Vice-President, Candelaria Mining Company, to C. I. Reeves, New York, 20 April 1909, in Thomas Wentworth Peirce, Jr., Papers, University of Texas at Austin, Benson Latin American Collection (hereafter cited as BLAC).

14. "Brillantes augurios. La Fundición," *El Hijo del Parral,* 20 Nov. 1904, 1: 1, in Hidalgo del Parral, Preventiva, AM, caja 1904A. American mine owners also complained about the effects of the "trust" on mining in Hidalgo District; see Frederic J. M. Rhodes, "Burdens on Mexican Mining," *EMJ,* 23 March 1905, p. 568.

15. "The Miner's Hope: A Stubborn Opposition Will Meet the Smelting Trust," *CE,* 15 Feb. 1902, 10: 3. Wasserman, *Capitalists, Caciques, and Revolution,* p. 77.

16. Wasserman, *Capitalists, Caciques, and Revolution,* p. 81. See also the table compiled by Wasserman on p. 82.

17. See the discussion of the South African case in Eakin, *British Enterprise in Brazil,* pp. 113–18 and 139–41.

18. Otis E. Young, Jr., *How They Dug the Gold: An Informal History of Frontier Prospecting, Placering, Lode-Mining and Milling in Arizona and the Southwest* (Tucson: Arizona Pioneers' Historical Society, 1967), p. 127; Eakin, *British Enterprise in Brazil,* p. 140; Bernstein, *Mexican Mining Industry,* p. 44.

19. H. T. Willis, "The Cyanidation of the Silver Ores of Parral," *MMJ,* May 1909, p. 18.

20. "Guanajuato Correspondence," *MMJ,* Oct. 1909, p. 36.

21. Willis, "The Cyanidation of the Silver Ores of Parral," *MMJ,* p. 19.

22. Bernstein, *Mexican Mining Industry,* p. 31.

23. *MMJ,* May 1909, p. 19. The need for a plant is also discussed in "Concession for Cyanide Plant: Granted AJ McQuatters and JI Long to be Built at Parral," *CE,* 29 May 1909, 1: 5.

24. Bernard MacDonald, "The Inauguration of the Cyanide Era in the Parral District," *MMJ,* August 1910, p. 9.

25. *MMJ,* August 1909, p. 13.

26. Although the arrival of larger companies with greater amounts of capital had begun before the end of 1907, the downturn set many of them back; see "Stronger Men into Parral: New Era Well Begun and Light Weights' Day Is Ending," *CE,* 19 Oct. 1907, 2: 1.

27. James Hyslop to F. Smith, 30 Sept. 1909, Hyslop Collection, UTEP, Box 3, FF 39. The plans of the Palmilla Milling Company are discussed in *MMJ,* Sept. 1909, p. 33.

28. "Parral and Durango Increases Equipment," *El Paso Morning Times*

(hereafter cited as *EPMT*) 30 Dec. 1910, 8: 5, University of Texas at El Paso, Reel 50.

29. "The Red Vein of Mexico: Veta Colorado Parral," *EPMT,* 17 Jan. 1911, 9: 5, Reel 50. Other articles also treat the resumption of mining in 1910; see "Progress on the Palmilla Mill," *EPMT,* 19 July 1910, 3: 3, Reel 49; "Special Correspondence: Parral," *MMJ,* April 1910, p. 35. See also Wasserman, *Capitalists, Caciques and Revolution,* p. 78.

30. W. H. Trewartha-James to Don Santiago Hyslop, 8 May 1908, Hyslop Collection, UTEP, Box 3, FF 108.

31. See the discussion by Richard Price on this subject, in his "Theories of Labour Process Formation," *Journal of Social History* (Fall 1984), p. 94. Wasserman points out that depression led to the introduction of labor-saving capital equipment; see his *Capitalists, Caciques, and Revolution,* p. 124.

32. Report of the Alvarado Group of Mines Consisting of La Palmilla and Anexas, 1908, Hyslop Collection, Box 3, FF 105. See also "Alvarado Is Becoming Poor," *EPMT,* 20 May 1909, 5: 1, Reel: April 1909–July 1909. Workers did not necessarily view taking ore as stealing. See Chapter 5 for a discussion of the "moral economy" of mine workers.

33. *Mexican Investor,* 17 Sept. 1904, p. 8, cited in Wasserman, *Capitalists, Caciques, and Revolution,* p. 124.

34. Historians of mining in North America agree that these broad changes characterized the period under consideration. See Derickson, *Workers' Health, Workers' Democracy,* pp. 9 and 190; Julian Laite, "Capitalist Development and Labour Organisation: Hard-Rock Miners in Ontario," in Greaves and Culver, *Miners and Mining in the Americas,* p. 93; Mark Wyman, *Hard Rock Epic: Western Miners and the Industrial Revolution, 1860–1910* (Berkeley: University of California Press, 1979), p. 17; Brown, *Hard-Rock Miners,* p. 65; and Michael Neuschatz, *The Golden Sword: The Coming of Capitalism to the Colorado Mining Frontier* (New York: Greenwood Press, 1986), p. 50.

35. "The Alvarado Consolidated Mines Co.," *CE,* 4 July 1908, 6: 1.

36. "Parral Will Improve," *EPMT,* 1 Nov. 1910, 7: 3, Reel 50; "Parral and Durango Line Sold to Dallas Men," *EPMT,* 17 Nov. 1910, 13: 2, Reel 50; "The Red Vein of Mexico: Veta Colorado Parral," *EPMT,* 17 Jan. 1911, 9: 5, Reel 50; "Heavy Expense of Alvarado Parral," *EPMT,* 6 July 1911, 3: 3, Reel 53. For a description of the organization of the Parral and Durango Railroad, see "New Railroad, From Parral to a Point in Durango," *CE,* 11 Feb. 1899, 3: 2. On the history of the Hidalgo Mining Company, see "The Hidalgo Mining Company: The Pioneer American Concern that Made the Parral District," *CE,* 27 June 1908, 5: 3.

37. James Hyslop to R. C. Peters, 5 Jan. 1925, Hyslop Collection, UTEP, Box 1, FF 94; Bernstein, *Mexican Mining Industry,* pp. 144–45.

38. Brown, *Hard-Rock Miners,* p. 65.

39. On El Rayo Development and Mining Company, see El Secretario, Secretaría del Gobierno del Estado, Ramo de Fomento, núm. 6638, to jefe político, Hidalgo District, 10 Oct. 1907, AM, caja 1907D; on San Francisco del Oro, see James Hyslop to Hugh Rose, 23 Feb. 1906, Hyslop Collection, UTEP, Box 3, FF 139; employment figures on Tecolotes y Anexas are from the Engineers Association of the Parral District, 12 Aug. 1910, Hyslop Collection, UTEP, Box 3, FF 98; for Villa Escobedo, see Informe que rinde el Jefe Municipal de Villa Escobedo, C. Manuel G. Martínez, 31 Dec. 1910, AM, caja 1910U; on Esmeraldo, see "Spend 600,000 in Development," *EPMT,* 24 Feb. 1911, 2: 5, Reel 51.

40. "The Return of the Mining Engineers," *EMJ,* 7 Dec. 1901, p. 747; *EPMT,* 23 April 1911, 9: 3, Reel 52.

41. Ralph McA. Ingersoll, *In and under Mexico* (New York: Century Company, 1924), p. 64.

42. General Manager, Mining Department, to H. R. Wagner, Executive Committee, Mexico City, 2 Sept. 1909, American Smelting and Refining Company Archive (hereafter cited as ASARCo Archive), Tucson, Drawer 11, File: 245–5, "Coahuila, La Paloma." I thank Mr. Andy Coumides, of ASARCo, for permission to read and cite material from this archive.

43. Brown, *Hard-Rock Miners.* For a discussion of the literature on the relationship between technological change and mine working conditions, see Larry D. Lankton and Jack K. Martin, "Technological Advance, Organizational Structure, and Underground Fatalities in the Upper Michigan Copper Mines, 1860–1929," *Technology and Culture* 28: 1 (January 1987), pp. 42 and 45.

44. Bernstein, *Mexican Mining Industry,* p. 42; Guadalupe Nava Oteo, "La minería bajo el porfiriato," in *México en el siglo XIX (1821–1910): Historia económica y de la estructura social,* ed. Ciro Cardoso (México: Editorial Nueva Imagen, S.A., 1983), p. 354.

45. Derickson, *Workers' Health, Workers' Democracy,* pp. 39–41.

46. Marcosson, *Metal Magic,* p. 196.

47. "The Changing Character of Mining Labor," *EMJ,* March 1913, p. 534.

48. Brown, *Hard-Rock Miners,* p. 132.

49. Cuauhtémoc Velasco Avila, "Labour Relations in Mining: Real del Monte and Pachuca, 1824–74," in Greaves and Culver, *Miners and Mining in the Americas,* pp. 53–55.

50. Ibid.

51. *MMJ,* December 1910, p. 30; for a description of hand drilling methods, see Young, *How They Dug the Gold,* p. 77.

52. Grant Shepherd, *The Silver Magnet: Fifty Years in a Mexican Silver Mine* (New York: E. P. Dutton and Co., 1938), p. 194. Also see the

description of the mining process in the 1880s by Santiago Ramírez as cited in Juan Luis Sariego Rodríguez, Luis Reygadas, Miguel Angel Gómez, and Javier Farrera, *El estado y la minería mexicana. Política, trabajo y sociedad durante el siglo XX* (México: Secretaría de Energía, Minas e Industria Paraestatal, Fondo de Cultura Económica, 1988), pp. 83–84.

53. Laite, "Capitalist Development and Labour Organisation," p. 93; Derickson, *Workers' Health, Workers' Democracy,* p. 40.

54. Young, *How They Dug the Gold,* p. 83.

55. Larry Lankton, "The Machine under the Garden: Rock Drills Arrive at the Lake Superior Copper Mines, 1868–1883," *Technology and Culture* 24: 1 (January 1983), pp. 22 and 32; Laite, "Capitalist Development and Labour Organisation," p. 93.

56. "Pilares Has Large Reserve," *EPMT,* 24 May 1911, 9: 1, Reel 52.

57. George Laird to Morgan, 22 March 1909, Thomas Wentworth Peirce, Jr., Papers, BLAC; Ingersoll, *In and under Mexico,* p. 62; Bernstein, *Mexican Mining Industry,* p. 42.

58. George Laird to Dwight, 26 July 1909, Thomas Wentworth Peirce, Jr., Papers, BLAC.

59. Números y ocupaciones de los trabajadores de la Negociación de Minas Tecolotes y Anexas á Sta. Bárbara, AM, caja 1901F; The Engineers Association of the Parral District, Hyslop Collection, UTEP, Box 3, FF 98.

60. Lankton, "Machine under the Garden," p. 29; and for a description of the arduous nature of sledging in the American West, see Brown, *Hard-Rock Miners,* p. 70.

61. Investigations into accidents are located in the Archivo Judicial, Hidalgo del Parral (hereafter cited as AJ).

62. See the statements of Bernardo Uribe, operario, and Juan Soltero, operario, in Criminal con motivo del accidente de la muerte de José Solis acaecida en la mina de Clarines, Santa Bárbara, 7 de julio de 1906, AJ, caja 1906V.

63. Basilio Portillo, poblador, in Averiguación criminal con motivo de las lesiones sufridas por Basilio Portillo, Santiago Enríquez Librado, Arriola y Matías Sandoval ocasionadas por la explosión de un barreno en la mina La Palmilla, 28 mayo 1901, AJ, caja 1901L.

64. Librado Arriola, minero, in Averiguación criminal con motivo de las lesiones sufridas por Basilio Portillo, Santiago Enríquez Librado, Arriola y Matías Sandoval ocasionadas por la explosión de un barreno en la mina La Palmilla, 28 mayo 1901, AJ, caja 1901L; Manuel Rivas, operario, in Averiguación con motivo al acontecimiento sucedido en la persona del joven Manuel Rivas, en la mina de "Clarines," Santa Bárbara, 11 feb. 1908, AJ, caja 1908L.

65. Merced Juárez, operario, Mauricio Carrillo, operario, Teofilo Calderón, operario, y José Gallegos, operario, in Averiguación con motivo

á la muerte del que en vida llevó por nombre Higinio Félix, Santa Bárbara, 27 de abril de 1913, AJ, caja 1913L.

66. See Appendix.

67. Ramón López, operario, in Averiguación: relativa al acontecimiento sucedido a Eusebio Orquiz y compañeros en la mina denominada 'Hesperides,' Santa Bárbara, 20 de mayo de 1901, AJ, caja 1901L.

68. Many descriptions of contract arrangements are located in the Archivo Judicial. Two secondary sources discuss the contract system, see Juan Luis Sariego Rodríguez and Raúl Santana Paucar, "Transición tecnológica y resistencia obrera en la minería mexicana," *Cuadernos políticos* 31 (1982), pp. 18–20; and Juan Luis Sariego Rodríguez, Luis Reygadas, Miguel Angel Gómez and Javier Farrera, *El estado y la minería mexicana*, pp. 88–91.

69. E. A. H. Tays, "Present Labor Conditions in Mexico," *EMJ*, 5 Oct. 1907, p. 624.

70. Hugh G. Elwes, "Points about Mexican Labor," *EMJ*, 1 Oct. 1910, p. 662; Evan Fraser-Campbell, "The Management of Mexican Labor," *EMJ*, 3 June 1911, pp. 1104–5; "Mexican Methods of Mine Management and Operation," *CE*, 24 June 1899, 2: 1, Tomo 4. See Appendix for a list of jobs and wage rates.

71. "Mexican Methods of Mine Management and Operation," *CE*, 24 June 1899, 2: 1, Tomo 4.

72. Sariego Rodríguez and Santana Paucar, "Transición tecnológica," p. 20. The two types of contract labor are discussed in Campbell, "The Management of Mexican Labor," *EMJ*, 3 June 1911, p. 1104; on the Palmilla mine, see n. 70.

73. The contract system for sorting ore is discussed in Criminal, averiguación contra Pablo Contreras por el delito de lesiones inferidas Florencio Vázquez, y de homicidio perpetrado en la persona de Sostenes Rosales, Santa Bárbara, 13 de junio de 1913, AJ, caja 1913L; for delivering lime, see Averiguación con motivo a la muerte del Sr. Marcelo Ontiveros en el mineral de Los Azules, Santa Bárbara, 23 de mayo de 1913, AJ.

74. Averiguación levantada con motivo de un cartucho de dinamita estallado en la casa habitación del C. Jefe Municipal de esta Villa, Santa Bárbara, 29 de mayo de 1905, AJ, caja 1905V.

75. See the statement of Tomás Rodríguez, operario, in Criminal en contra de Tomás Rodríguez por el delito de robo de herramientas y metales á la mina denominada La "Capitaneña," Santa Bárbara, 22 de diciembre de 1910, AJ, caja 1910R.

76. ASARCo's arrangements with contratistas are discussed in Ejecutoria dictada en el toca a la apelación interpuesta en la causa instruida en contra de Jorge Pérez y Andrés Domínguez, por el delito de robo, Parral, 24 de oct. de 1925, AJ, caja 1925R.

77. Hugh G. Elwes, "Points about Mexican Labor," *EMJ*, 1 Oct. 1910, p. 662.

78. See the statement of José Gallegos, perforista, in Averiguación con motivo a la muerte del que en vida llevó por nombre Higinio Félix, Santa Bárbara, 27 de abril de 1913, AJ, caja 1913L.

79. Derickson, *Workers' Health, Workers' Democracy*, pp. 9 and 41.

80. Guadalupe Nava Oteo, "La minería," in *Historia moderna de México: El Porfiriato, La vida económica*, ed. Daniel Cosío Villegas, vol. 6, no. 1 (México: Editorial Hermes, 1965), p. 248.

81. Sariego Rodríguez and Santana Paucar, "Transición tecnológica," p. 18; Juan Luis Sariego Rodríguez, "La cultura minera en crisis. Aproximación a algunos elementos de la identidad de un grupo obrero," in *Coloquio sobre cultura obrera*, ed. Victoria Novelo (Tlalpan, México: Secretaría de Educación Pública, Centro de Investigaciones y Estudios Superiores en Antropología Social, 1987), p. 140; and Juan Luis Sariego Rodríguez, *Enclaves y minerales en el norte de México: Historia social de los mineros de Cananea y Nueva Rosita, 1900–1970* (México: Centro de Investigaciones y Estudios Superiores en Antropología Social, 1988), p. 110.

82. "El Parral necesita de un instituto minero," *La Nueva Era*, 16 Nov. 1899, 1: 1, AM.

83. ASARCo, Mexican Mining Department, Santa Bárbara Unit, August 1920, in Archivo General de la Nación, Fondo: Trabajo, Volumen 211, Expediente 14, Folio 100. I thank Jesús Vargas of the Centro de Investigaciones del Estado de Chihuahua for his generosity in sharing this material.

84. All figures that follow, unless otherwise indicated, are from the yearly reports of the jefe político, Hidalgo District, *El Hijo del Parral*, and other correspondence located in the AM, Parral.

85. S. E. Gill, "Mineral District of Hidalgo de Parral," *EMJ*, 22 May 1897, p. 509, cited in Wasserman, *Capitalists, Caciques, and Revolution*, p. 76.

86. Agustín Páez, jefe municipal, Santa Bárbara, to jefe político, Hidalgo District, 14 August 1909: "Y habiéndose celebrado un acuerdo tácite por parte de las dos ó tres compañías en movimiento, para la rebaja en los salarios de todos los empleados y trabajadores . . . "; AM, caja 1909D. On wages increasing in 1910, see Agustín Páez to jefe político, 3 August 1910: "cada día aumentan el número de sus operarios y hacen una pequeña alza en los jornales de sus trabajadores," in AM, caja 1910P. According to the *Chihuahua Enterprise*, mining wages in the district had been reduced since late 1907; see "Cut Miners' Wages: The Low Metal Prices and Increased Labor Supply Doing It," *CE*, 28 Dec. 1907, 10: 3.

87. "Parral New England City," *EPMT*, 25 Nov. 1911, 5: 5, Reel 54.

Chapter 2

1. On the English working class, see Thompson, "Time, Work-Discipline, and Industrial Capitalism," p. 90, and Pollard, *Genesis of Modern Management,* especially the fifth chapter entitled "The Adaptation of the Labour Force." On Piedmont textile mills, see Jacquelyn Dowd Hall et al., *Like a Family: The Making of a Southern Cotton Mill World* (Chapel Hill: University of North Carolina Press, 1987), pp. 31, 123, and 133. Gutman sets out his argument in *Work, Culture, and Society in Industrializing America,* p. 9. On France, see Michelle Perrot, "On the Formation of the French Working Class," in Katznelson and Zolberg, *Working-Class Formation,* p. 79. Donald Reid also describes mine workers in Decazeville, France, as "peasant workers," in his "Labour Management and Labour Conflict in Rural France: The Aubin Miners' Strike of 1869," *Social History* 13: 1 (January 1988), p. 29.

2. Stephen Meyer discusses Ford in *The Five Dollar Day: Labor Management and Social Control in the Ford Motor Company 1908–1921* (Albany: State University of New York Press, 1981), pp. 74, 157, and 160. The British experience is set out in Pollard, *Genesis of Modern Management,* p. 186. For another case, see the discussion of employers in Charles F. Sabel, *Work and Politics: The Division of Labor in Industry* (Cambridge: Cambridge University Press, 1982), p. 109.

3. Friedrich Katz, "Rural Rebellions after 1810," in *Riot, Rebellion, and Revolution: Rural Social Conflict in Mexico,* ed. Katz (Princeton, N.J.: Princeton University Press, 1988), p. 533. Alan Knight also discusses the concentration of land ownership during the Porfiriato, in *The Mexican Revolution,* vol. 1: *Porfirians, Liberals and Peasants* (Cambridge: Cambridge University Press, 1986), p. 95. On land expropriation and community protest accompanying railroad construction, see John H. Coatsworth, "Railroads, Landholding and Agrarian Protest in the Early Porfiriato," *Hispanic American Historical Review* 54 (1974), pp. 48–71.

4. Wasserman, *Capitalists, Caciques, and Revolution,* pp. 44–49, 109, 112, and 135–36. On the effects of political centralization, see also Katz, "Rural Rebellions after 1810," p. 537.

5. Jane-Dale Lloyd, *El proceso de modernización capitalista en el noroeste de Chihuahua (1880–1910)* (México: Universidad Iberoamericana, 1987), pp. 62, 80, and 100–101. Robert H. Holden disputes what he calls the "black legend" of survey companies portrayed by Lloyd and others, in his article "Priorities of the State in the Survey of the Public Land in Mexico, 1876–1911," *Hispanic American Historical Review* 70: 4 (November 1990), pp. 579–608.

6. The dispute between Alvarado and the residents of Las Animas is discussed in Isidro Aguilera, Rancho de Las Animas, 6 Aug. 1906, AM,

caja 1906M. On the abuse of the Municipal Land Law in Villa Escobedo, see Francisco de la Garza, jefe municipal, Villa Escobedo, 2 Nov. 1907, AM, caja 1907Z.

7. On Villa Escobedo, see Presidente municipal, Minas Nuevas, to jefe político, 20 Dec. 1901, AM, caja 1901F; jefe municipal, Villa Escobedo, AM, caja 1903M; jefe municipal, Villa Escobedo, AM, caja 1906H. For Santa Bárbara, see jefe municipal, Santa Bárbara, AM, caja 1903I; jefe municipal, AM, caja 1906K; Agustín Páez discusses the high price of food in the mining town of Santa Bárbara in jefe municipal, Santa Bárbara, 7 Sept. 1907, AM, caja 1907D. For San Francisco del Oro, see jefe municipal, AM, caja 1906C.

8. For Huejotitan, see Año de 1901: Producción de Frutas y Legumbres: Huejotitan, AM, caja 1902B. On the other regions, see Francisco Chávez L., jefe municipal, Valle de Zaragoza to jefe político, Parral, 17 Oct. 1908, AM, caja 1908Q; Emiliano Moreno, jefe municipal, San Antonio del Tule, to jefe político, 17 Oct. 1908, AM, caja 1908V; and Jesús Solis, jefe municipal, San Isidro de las Cuevas, to jefe político, 31 Dec. 1909, AM, caja 1909M.

9. Population figures for the municipalities in Hidalgo District in 1900 are as follows: Huejotitan, 954; Valle de Rosario, 1,484; San Antonio del Tule, 2,533; Valle de Olivos, 2,324; Valle de Zaragoza, 4,172; Balleza, 4,651; and San Isidro de las Cuevas, 4,788. The remarks of the jefe político are located in his report entitled Visita á Balleza, San Antonio del Tule, Huejotitan, Valle de Olivos, Valle del Rosario y Valle de Zaragoza, July 1906, AM, caja 1905E.

10. Petition from 30 vecinos, Hacienda de San José de Gracia, Municipalidad del Rosario, Hidalgo District, 25 Jan. 1902, AM, caja 1904O. For a discussion of the 1883 Ley de Terrenos Baldíos, see Katz, "Rural Rebellions after 1810," p. 534. On Galeana District, see Lloyd, El proceso de modernización capitalista, pp. 71–74.

11. Holden concludes that no land was awarded to survey companies in compensation for work carried out in Hidalgo District between 1876 and 1911; see his "Priorities of the State," p. 589.

12. Presidente municipal, Balleza, to jefe político, 17 June 1903, AM, caja 1903J.

13. Jefe político, Visita á Balleza, San Antonio del Tule, Huejotitan, Valle de Olivos, Valle del Rosario y Valle de Zaragoza, July 1906, AM, caja 1905E.

14. Numerous petitions were sent in 1903 and 1904; see José Pallán, Gobernadorcillo, Pueblo de Guazárachic, and 47 others to jefe político, Hidalgo District, 20 Feb. 1903, AM, caja 1903E; Pallán and 50 signatories to jefe político, 22 Sept. 1903, AM, caja 1903E; Pallán and 50 signatories to Gobernador del Estado de Chihuahua, 21 Aug. 1903, AM, caja

1903E; Pallán and 30 others to jefe político, 4 Feb. 1904, AM, caja 1904C.

15. Carl Lumholtz, *Unknown Mexico: A Record of Five Years' Exploration among the Tribes of the Western Sierra Madre; in the Tierra Caliente of Tepic and Jalisco; and among the Tarascos of Michoacan*, 2 vols. (London: Macmillan and Company, 1903), vol. 1, pp. 119, 120, and 198.

16. Residents of Pueblo of Guazárachic to El Secretario, Secretaría del Gobierno del Estado, Ramo de Fomento, 11 May 1908, AM, caja 1908Ch. See also 6 vecinos del Rancho de la Guitarrilla to jefe político, 4 Jan. 1908, AM, caja 1908V. Petitioners referred to themselves as "vecinos de razón" and "gente castellana."

17. On the revolutionary movement, see de la Garza, jefe municipal interino, Balleza, to jefe político, Hidalgo District, 27 Oct. 1908, AM, caja 1908D. Tarahumara-Mexican relations are also discussed in M. de la Garza, Balleza, 25 March 1908, AM, caja 1908J; M. de la Garza, Balleza, 27 April 1908, AM, caja 1908Ch; and M. de la Garza, Balleza, 28 May 1908, AM, caja 1908D. Lumholtz's remark appears in *Unknown Mexico*, vol. 1, p. 431.

18. R. Garza Cantú to jefe político, 30 Nov. 1903, AM, caja 1903A; Petition from 20 indígenas, San Javier to jefe político, 22 June 1904, AM, caja 1904J; Joaquín Cortazar, Secretaría del Gobierno, Ramo de Fomento, núm. 4618, to jefe político, 25 Oct. 1905, AM, caja 1905T; 18 indígenas, San Pablo de Balleza, to Gobernador del Estado, 10 Nov. 1907, AM, caja 1907AA; Indígenas, San Mateo, to jefe político, 29 July 1907, AM, caja 1907O; Secretaría del Gobierno del Estado, Ramo de Fomento, núm. 7070, to jefe político, 29 Oct. 1907, AM, caja 1907A; and seven documents from indígenas, Pueblo de San Francisco Javier, AM, caja 1907J.

19. Opinions of the jefe político were expressed during the course of his visita to Balleza, July 1906, located in caja 1905E. For the response of the state government, see Joaquín Cortazar, Secretaría del Estado, to jefe político, 11 March 1904, AM, caja 1904E; El Oficial Mayor, Chihuahua, Secretaría del Gobierno del Estado, Ramo de Fomento, to jefe político, 23 June 1905, AM, caja 1905I.

20. Presidente municipal, Valle de Zaragoza, to jefe político, 28 Jan. 1904, AM, caja 1904A and Presidente municipal, San Isidro de las Cuevas, to jefe político, 21 Oct. 1902, AM, caja 1902G. On livestock holdings in Zaragoza, see Expediente: Varios correspondientes al mes de Octubre 1907, Zaragoza, 9 Oct. 1907, AM, caja 1907K.

21. M. de la Garza, jefe municipal interino, Balleza, 24 June 1908, AM, caja 1908D. See also Jesús Solis, jefe municipal, San Isidro de las Cuevas, 31 Dec. 1909, AM, Caja 1909M; Francisco Chávez L., jefe municipal, Valle de Zaragoza, 26 June 1908, AM, caja 1908Q; Francisco Chávez L., 17 Oct. 1908, AM, caja 1908Q; and Jesús J. Solis, 17 June 1908, AM, caja 1908Z.

22. Sixto Flores, presidente municipal, San Isidro de las Cuevas, to jefe político, 20 Jan. 1902, AM, caja 1902A. On the need for winter rains, see Memoria que rinde el C. José Muñoz, jefe municipal, Santa Bárbara, en cumplimiento de la fracción VIII del Artículo 14 de la Ley Reglamentaria para la Organización de los Distritos del Estado, Año de 1905, 5 Jan. 1906, AM, caja 1906C. The agricultural cycle in the district is described in Jefe municipal, Valle de Rosario, 14 Oct. 1907; jefe municipal, Valle de Olivos, 18 Oct. 1907; jefe municipal, Balleza, 9 Oct. 1907; and jefe municipal, Santa Bárbara, 14 Oct. 1907, all in AM, caja 1907K. See also Lumholtz, *Unknown Mexico*, vol. 1, pp. 206–7.

23. Francisco Chávez, jefe municipal, Zaragoza, 18 Sept. 1906, AM, caja 1906N.

24. Letters of resignation from the post of comisario de policía include D. Villalovos, Comisario Propietario, San Nicolas del Terrero, 12 Feb. 1903, AM, caja 1903E; Dulces N. Piñon, Valle del Rosario, 17 Dec. 1904, AM, caja 1904A; Jorge Loya, El Comisario, San Antonio del Tule, 1 Dec. 1902, AM, caja 1902H; Amadeo Loya, Comisario Rural de Baqueteros, 31 Aug. 1904, AM, caja 1904C. Even a presidente municipal resigned to look for wage labor; see Antonio Aguirres, presidente municipal, Guazárachic, 12 Dec. 1903, AM, caja 1903E.

25. Lloyd, *El proceso de modernización capitalista,* pp. 50 and 100–104.

26. Douglas R. Holmes and Jean H. Quataert, "An Approach to Modern Labor: Worker Peasantries in Historic Saxony and the Friuli Region over Three Centuries," *Comparative Studies in Society and History* 28: 2 (April 1986), p. 192. Michael J. Piore discusses migration and peasant workers, in his *Birds of Passage: Migrant Labor and Industrial Societies* (Cambridge: Cambridge University Press, 1979), pp. 88–91.

27. Miguel Armendariz, jefe municipal, Balleza, to jefe político, 16 Aug. 1905, AM, caja 1905I. On population increase during planting and harvesting, see Sixto Flores, presidente municipal, San Isidro de las Cuevas, 7 Jan. 1904, AM, caja 1904I.

28. Armendariz, jefe municipal, Balleza, 22 July 1907, AM, caja 1907Z, and the official response in Secretaría del Gobierno del Estado, Ramo de Instrucción Pública, 8 Aug. 1907, AM, caja 1907P.

29. Francisco Chávez F., jefe municipal, Valle de Zaragoza, 5 Aug. 1908, AM, caja 1908E.

30. El Canciller encargado del Consulado de México, en Los Angeles, found in J. Cortazar, Secretaría del Gobierno, to jefe político, Distrito Hidalgo, 21 Oct. 1904, AM, caja 1904G. See also Cortazar to jefe político, 26 May 1904, AM, caja 1904E, and Cortazar to jefe político, 19 Aug. 1904, AM, caja 1904H.

31. On the difference between Mexican and American wages, see

Wasserman, *Capitalists, Caciques, and Revolution,* p. 122.

32. William K. Meyers, "Second Division of the North: Formation and Fragmentation of the Laguna's Popular Movement, 1910–11," in Katz, *Riot, Rebellion, and Revolution,* p. 458. For a recent study of the factors influencing mine workers and others to leave Zacatecas to search elsewhere for work, see Armando Márquez Herrera, "Las transformaciones de la minería zacatecana durante el porfiriato," in *Minería regional mexicana: Primera reunión de historiadores de la minería latinoamericana (IV),* eds. Dolores Avila, Inés Herrera and Rina Ortiz (México: Instituto Nacional de Antropología e Historia, 1994).

33. The Dillingham Commission figures in Mario T. García, *Desert Immigrants: The Mexicans of El Paso, 1880–1920* (New Haven: Yale University Press, 1981), p. 62; Bureau of Labor figures appear in "Mexican Labor and Its Place in This Country," *EPMT,* 17 Dec. 1908, p. 8, col. 4, Reel 44. Jane-Dale Lloyd describes how Galeana District became a passageway for migrants on their way to the United States, in her *El proceso de modernización capitalista,* p. 46. On the development of El Paso as a labor supply center and on the activities of the labor contractors, or *renganchistas,* see García, *Desert Immigrants,* pp. 33, 35, 51, and 62.

34. The *EPMT* made much of this yearly migration pattern; see "Mexican Laborers Returning Home," *EPMT,* 22 Nov. 1910, p. 3, col. 7, Reel 50, and "Influx of Mexican Laborers Is Beginning," *EPMT,* 28 Oct. 1911, p. 10, col. 2, Reel 54. Katz also points to the heterogeneous wage-labor force in "Rural Rebellions after 1810," p. 544. According to Wasserman, the percentage of the total workforce in agriculture declined from 24.5 percent in 1895 to 21.4 percent in 1910; see his *Capitalists, Caciques, and Revolution,* p. 123.

35. All of these comments, made by mine managers, appear in interviews with American mine managers located in the Edward L. Doheny Research Fund Collection, Occidental College, Los Angeles. My thanks to Jonathan Brown for his generosity in sharing this material with me.

36. Shepherd, *Silver Magnet,* p. 141.

37. Candelaria mines are discussed in Morris B. Parker, *Mules, Mines and Me in Mexico, 1895–1932* (Tucson: University of Arizona Press, 1979), p. 74, and in Laird to Dwight, 30 April 1909, Thomas Wentworth Peirce, Jr., Papers, BLAC.

38. Piore, *Birds of Passage,* pp. 54 and 88. For more on the activities of worker peasantries, see Douglas R. Holmes, *Cultural Disenchantments: Worker Peasantries in Northeast Italy* (Princeton, N.J.: Princeton University Press, 1989).

39. "El Ferro-Carril á Guanaceví. Emigración de trabajadores," *El Hijo del Parral,* 22 June 1902, AM, caja 1902D.

40. Mining companies in Chihuahua offered high wages to attract skilled workers from other Mexican states. This is discussed in File: Chihuahua: Porvenir, near San Pedro, Report, 26 June 1910, ASARCo Archive, Tucson. On agricultural wages in Hidalgo District, see Presidente municipal, Valle de Zaragoza to jefe político, AM, caja 1900D; Presidente municipal, Valle de Olivos, caja 1900; Presidente municipal, San Ygnacio, caja 1900; Presidente municipal, Olivos, to jefe político, 6 Feb. 1903, AM, caja 1903A; Jefe municipal, Balleza, 24 June 1908, AM, caja 1908D; Jefe municipal, Valle de Zaragoza, 26 June 1908, AM, caja 1908Q; and Jefe municipal, San Isidro de las Cuevas, 17 June 1908, AM, caja 1908Z.

41. "Labor Conditions in Mines," Doheny Research Fund Collection, pp. 1–2. The Doheny collection contains interviews conducted during the Mexican Revolution with several managers who had extensive experience in copper and lead-silver mining in northern Mexico during the Porfiriato. While managers attempted to portray themselves in the best light possible, the interviews, used cautiously, can deliver valid conclusions concerning the organization of mine work and management policies toward labor.

42. Adrian Shuber, *The Road to Revolution in Spain: The Coal Miners of Asturias, 1860–1934* (Urbana: University of Illinois Press, 1987), pp. 36–37; Peter N. Stearns, *Paths to Authority: The Middle Class and the Industrial Labor Force in France, 1820–48* (Urbana: University of Illinois Press, 1978), p. 50; and on migrants as target earners, see Piore, *Birds of Passage*, p. 95.

43. "Railroads Shipping Mexicans," *EPMT,* 1 April 1910, p. 8, Reel 48.

44. Donald Reid, "Industrial Paternalism: Discourse and Practice in Nineteenth-Century French Mining and Metallurgy," *Comparative Studies in Society and History* 27: 4 (1985), p. 583. Railroad companies using this tactic are discussed in William E. French, "Business as Usual: Mexico North Western Railway Managers Confront the Mexican Revolution," *Mexican Studies/Estudios Mexicanos* 5: 2 (Summer 1989), p. 226.

45. "Interview with Willard Morse of ASARCo," Doheny Research Fund Collection.

46. "Questionnaires of R. G. Cleland. Answers," Doheny Research Fund Collection.

47. Interview with Douglas, in "Great Need to Dealing Carefully and Intelligently with Mexico," *EPMT,* 18 Dec. 1910, p. 8, Reel 50.

48. "Informant: American for 15 Years, Manager of Mine in Western Mexico," Doheny Research Fund Collection.

49. P. V. Fishback, "Did Coal Miners 'Owe Their Souls to the Company Store'? Theory and Evidence from the Early 1900s," *The Journal of Economic History* 46: 4 (December 1986), pp. 1012 and 1029.

50. Hall, *Like a Family*, p. 129, and Cathy L. McHugh, *Mill Family: The Labor System in the Southern Cotton Textile Industry, 1880–1915* (New York: Oxford University Press, 1988), pp. 19–20.

51. Ramón Eduardo Ruiz, *The People of Sonora and Yankee Capitalists* (Tucson: University of Arizona Press, 1988), p. 76.

52. French, "Business as Usual," p. 226.

53. D. E. Woodbridge, "Labor Data of Northern Mexico Mine," *MMJ*, July 1913, pp. 348–49. One mine manager interviewed in the Doheny Collection identified company stores run by Spaniards in southern Sinaloa as the worst offenders against Mexican workers. He also stated that mine owners, including some Americans, made at least 25 percent profit on items in their stores there. See "Labor Conditions. Southern Sinaloa," Doheny Research Fund Collection.

54. Contract between W. S. Harrison, San Francisco del Oro Mining Company Limited, and G. C. Beckmann, 1 July 1910, located in Hyslop Papers, FF1, Box 4. The operation of the store is discussed further in Hyslop to Calvert G. Schobell, British Vice-Consul, Chihuahua, 16 Aug. 1911, Hyslop Papers, FF 36, Box 2.

55. For a discussion of the economic risks involved in opening a company store under such circumstances, see Fishback, "Did Coal Miners 'Owe Their Souls to the Company Store'?," p. 1014. The system of granting credit based on work already accomplished, used in Sonora, is discussed in Ingersoll, *In and under Mexico*, p. 44.

56. Baca's behavior is discussed in J. M. Delgado, jefe municipal, Villa Escobedo, to jefe político, 30 April 1908, AM, caja 1908A; and Jorge Maul, jefe municipal, Villa Escobedo, to jefe político, 5 March 1909, AM, caja 1909B. The difficult economic times are outlined by the Parral Grocery Company (El Centro Minero) to jefe político, 8 Feb. 1909, AM, caja 1909B.

57. See the coverage given this question in letters from mine workers in *El Correo de Chihuahua* (hereafter cited as *El Correo*), including "Remetido," *El Correo*, 18 Feb. 1907, University of Texas, Austin, BLAC, MF 479, Reel 6 (all subsequent citations of *El Correo* are from the BLAC); "Las tiendas de raya en Santa Eulalia," *El Correo*, 22 Feb. 1907, Reel 6; "Las tiendas de raya," *El Correo*, 4 March 1907, Reel 6; "Noticias de Santa Eulalia," *El Correo*, 6 March 1907, Reel 6; and "Lo de las tiendas de raya," *El Correo*, 9 March 1907, Reel 6.

58. Circular núm. 2044, 19 June 1905, in El O. M. E. de la Sria., Secretaría del Gobierno del Estado, Ramo de Hacienda, núm. 3536, to jefe político, Distrito Hidalgo, 18 Sept. 1908, AM, caja 1908X; Secretaría del Gobierno del Estado, Ramo de Gobernación, núm. 147, to jefe político, Parral, 30 March 1909, AM, caja 1909A.

59. French, "Business as Usual," p. 231.

60. The movement to enforce Sunday closing and merchant reactions

are documented in Agustín Páez, jefe municipal, Santa Bárbara, to jefe político, Parral, 25 Dec. 1908, AM, caja 1908Ll. Fishback argues that the issuance of company scrip is the most frequently misunderstood practice of the mining company. In his opinion, scrip was a convenience for workers, offering them the opportunity to draw wages as they were earned. See Fishback, "Did Coal Miners 'Owe Their Souls to the Company Store'?," pp. 1022 and 1029.

61. Ingersoll observes that workers in Mexico did not resist paternalism in the same way as workers in the United States; see his *In and under Mexico*, p. 116.

62. "Questionnaires of R. G. Cleland. Answers," Doheny Research Fund Collection.

63. "Informant: Officer of Moctezuma Copper Company of Sonora," Doheny Research Fund Collection.

64. Secretaría del Gobierno del Estado, Ramo de Fomento, 10 Oct. 1907, AM, caja 1907D; Agustín Páez, jefe municipal, Santa Bárbara, to jefe político, Parral, 29 August 1910, AM, caja 1910J.

65. "Smelter at Aguas Calientes," Doheny Research Fund Collection.

66. "Parral Notes," *CE*, 12 Nov. 1898, 3: 1. See the following chapter for a discussion of the importance of education to middle-class Chihuahuans.

67. Informe rendido por el Sr. Rodolfo Valles, jefe político del Distrito Hidalgo, en al I. Ayuntamiento de Hidalgo del Parral, el día 1o de enero de 1907, AM, caja 1907J. Figures on school attendance in Parral are from the same document. For schools in other mining towns, see Noticia del 1o de enero 1906 ál 31 de mayo de 1906: Noticia mensual que rinde la J. M. de San Francisco del Oro, 31 May 1906, AM, caja 1906C; Noticias mensuales—Villa Escobedo and Santa Bárbara, 1 April 1906, AM, caja 1906H.

68. On the safety movement in the United States, see Daniel Nelson, *Managers and Workers: Origins of the New Factory System in the United States, 1880–1920* (Madison: University of Wisconsin Press, 1975), p. 33. On safety standards and health care in mining, see Derickson, *Workers' Health, Workers' Democracy*, p. 190. An analysis of the timing of these changes in the lumber industry in the United States is found in Daniel A. Cornford, *Workers and Dissent in the Redwood Empire* (Philadelphia: Temple University Press, 1987), p. 206.

69. David G. Backer, "The Workers of the Modern Mines in Southern Peru," in Greaves and Culver, *Miners and mining in the Americas*, p. 253.

70. "Interview with Willard Morse, ASARCo," Doheny Research Fund Collection.

71. *MMJ* 9: 1 (July 1909), p. 1.

72. Agustín Páez, jefe municipal, Santa Bárbara, to jefe político, 4 Janu-

ary 1910, AM, caja 1910B. The actions of the Tecolotes Mining Company during the epidemic in 1909 are discussed in Páez to jefe político, 5 Nov. 1909, AM, caja 1909A, and Páez to jefe político, 2 Dec. 1909, AM, caja 1909A. The number of American doctors is listed in Páez to jefe político, 15 Dec. 1907, AM, caja 1907H.

73. "Correspondencia del Parral," *El Correo,* 11 May 1905, Reel 4.

74. Shepherd, *Silver Magnet,* p. 218.

75. "Interview with Willard Morse, ASARCo," Doheny Research Fund Collection.

76. David Crew, *Town in the Ruhr: A Social History of Bochum, 1860-1914* (New York: Columbia University Press, 1979), p. 153. The use of personal contact to form a bond of loyalty between employers and workers is discussed in Dowd Hall, *Like a Family,* p. 92. Peter Stearns also stresses that nineteenth-century French industrialists expected "lively gratitude" and loyalty from workers in exchange for paternalistic measures; see his *Paths to Authority,* p. 101.

77. Ingersoll, *In and under Mexico,* p. 116. Other examples of mine managers referring to Mexicans as children include "Interview with Willard Morse, ASARCo," Doheny Research Fund Collection; "Labor Conditions in Mine," Doheny Research Fund Collection; and T. Lane Carter, "The Peon and the Kaffir," *EPMT,* 15 Oct. 1911, Reel 54.

78. Ingersoll, *In and under Mexico,* p. 117. Morse uses the phrases "fatherly interest" and "big parent" in his interview in the Doheny Research Fund Collection.

79. T. Lane Carter, "The Peon and the Kaffir—A Comparison," *EPMT,* 15 Oct. 1911, Reel 54.

80. M. Cavazos, jefe municipal, Santa Bárbara, to jefe político, Parral, 23 Nov. 1911, AM, caja 1911F.

81. Hyslop to Calvert G. Schobell, British Vice-Consul, Chihuahua, 21 August 1911, James E. Hyslop Collection, Box 2, FF 36.

82. Knight, *Mexican Revolution,* vol. 1, p. 144. See Reid's discussion of a comparable situation in France, in his "Industrial Paternalism," pp. 585-86.

83. For the process of choosing an encargado in Santa Bárbara, see J. J. Gutiérrez, presidente municipal, Santa Bárbara, to jefe político, Parral, 23 August 1901, AM, caja 1901F. For an example of an encargado sending workers to jail, see Matteo A. Pagano, encargado, Palmilla Milling Company, Parral, to jefe político, AM, caja 1909F.

84. "Great Excitement," *CE,* 19 July 1902.

85. "Workers Plan Gigantic Union," *EPMT,* 8 July 1911; "General Orozco in Chihuahua," *EPMT,* 5 July 1911; and "Women Strike in Chihuahua," *EPMT,* 10 July 1911.

86. "A traves del estado: Parral," *El Correo,* 21 Dec. 1902, Reel 1; "A

traves del estado: Parral," *El Correo*, 25 Dec. 1902, Reel 1; "A traves del estado: Parral," *El Correo*, 16 Jan. 1903, Reel 2; "A traves del estado: Parral," *El Correo*, 11 Sept 1903, Reel 2; and "Nueva Acordada," *La Nueva Era*, 18 Oct. 1903, AM, caja 1903C.

87. Activities of the force are discussed in Ynocencia Palma, El jefe de la policía rural, Santa Bárbara, to jefe político, Parral, 10 Nov. 1903, AM, caja 1903K; Expediente de los negocios pertenecientes a la Municipalidad de Parral y que corresponden ál mes de agosto de 1904, AM, caja 1904H; Jefe de la primera sección de Policía Rural to jefe político, 4 Sept. 1904, AM, caja 1904H; Ynocencia Palma, Los Azules, to jefe político, Parral, 13 Dec. 1907, AM, caja 1907ñ.

88. Table 2.1 was compiled from correspondence between officials in Santa Bárbara, Villa Escobedo, Los Azules, and San Francisco del Oro with jefe político, Hidalgo District. See especially Presidente municipal, Santa Bárbara, 12 Dec. 1903, AM, caja 1903I; Albino Padilla, presidente municipal, Santa Bárbara, 11 Oct. 1904, AM, caja 1904B; F. Villegas, jefe municipal, Santa Bárbara, 14 Aug. 1906, AM, caja 1906T; Agustín Páez, jefe municipal, Santa Bárbara, 26 Dec. 1907, AM, caja 1907ñ; E. de la Fuente, Villa Escobedo, 8 Feb. 1908, AM, caja 1908C; J. M. Delgado, jefe municipal, Villa Escobedo, 2 April 1908, AM, caja 1908C; Jorge Maul, jefe municipal, Villa Escobedo, 3 June 1908, AM, caja 1908ñ; Agustín Páez, 8 Dec. 1909, AM, caja 1909A; F. Gaudan, Tesorero Municipal, Santa Bárbara, 15 March 1910, AM, caja 1910H; Agustín Páez, 10 Feb. 1910, AM, caja 1910H; Páez, 7 Dec. 1910, AM, caja 1910P; and Páez, 5 March 1911, AM, caja 1911B.

89. Presidente municipal, Santa Bárbara, to jefe político, Parral, 17 May 1900, AM, caja 1900 SUSY; presidente municipal, Santa Bárbara, to jefe político, Parral, 22 May 1903, AM, caja 1903I; presidente municipal, Santa Bárbara, to jefe político, Parral, 9 July 1903, AM, caja 1903I; Agustín Páez, jefe municipal, Santa Bárbara, 19 Sept. 1906, AM, caja 1906Y; Páez, 9 May 1907, AM, caja 1907A.

90. The jefe político in Parral justified this reduction by citing the formula used in Mexico City to determine the number of police: the ratio was to be one for every five hundred inhabitants; see his Informe, Hidalgo del Parral, AM, caja 1908H. For Santa Bárbara, see Informe Oficial, rendido por el C. Agustín Páez, jefe municipal, Santa Bárbara, 31 Dec. 1909, AM, caja 1909A.

91. Páez, Santa Bárbara, 25 Feb. 1909, AM, caja 1909D; Páez, 7 April 1909, AM, caja 1909D.

92. G. Porras, Ramo de Gobernación, to jefe político, Parral, 15 March 1909, AM, caja 1909D; Páez, 2 April 1909, AM, caja 1909D; G. Porras to jefe político, 5 Nov. 1910, AM, caja 1910G.

93. F. Villegas, jefe municipal, Santa Bárbara, to jefe político, Parral, 4

August 1906, AM, caja 1906T; V. Salado Alvarez, Secretaría del Gobierno del Estado, Ramo de Gobernación, 13 August 1906, AM, caja 1906T.

94. This phrase is quoted from Páez, 3 Oct. 1906, AM, caja 1906T.

95. Ignacio Sandoval, jefe municipal, Villa Escobedo, and representatives of six mining companies, 21 March 1907, AM, caja 1907Z.

96. Nieves Heredia to jefe político, Parral, 10 Dec. 1908, AM, caja 1908X.

97. Páez to jefe político, Parral, 26 Nov. 1907, AM, caja 1907D; Páez to jefe político, 17 Oct. 1908, AM, caja 1908AA.

98. A. H. Martin, "Successful Mine Management," *MMJ* 11: 6 (December 1910), p. 20. Another example of this type of article is J. E. Wilson, "The Handling of Mexican Labor," *MMJ* 11:7 (Jan. 1911).

99. "Ecos de Villa Escobedo," *El Padre Padilla*, 15 Nov. 1905, p. 1, AM.

Chapter 3

1. Alan Knight uses the term *developmentalist ideology* to describe beliefs shared by respectable Porfirians, particularly an emphasis on time discipline, thrift, hard work, hygiene, and progress. See Knight, *Mexican Revolution*, 2 vols. (Cambridge: Cambridge University Press, 1986), vol. 1, pp. 23, 84. On the inculcation of work discipline, see Thompson, "Time, Work-Discipline, and Industrial Capitalism." For the case of the Mexican working class and time discipline, see Alan Knight, "The Working Class and the Mexican Revolution, c. 1900–1920," *Journal of Latin American Studies* 16 (May 1984), pp. 51–97. Also on developmentalist ideology in Latin America, see David McCreery, "'This Life of Misery and Shame': Female Prostitution in Guatemala City, 1880–1920," *Journal of Latin American Studies* 18: 2 (November 1986), pp. 333–53.

2. Stearns, *Paths to Authority*, p. 150.

3. Meyer, *Five Dollar Day*, p. 151.

4. Philip Corrigan and Derek Sayer, *The Great Arch: English State Formation as Cultural Revolution* (Oxford: Basil Blackwell, 1985), pp. 61, 117–19, 129, 132, 140, 155, 171, 184, and 200. For a discussion of the "Great Arch" in the Mexican context, see Alan Knight, "The Peculiarities of Mexican History: Mexico Compared to Latin America, 1821–1992," *Journal of Latin American Studies* 24 (Quincentenary Supplement 1992), pp. 134–44.

5. Max Weber, cited in Robert Moore, "History, Economics and Religion: A Review of 'The Max Weber Thesis,'" in *Max Weber and Modern Sociology*, ed. Arun Sahay (London: Routledge and Kegan Paul, 1971), p. 86.

6. Alan Knight discusses these "American" values in *Mexican Revolution,* vol. 1, p. 69. A recent work judges these values to be "negative." See Ruiz, *People of Sonora and Yankee Capitalists,* pp. 20, 194–96.

7. Doris M. Ladd, *The Making of a Strike: Mexican Silver Workers' Struggles in Real del Monte, 1766–1775* (Lincoln: University of Nebraska Press, 1988), pp. 43 and 74. Cheryl Martin discusses the attempts to limit the festive calendar of mine workers in colonial Chihuahua, in her "Public Celebrations, Popular Culture and Labor Discipline in Eighteenth-Century Chihuahua," in *Rituals of Rule, Rituals of Resistance: Public Celebrations and Popular Culture in Mexico,* ed. William H. Beezley, Cheryl E. Martin, and William E. French (Wilmington, Del.: Scholarly Resources, 1994).

8. Viqueira Albán, *¿Relajados o reprimidos?* Moral reform in Bourbon New Spain is a subject with a growing historiography; for some recent works, see Pamela Voekel, "Peeing on the Palace: Bodily Resistance to Bourbon Reforms in Mexico," *Journal of Historical Sociology* 5: 2 (June 1992); and Susan Deans-Smith, "The Working Poor and the Eighteenth-Century Colonial State: Gender, Public Order and Work Discipline," in Beezley, Martin, and French, *Rituals of Rule, Rituals of Resistance,* pp. 47–75.

9. Jean Franco, *Plotting Women: Gender and Representation in Mexico* (New York: Columbia University Press, 1989), p. 79.

10. Anne Staples, "'Policia y buen gobierno': Nineteenth-Century Efforts to Regulate Public Behavior," in Beezley, Martin, and French, *Rituals of Rule, Rituals of Resistance,* pp. 115–126.

11. Officials and residents in Parral and smaller mining centers constantly referred to arriving workers and other newcomers as outsiders or unknown people (*gente desconocida*). For two examples, see Presidente municipal, Santa Bárbara, to jefe político, Distrito de Hidalgo, 25 Sept. 1903, AM, caja 1903I, and 29 residents to the jefe político, Distrito de Hidalgo, 10 June 1903, AM, caja 1903M. Laurence Rohlfes maintains that during the final decade of Porfirian rule, residents of Mexico City also perceived an increasing "crime problem" in their city. See his "Police and Penal Correction in Mexico City, 1876–1911: A Study of Order and Progress in Porfirian Mexico" (Ph.D. diss., Tulane University, 1983), p. 139.

12. Jefe de la Seguridad Pública, Los Azules, to jefe político, Hidalgo District, 21 June 1904, AM, caja 1904G; Presidente municipal, Santa Bárbara, to jefe político, 25 June 1904, AM, caja 1904O; Agustín Páez, jefe municipal, Santa Bárbara, to jefe político, 3 Oct. 1908, AM, caja 1908AA. For Villa Escobedo, see Presidente municipal, Villa Escobedo, to jefe político, 27 Sept. 1904, and 9 Nov. 1904, AM, caja 1904C. Re-

ports from San Francisco del Oro in Presidente municipal, San Francisco del Oro, to jefe político, 13 Apr 1906, AM, caja 1906C; Páez to jefe político, 2 Jan. 1911, AM, caja 1911B. On railroad workers, see J. J. Gutiérrez, presidente municipal, Santa Bárbara, to jefe político, 17 Dec. 1900, AM, caja 1900SUSY.

13. This phrase began to appear in Chihuahua newspapers and in Hidalgo District reports soon after the turn of the century. For an early usage, see "El Ferro-Carril a Guanaceví. Emigración de trabajadores," *El Hijo del Parral,* 22 June 1902, p. 1, AM, caja 1902D.

14. This figure is from José Iturriaga, as cited in Knight, *Mexican Revolution,* vol. 1, p. 43. On the middle class and moral reform, see ibid., pp. 63–68. On the middle class in Chihuahua, see Wasserman, *Capitalists, Caciques, and Revolution,* pp. 95–97.

15. Rodolfo Valles, jefe político, to C. C. Miembros de la Asamblea Municipal, Parral, 2 July 1906, AM, caja 1906N.

16. "El Ferro-Carril á Guanaceví. Emigración de trabajadores," *El Hijo del Parral,* 22 June 1902, p. 1, AM, caja 1902D.

17. "Como debe ser un obrero," *El Correo,* 15 July 1904, p. 3.

18. "Las clases trabajadores: cooperación y ahorro," *La Nueva Era* (Santa Bárbara), 1 May 1904, p. 1, AM, caja 1904F. For an interesting discussion of the social divide between the *gente decente* and workers, also conceptualized in cultural terms and in a comparative context, that of Lima, see David S. Parker, "White-Collar Lima, 1910–1929: Commercial Employees and the Rise of the Peruvian Middle Class," *Hispanic American Historical Review* 72: 1 (February 1992), esp. pp. 52–57.

19. The material on social Catholicism is from Jorge Adame Goddard, *El pensamiento político y social de los católicos mexicanos, 1867–1914* (México: Universidad Nacional Autónoma de México, 1981), pp. 117, 145–49, 190–91, 206, 219.

20. In Hidalgo District, liberal papers such as *El Hijo del Parral* and *La Nueva Era* devoted considerable attention to these issues. Goddard puts it as follows: "El tema de la 'desmoralización de las masas' fue un tópico tratado constantemente por católicos y liberales [The theme of the 'corruption of the masses' was a topic treated constantly by Catholics and liberals]" (*El pensamiento político,* p. 206; see also pp. 114–15).

21. "La embriaguez," *El Hijo del Parral,* 29 April 1900, p. 1, AM, caja 1900.

22. "Desastrosos efectos de la embriaguez," *El Correo,* 14 March 1905, p. 1, Reel 4.

23. Rohlfes, "Police and Penal Correction in Mexico City," p. 139. In Chihuahua, governmental authorities and their respectable critics linked criminality with alcohol. For examples of this viewpoint, see J. Cortazar, Ramo de Gobernación, Estado de Chihuahua, to Jefe Político, Hidalgo

District, 16 June 1903, AM, caja 1903A, and "Iniciativa contra el alcoholismo . . .," *El Correo*, 2 May 1903, p. 2, Reel 2. On the link between alcohol and crime in Mexico City, see Carlos Roumagnac, *Los criminales en México: Ensayo de psicología criminal* (México: Tipografía "El Fénix," 1904), esp. pp. 47–53, and Miguel Macedo, *La criminalidad en México: Medios de combatirla* (México: Secretaría de Fomento, 1897), pp. 31–32.

24. "México," *El Correo*, 7 Feb. 1903, p. 3, Reel 2.

25. For a discussion of the impact of Lamarckianism in Latin America, alcohol's role as a racial poison, and race, see Nancy Leys Stepan, *"The Hour of Eugenics": Race, Gender and Nation in Latin America* (Ithaca: Cornell University Press, 1991), especially pp. 63–101.

26. Silvestre Terrazas, "El alcoholismo," *El Correo*, 11 June 1902, p. 1, Reel 1; "Iniciativa contra el alcoholismo . . .," *El Correo*, 2 May 1903, p. 2, Reel 2.

27. Alfonzo Cinelti, "El Trabajo," *El Hijo del Parral*, 9 Dec. 1900, p. 1, AM, caja 1902G. See also "La embriaguez," *El Hijo del Parral*, 29 April 1900, p. 1, AM, caja 1900.

28. For a discussion of prostitution's effect on corrupting public morals in Hidalgo District, see "La prostitución y los menores de edad," *El Hijo del Parral*, 2 Sept. 1900, p. 1, AM, caja 1902D.

29. *El Correo* constantly complained of alcohol sales in brothels. For one example, see "Ventas clandestinas," *El Correo*, 21 Jan. 1908, p. 1, Reel 7.

30. Cinco vecinos ál C. C. Presidente y Vocales del C. Ayuntamiento del Hidalgo del Parral, 21 July 1903, in Expediente que contiene negocios correspondientes al mes de julio, Año 1903, Parral, AM, caja 1903H.

31. "Necesidad de reglamentar la prostitución," *El Hijo del Parral*, 30 April 1899, p. 2, AM, caja 1900I. See "Iniciativa contra el alcoholismo y la prostitución . . .," *El Correo*, 2 May 1903, p. 2, Reel 2.

32. See the discussion of brothel regulations in Mexico City and a short summary of regulation in Mexico in Sergio González Rodríguez, *Los bajos fondos: El antro, la bohemia y el café* (México: Cal y Arena, 1989), pp. 32, 34, and 61–68.

33. "A traves del Estado: Parral," *El Correo*, 8 July 1902, p. 2, Reel 1.

34. "A dónde podrian ser trasladadas," *El Correo*, 17 Dec. 1907, p. 1, Reel 6.

35. Originally published in *El Hijo del Parral* and reprinted as "A traves del Estado: Parral," *El Correo*, 29 Aug. 1902, p. 1, Reel 1.

36. Ibid.

37. "El juego," *El Correo*, 21 June 1905, p. 2, Reel 4.

38. "El juego," *El Hijo del Parral*, 15 June 1902, p. 1, AM, caja 1902D.

39. J. Reyes Zavala, "El juego," *El Correo*, 25 Jan. 1907, p. 2, Reel 6.

40. "Faltan brazos y sobran vagos," *El Correo,* 10 Jan. 1906, p. 2, Reel 5. On ideas about prisons and prison reform in Mexico, see Robert Buffington, "Revolutionary Reform: The Mexican Revolution and the Discourse on Prison Reform," *Mexican Studies/Estudios Mexicanos* 9: 1 (Winter 1993), esp. pp. 74–87.

41. "La vagancia," *El Correo,* 8 Feb. 1907, Reel 6.

42. Moisés González Navarro, *La vida social,* in Cosío Villegas, *Historia moderna de México,* vol. 4 (México: Editorial Hermes, 1957), p. 422. Calls for vagrancy regulation in Parral were extensive; as examples, see "Dos verguenzas," *El Hijo del Parral,* 9 July 1899, p. 1, AM, caja 1901C; "Menesteros ó flojos," *La Nueva Era,* 5 Jan. 1902, p. 1, AM, caja 1902D; and "Perder el tiempo," *El Hijo del Parral,* 23 July 1905, p. 1, AM, caja 1905F.

43. "Notas oficiales," *El Correo,* 8 Nov. 1904, p. 1, Reel 3.

44. Luis Terrazas, Gobernador, ál jefe político, D. Rodolfo Valles, Parral, 25 June 1904, AM, caja 1900A.

45. "To Encourage Laboring Men: Gov. Creel Planning to Help Them to Get Their Own Homes," *CE,* 14 Nov. 1908, p. 1.

46. Francisco Díaz, "Los artesanos informales," *El Correo,* 1 May 1905, p. 2, Reel 4.

47. "Castigo para los artesanos informales," *El Correo,* 1 March 1906, p. 2, Reel 5.

48. "Los vagos," *El Hijo del Parral,* 25 Oct. 1903, p. 1, AM, caja 1903C.

49. "Franquezas populares," *El Correo,* 14 Aug. 1906, p. 1, Reel 5.

50. "Las fiestas de navidad," *El Hijo del Parral,* 14 Oct. 1900, p. 1, AM, caja 1902D. See also "Los fiestas anuales," *La Nueva Era,* 29 Sept. 1901, p. 1, AM, caja 1903H.

51. For a discussion of Terrazas's relationship with Díaz and his terms as governor, see Wasserman, *Capitalists, Caciques, and Revolution,* pp. 36–42.

52. "Hace treinta años y despues de treinta años," *El Correo,* 13 April 1904, p. 1, Reel 3.

53. Silvestre Terrazas, "Iniciativa contra el alcoholismo y la prostitución, presentada al I. Ayuntamiento por el Regidor 6° C. S. Terrazas," *El Correo,* 2 May 1903, p. 2, Reel 2.

54. Ramo de Gobernación, núm. 858, 16 June 1903, in AM, caja 1903A.

55. "Reglamento de cantinas," *El Correo,* 9 July 1903, p. 2, Reel 2. See also "Un decreto del Congreso del Estado," *El Correo,* 3 July 1903, p. 1, Reel 2; "¡Ahora ó nunca!," *El Correo,* 21 June 1903, p. 1, Reel 2; "Decreto sobre las cantinas," *El Correo,* 8 July 1903, p. 1, Reel 2; and "Las cantinas," *El Correo,* 15 July 1903, p. 1, Reel 2.

56. "Las primeras medidas," *El Correo,* 4 June 1903, p. 1, Reel 2;

"Un decreto del Congreso del Estado," *El Correo*, 3 July 1903, p. 1, Reel 2; "Reglamento de juego," *El Correo*, 9 July 1904, p. 2, Reel 3; and "Reglamento de juego," *El Correo*, 11 July 1904, p. 2, Reel 3.

57. "En el Ayuntamiento," *El Correo*, 26 Sept. 1903, p. 1, Reel 2; "El Reglamento de Tolerancia," *El Correo*, 27 Sept. 1903, p. 1, Reel 2; "El Reglamento de Tolerancia, " *El Correo*, 3 Oct. 1903, p. 1, Reel 2.

58. On Creel's rule in Chihuahua, see Wasserman, *Capitalists, Caciques, and Revolution*, pp. 131–38.

59. "Notas oficiales," *El Correo*, 19 Jan. 1905, p. 1, Reel 4, and "Informe leido el 1° de junio de 1905 por el Gobernador Interino Constitucional del Estado C. Enrique C. Creel," *El Correo*, 2 June 1905, p. 2, Reel 4.

60. "Aprehensiones," *El Correo*, 19 June 1905, p. 1, Reel 4.

61. "Magnífica disposición," *El Correo*, 14 July 1904, p. 1, Reel 3. For examples of complaints against cantinas and billiard halls, see "Las cantinas," *El Correo*, 18 July 1903, p. 1, Reel 2; "Alarma entre los comerciantes," *El Correo*, 24 Jan. 1905, p. 1, Reel 4; "El cierre del comercio en pequeño y los expendios de licores," *El Correo*, 26 Jan. 1905, p. 2, Reel 4; "Billares y cantinas," *El Correo*, 1 Aug. 1905, p. 2, Reel 4; "El cierre de las cantinas: Reformas al reglamento," *El Hijo del Parral*, 20 Nov. 1904, p. 2, AM, caja 1904A.

62. González Navarro, *La vida social*, p. 79.

63. "Contra la embriaguez," *El Correo*, 11 Aug. 1906, p. 1, Reel 5.

64. "Contra el alcoholismo (discurso pronunciado por su autor en la Velada que organizó la Liga Antialcohólica en el Teatro de los Héroes)," *El Correo*, 14 Dec. 1906, p. 2, Reel 5.

65. Agustín Páez, jefe municipal, Santa Bárbara, to jefe político, Distrito de Hidalgo, 14 March 1908, in AM, caja 1908C.

66. Presidente municipal, Valle de Zaragoza, to jefe político, Distrito de Hidalgo, 12 April 1904, AM, caja 1904A, and presidente municipal, Valle de Zaragoza, to jefe político, 20 Oct. 1904, AM, caja 1904J.

67. Miguel Domínguez to Ayuntamiento, Parral, 4 Aug. 1903, AM, caja 1903E.

68. Luis Terrazas, Governor, to Rodolfo Valles, jefe político, Distrito de Hidalgo, 25 June 1904, in AM, caja Decade 1900A.

69. Presidente municipal, Santa Bárbara, to jefe político, 8 June 1903, in AM, caja 1903I.

70. Borrador de Acuerdos del Ayuntamiento—1900: Sesión ordinaria del día 21 de abril de 1900, in AM, caja 1900 Legislación.

71. Alain Corbin, *Women for Hire: Prostitution and Sexuality in France after 1850*, trans. Alan Sheridan (Cambridge: Harvard University Press, 1990), pp. 9–10.

72. Presidente municipal, Santa Bárbara, to jefe político, Distrito de Hidalgo, 19 June 1903, in AM, caja 1903I.

73. Octaviana Ruiz to C. C Presidente y Vocales de la Junta Calificadora Municipal, 26 March 1900, in AM, caja 1900G; Padrón de las meretrices inscritas en el ramo de Tolerancia 1902, AM, caja 1902F.

74. Reglamento de Cantinas aprobado por el Y. Ayuntamiento de Hidalgo del Parral, in Ramo de Gobernación, núm. 858, 16 June 1903, in AM, caja 1903A.

75. Presidente municipal, Huejotitan, to jefe político, Distrito de Hidalgo, 23 June 1903, AM, caja 1903J; on Santa Bárbara, see presidente municipal, Santa Bárbara, to jefe político, 8 June 1903, AM, caja 1903I.

76. Presidente municipal, Santa Bárbara, to jefe político, 2 Aug. 1903, AM, caja 1903I.

77. Presidente municipal, San Isidro de las Cuevas, to jefe político, 6 Aug. 1903, AM, caja 1903F, and presidente municipal, Valle de Zaragoza, to jefe político, 21 June 1903, AM, caja 1903I.

78. Miguel Armendariz, presidente municipal, Balleza, to jefe político, 14 Oct. 1903, AM, caja 1903G.

79. President municipal, Santa Bárbara, to jefe político, 16 Oct. 1903, caja 1903I. For evidence of this new concern with alcohol, see Presidente municipal, Santa Bárbara, to jefe político, 8 June 1903, AM, caja 1903I; "Escandalitos en Santa Bárbara," La Nueva Era, 28 July 1904, p. 3, AM, caja 1904A, and Presidente municipal, Valle de Zaragoza, to jefe político, 20 Oct. 1904, AM, caja 1904J.

80. "Ventas clandestinamente," El Correo, 21 Jan. 1908, p. 1, Reel 7, and Expediente: Varios correspondientes al mes de diciembre 1907, AM, caja 1907H.

81. Informe rendido por el Sr. Rodolfo Valles, jefe político del Distrito Hidalgo, ante el I. Ayuntamiento de Hidalgo del Parral, el día 1º de enero de 1907, in AM, caja 1907J.

82. Christopher Hill, Society and Puritanism in Pre-Revolutionary England (London: Secker and Warburg, 1964), pp. 257–58.

83. For an example of state measures designed to "moralize" public officials in Hidalgo District, see J. Cortazar to jefe político, Distrito de Hidalgo, 3 Aug. 1903, in Expediente: Parral, agosto 1903, AM, caja 1903L. Mark Wasserman concludes that despite "progressive" reforms and benevolent projects, Creel presided over "a morass of corruption and governmental abuse" (Capitalists, Caciques, and Revolution, p. 133).

84. The uproar surrounding the robbery of the Banco Minero de Chihuahua, a Terrazas family enterprise, in March 1908, and the attention it received in El Correo makes more sense if interpreted in light of this preoccupation with moral reform. See Wasserman, Capitalists, Caciques, and Revolution, pp. 53–58.

85. Knight, Mexican Revolution, vol. 1, p. 30.

Chapter 4

1. Lion Murard and Patrick Zylberman, *Le petit travailleur infatigable. Recherches*, no. 25 (1976), as discussed in Corbin, *Women for Hire*, pp. 188–93.

2. Peter Stallybrass and Allon White, *The Politics and Poetics of Transgression* (London: Methuen, 1986), p. 94.

3. Pierre Bourdieu, *Outline of a Theory of Practice*, trans. Richard Nice (Cambridge: Cambridge University Press, 1977), pp. 94–95.

4. Voekel, "Peeing on the Palace," p. 201.

5. Franco, *Plotting Women;* see especially her discussion of Lizardi's novel *La quijotita y su prima*, pp. 83–85. Enlightened reformers often encouraged women to work outside the home as a means of overcoming Spain's economic backwardness; see David Brading, *The First America: The Spanish Monarchy, Creole Patriots, and the Liberal State, 1492–1867* (Cambridge: Cambridge University Press, 1991), pp. 505–6.

6. Joan B. Landes, *Women and the Public Sphere in the Age of the French Revolution* (Ithaca: Cornell University Press, 1988), pp. 148 and 171.

7. Julio Guerrero, *La génesis del crimen en México* (1901; México: Editorial Porrúa, 1977), pp. 157–82.

8. Guerrero uses the term in ibid., p. 181. His discussion of the middle categories is also interesting. For example, he viewed *soldaderas* (group B) as the "first stage of civilization" because of their absolute faithfulness and unconditional abnegation to their husbands or lovers; female servants, on the other hand, although in group D, he describes as possessing very "relaxed" morals and as the favorite target of the *policía de sanidad.*

9. Guerrero, *La génesis del crimen en México*, pp. 177–82 and 337–39.

10. Carmen Ramos Escandón, "Señoritas porfirianas: mujer e ideología en el México progresista, 1880–1910," in *Presencia y transparencia: La mujer en la historia de México,* ed. Ramos Escandón (Mexico City: El Colegio de México, Programa Interdisciplinario de Estudios de la Mujer, 1987), pp. 149, 150, 152, and 159. See also her working paper, "Gender Construction in a Progressive Society: Mexico, 1870–1917," *Texas Papers on Mexico*, no. 90–07 (Austin: Mexican Center, Institute of Latin American Studies, University of Texas, 1990).

11. Jean-Pierre Bastian, "Modelos de mujer protestante: Ideología religiosa y educación femenina, 1880–1910," in Ramos Escandón, *Presencia y transparencia*, pp. 173 and 179.

12. Verena Radkau, *"Por la debilidad de nuestro ser": Mujeres del pueblo en la paz porfiriana* (Mexico City: Centro de Investigaciones y Estudios Superiores en Antropología Social, Secretaría de Educación Pública, 1989), pp. 87–90.

13. On women and education during the late colonial period and the first half of the nineteenth century, see Silvia Marina Arrom, *The Women of Mexico City, 1790–1857* (Stanford, Calif.: Stanford University Press, 1985), pp. 15–24.

14. Valles's comments appear in Informe rendido por el Sr. Rodolfo Valles, jefe político del Distrito Hidalgo, 1 Jan. 1907, in AM, caja 1907J. Figures on school attendance in Parral are from the same document. For schools in other mining towns, see Noticia del 1° de enero 1906 al 31 mayo de 1906: noticia mensual que rinde el J[efe] M[unicipal] de San Francisco del Oro, 31 mayo de 1906, AM, caja 1906C; Noticias mensuales—Villa Escobedo y Santa Bárbara, 1 April 1906, AM, caja 1906H. For a discussion of the role of education in the inculcation of the work ethic, see Mary Kay Vaughan, "Primary Education and Literacy in Nineteenth-Century Mexico: Research Trends, 1968–1988," *Latin American Research Review* 25: 1 (1990), pp. 31–66.

15. Text of a speech given by Luz Fernández M., 8 December 1908, AM, caja 1908H. Arrom discusses the increased emphasis on motherhood at the end of the nineteenth century, in *Women of Mexico City*, pp. 261–63.

16. Zuleiman, "La educación de la mujer y su estado civil," *El Hijo del Parral*, 30 March 1902, p. 1, AM, caja 1903; Rafael Martínez, "Educación del pueblo como medio; progreso de la patria como fin," *El Hijo del Parral*, 17 December 1905, p. 1, AM, caja 1906G. For a petition against sending female students to male teachers, see Miguel Armendariz, jefe municipal, Balleza, to jefe político, Distrito de Hidalgo, 16 April 1906, AM, caja 1906Y.

17. Quoted in Doctor Salustio, "La mujer tal como debe ser; resultados de la buena educación. Delicias verdaderas del hogar," *El Correo*, 18 January 1906, p. 2, Reel 5.

18. Mark Thomas Connelly observes that during the Progressive era, prostitution reformers in the United States shared these assumptions. See Connelly, *The Response to Prostitution in the Progressive Era* (Chapel Hill: University of North Carolina Press, 1980), p. 23. Note also the similarity of views on the role of habit between Luis Lara y Pardo and those dealing with education. For Lara y Pardo, habit and example explained why working-class women became prostitutes. See Lara y Pardo, *La prostitución en México* (México: Librería de la Vda. de Ch. Bouret, 1908). Lara y Pardo's attitudes are discussed at greater length later in this chapter and in note 44 as well.

19. "El gran problema: la educación de la familia," *El Correo*, 7 Nov. 1902, p. 1, Reel 1.

20. "La educación de los hijos de millonarios," *El Hijo del Parral*, 18 Feb. 1906, p. 2, AM, caja 1906R. Another allegorical story is found in

"¡Viva el trabajo!" *El Hijo del Parral,* 8 Dec. 1901, p. 1, AM, caja 1902G.

21. Aurelia Torres, Escuela Industrial para Señoritas, Parral, to jefe político, Distrito de Hidalgo, 18 Jan. 1908, AM, caja 1908B. The founding of the school is discussed by Luz Fernández M. in her speech, 8 Dec. 1908, AM, caja 1908H. Subjects taught in the school are discussed in "Certificates Distributed: Exercises at the Escuela Industrial para Señoritas: Gov. Ahumada Congratulates the Graduates on their Success," *CE,* 29 Oct. 1898, p. 1; and "The Year in Parral: J. P. Valles Submits a Strong Annual Report," *CE,* 25 Jan. 1908, p. 9.

22. J. S. de Anda. "Las mujeres sin educación," *El Correo,* 27 Oct. 1904, p. 2, Reel 3. Verena Radkau makes the same point regarding the conservative consequences of educating women (*Por la debilidad,* p. 42).

23. "Las buenas madres," *El Correo,* 30 Sept. 1902, p. 1, Reel 1; "Las madres de familia," *El Correo,* 16 May 1903, p. 2, Reel 2.

24. "El gran problema," *El Correo,* 7 Nov. 1902, Reel 1; "Las madres de familia," *El Correo,* 16 May 1903, Reel 2.

25. Mary Gibson draws similar conclusions in her study of nineteenth- and twentieth-century Italy, in *Prostitution and the State in Italy, 1860–1915* (New Brunswick: Rutgers University Press, 1986), p. 22.

26. Zuleiman, "La educación de la mujer y su estado civil," *El Hijo del Parral,* 30 March 1902, p. 1, AM, caja 1903H.

27. The education of women was a dominant theme. In addition to ibid., see "Educar a la mujer para el hogar," *El Correo,* 3 Sept.1903, p. 2, Reel 2; Rafael Martínez, "Educación del pueblo como medio; Progreso de la patria como fin," *El Hijo del Parral,* 17 Dec. 1905, p. 1, AM, caja 1906G; Rafael Martínez, "Influencia de la mujer en su hogar," *La Nueva Era,* 14 Dec. 1905, AM, caja 1906R.

28. M. A. Sanz, *La mujer mexicana en el santuario del hogar* (México: Lacaud, 1907), pp. 13, 18, 19, and 25.

29. The term is found in "Educar a la mujer para el hogar," *El Correo,* 3 Sept. 1903, p. 2, Reel 2.

30. Sanz, *La mujer mexicana* , pp. 14, 15, 32–35, 37, and 64.

31. Doctor Salustio, "La mujer tal como debe ser," *El Correo,* 18 Jan. 1906, Reel 5.

32. "Temas: La educación de la mujer—pensamientos del Doctor Rivera," *El Correo,* 22 Jan. 1902, p. 1, Reel 1.

33. "La modestía de la mujer mexicana," *El Correo,* 8 March 1902, p. 1, Reel 1.

34. "El amor y la mujer," *El Correo,* 27 Aug. 1902, p. 1, Reel 1; Doctor Salustio, "La mujer tal como debe ser," *El Correo,* 18 Jan. 1906, Reel 5.

35. Páez to jefe político, Distrito de Hidalgo, 10 Dec. 1907, in Expediente: Varios correspondientes al mes de diciembre 1907, AM, caja 1907H.

36. S. Terrazas actively opposed prostitution and luxury in a column entitled "Esas . . ." See "Prostitución y libertinaje: la ostentación del vicio," *El Correo*, 22 July 1902, p. 1, Reel 1; "Las mesalinas," *El Correo*, 3 Sept. 1903, p. 1, Reel 2; and "Esas . . .," 20 Oct. 1903, p. 1, Reel 2; 17 March 1904, p. 1, Reel 3, 18 March 1904, p. 1, Reel 3, and 7 Sept. 1905, p. 1, Reel 4.

37. For a discussion of the discourse surrounding clothing in another context, see Mariana Valverde, "The Love of Finery: Fashion and the Fallen Woman in Nineteenth-Century Social Discourse," *Victorian Studies* 32: 2 (Winter 1989), pp. 168–88.

38. María, "Para las señoritas: El matrimonio," *El Correo*, 21 Sept. 1905, p. 2, Reel 4.

39. Soledad Acosta de Samper, "La mujer en su casa," *El Correo*, 11 Sept. 1905, p. 2, Reel 4.

40. "Diálogos acerca de la mujer," *El Correo*, 20 July 1904, p. 3, Reel 3.

41. "Uno de nuestros defectos," *El Correo*, 12 May 1905, p. 2, Reel 4. William H. Beezley coined the phrase "Porfirian persuasion" to refer to the Mexican elite and their belief in progress and efficiency. See his *Judas at the Jockey Club and Other Episodes of Porfirian Mexico* (Lincoln: University of Nebraska Press, 1987), p. 13.

42. Lara y Pardo, *La prostitución en México*, pp. 73, 88–90, 108, and 146–47. For a discussion of the "scientific" theories that probed the supposedly "innate predisposition" to prostitution around the turn of the century, see Corbin, *Women for Hire*, pp. 298–308.

43. Lara y Pardo, *La prostitución en México*, pp. 25, 26, 39, and 48.

44. Ibid., pp. 39, 57–58, 115, and 120–21. For a further discussion of Lara y Pardo and prostitution in Mexico, see Carlos Monsiváis, "La mujer en la cultura mexicana," in *Mujer y sociedad en América Latina*, ed. Lucía Guerra-Cunningham (Irvine: University of California, Editorial Pacífico, 1980), pp. 101–17.

45. Jeffrey Weeks, *Sex, Politics, and Society: The Regulation of Sexuality since 1800* (New York: Longman, 1981), p. 20.

46. Judith R. Walkowitz, *City of Dreadful Delight: Narratives of Sexual Danger in Late-Victorian London* (Chicago: University of Chicago Press, 1992), pp. 16 and 20.

47. Sanz, *La mujer mexicana*, p. 68; see Guerrero, *La génesis del crimen en México*, pp. 157–82; see also Roumagnac, *Los criminales en México*, esp. pp. 40–46, and pt. 2.

48. J. S. de Anda, "La mujer trabajadora y los haraganes," *El Correo*, 18 Oct. 1905, p. 2. For the contrast between city and countryside, see "Siempre el alcohol," *El Correo*, 8 Nov. 1905, p. 1, Reel 4.

49. Gibson, *Prostitution and the State in Italy*, p. 20.

50. Corbin, *Women for Hire*, pp. 204–6. Other European and U.S. historians have concluded that attitudes toward morality and sexuality

often express, in symbolic and cultural terms, fundamental social and economic divisions. In addition to ibid.; Gibson, *Prostitution and the State in Italy;* and Weeks, *Sex, Politics, and Society;* see Joan Wallach Scott, "Statistical Representations of Work: The Politics of the Chamber of Commerce's Statistique de l'industrie á Paris, 1847–48," in *Work in France: Representations, Meaning, Organization, and Practice,* ed. Steven Laurence Kaplan and Cynthia J. Koepp (Ithaca: Cornell University Press, 1986); Joan Wallach Scott, "'L'ouvrière! Mot impie, sordide . . .': Women Workers in the Discourse of French Political Economy, 1840–1860," in *The Historical Meanings of Work,* ed. Patrick Joyce (Cambridge: Cambridge University Press, 1987); Helmut Gruber, "Sexuality in 'Red Vienna': Socialist Party Conceptions and Programs and Working-Class Life, 1920–34," *International Labor and Working-Class History* 31 (Spring 1987), 37–68; Paul Boyer, *Urban Masses and Moral Order in America, 1820–1920* (Cambridge: Harvard University Press, 1978); Connelly, *Response to Prostitution in the Progressive Era;* Ellen Ross and Rayna Rapp, "Sex and Society: A Research Note from Social History and Anthropology," *Comparative Studies in Society and History* 23 (January 1981), pp. 51–72; and Jed Dannenbaum, *Drink and Disorder: Temperance Reform in Cincinnati from the Washingtonian Revival to the WCTU* (Urbana: University of Illinois Press, 1984).

51. Mary Kay Vaughan, *The State, Education, and Social Class in Mexico, 1880–1928* (DeKalb: Northern Illinois University Press, 1982), pp. 22–38. See also Vaughan's "Women, Class, and Education in Mexico, 1880–1928," *Latin American Perspectives* 12–13 (1977), pp. 150–68.

52. "¿La taberna o el hogar?," *El Correo,* 15 Feb. 1908, p. 1, Reel 7.

53. For three references to this transformation, see Demaistre, "La mujer," *El Correo,* 5 July 1902, p. 4, Reel 1; "Brujas en Parral," *La Nueva Era,* 5 March 1903, p. 6, AM, caja 1903C; and de Anda, "La mujer trabajadora y los haraganes," *El Correo,* 18 Oct. 1905, p. 2, Reel 4.

54. Demaistre, "La mujer," *El Correo,* 5 July 1902, p. 4, Reel 1.

55. "Influencia de la madre en la educación de sus hijos," *El Correo,* 7 Nov. 1904, p. 2, Reel 3.

56. "El trabajo y la mujer," *El Hijo del Parral,* 16 April 1905, p. 1, AM, caja 1905D. Jean-Baptiste Say used the term *natural dependents* to refer to women and children. Quoted in Joan W. Scott, "Statistical Representations of Work," p. 354. Scott also discusses how the meaning of *worker* was established through a contrast between "natural" qualities of men and women, in *Gender and the Politics of History,* p. 175.

57. Donald Reid, *The Miners of Decazeville: A Genealogy of Deindustrialization* (Cambridge: Harvard University Press, 1985), p. 38. For stages of discipline in French industry, see Michelle Perrot, "The Three Ages of Industrial Discipline in Nineteenth-Century France," in *Consciousness and Class Experience in Nineteenth-Century Europe,* ed. John M.

Merriman (New York: Holmes and Meier, 1979).

58. Dr. Manuel Flores, "Bellas y feas: ¿quienes son más virtuosas y felices?," *El Hijo del Parral*, 13 April 1902, p. 1, AM, caja 1902G.

59. Woman as guardian angel of the home was a dominant theme of middle-class rhetoric. For two examples, see Dolores B. de Bustamante, "Temas: Educación de la mujer," *El Correo*, 4 March 1902, p. 1, Reel 1; Zuleiman, "La educación de la mujer y su estado civil," *El Hijo del Parral*, 30 March 1902. Reference to good mothers forming Christian families can be found in "Las buenas madres," *El Correo*, 30 Sept. 1902, Reel 1. For mother as God on earth, see Vesper, "La madre," *El Correo*, 31 Oct. 1904, p. 2, Reel 3.

60. "Lo que debe saber una buena madre," *El Correo*, 31 Oct. 1904, p. 2, Reel 3.

61. "Diez notas de higiene," *El Correo*, 20 March 1905, p. 2, Reel 4.

62. For an article that touches upon all these themes, see Doctor Salustio, "La mujer tal como debe ser," *El Correo*, 18 Jan. 1906, Reel 5.

63. Soledad Acosta de Samper, "La mujer en su casa," *El Correo*, 11 Sept. 1905, p. 2, Reel 4.

64. María, "Para las señoritas," *El Correo*, 21 Sept. 1905, Reel 4.

65. Connelly, *Response to Prostitution in the Progressive Era*, p. 75.

66. Boyer, *Urban Masses and Moral Order*, p. 61.

67. Weeks, *Sex, Politics, and Society*, p. 28.

68. Scott, "Statistical Representations of Work," p. 362, esp. n. 83.

69. "Ecos de Villa Escobedo," *El Padre Padilla*, 15 Nov. 1905, p. 1, AM, caja 1906T.

70. For one such article, see "Las angustias del pueblo," *El Correo*, 12 June 1902, p. 1, Reel 1.

71. "El descanso dominical," *El Correo*, 1 Jan. 1903, p. 2, Reel 2.

72. "El cierre dominical," *El Correo*, 6 April 1905, p. 2, Reel 4.

73. Seven comerciantes, Parral, to jefe político, 18 April 1906, AM, caja 1906H; "El cierre de las casas comerciales," *El Hijo del Parral*, 26 Nov. 1905, p. 1, AM, caja 1906G.

74. Seven petitioners, Parral, to Governor, Chihuahua, 22 January 1906, AM, caja 1906X.

75. Franco, *Plotting Women*, p. 100.

76. Katherine A. Lynch, *Family, Class, and Ideology in Early Industrial France: Social Policy and the Working-Class Family, 1825–1848* (Madison: University of Wisconsin Press, 1988), p. 8.

77. Rafael Díaz, Parral, to Governor, 27 May 1908, AM, caja 1908A. The term *progreso forzado* was used by a seventy-three-year-old complainant, Crescencio Sáenz. See his letter: Sáenz, Parral, to Secretaría del Gobierno del Estado, 24 June 1908, AM, caja 1908B.

Chapter 5

1. For a discussion of Marx's conception of class (based on its relationship to the means of production), see Anthony Giddens, *Capitalism and Modern Social Theory: An Analysis of the Writings of Marx, Durkheim and Max Weber* (Cambridge: Cambridge University Press, 1971), pp. 35–45. Weber's definition of class stresses the "market situation"; see H. H. Gerth and C. Wright Mills, eds., *From Max Weber: Essays in Sociology* (London: Kegan Paul, 1947), pp. 180–95.

2. E. P. Thompson, *The Making of the English Working Class* (New York: Vintage Books, 1966), pp. 9–14.

3. Richard Price, *Labour in British Society: An Interpretative History* (London: Croom Helm, 1986), p. 7. Price discusses Thompson's critics on pp. 1–14.

4. Ira Katznelson, "Working-Class Formation: Constructing Cases and Comparisons," in Katznelson and Zolberg, *Working-Class Formation*, p. 14.

5. Derickson, *Workers' Health, Workers' Democracy*, pp. 37–39.

6. "Las minas y los mineros," *El Hijo del Parral*, 15 Oct. 1899, AM, caja 1900F; "¡Pobres mineros!," *El Hijo del Parral*, 6 May 1900, AM, caja 1900; "¡Pobres mineros!," *El Hijo del Parral*, 15 July 1900, AM, caja 1900; "Desgracia en la mina del Refugio," *El Hijo del Parral*, 11 Feb. 1906, AM, caja 1906R.

7. "¡Pobres mineros!," *El Hijo del Parral*, 15 July 1900, AM, caja 1900.

8. "Desgracia en la mina del Refugio," *El Hijo del Parral*, 11 Feb. 1906, p. 3, AM, caja 1906R. On Villa Escobedo, see Ignacio Sandoval, presidente municipal, Villa Escobedo to jefe político, 29 Oct. 1904, AM, caja 1904C. The Palmilla Mine is discussed in "Por Hidalgo del Parral," *El Correo*, 7 Sept. 1905, p. 2, Reel 4. Many other accident reports were located in the Archivo Municipal in Parral.

9. El Comandante de Policía, Parral to Juez 2° Menor, 25 Dec. 1900, quoting Alberto Moreno, Villa de Allende, operario, Mine La Preseña, AM, caja 1900E.

10. "Un deber de humanidad: Indemnización á los obreros," *El Hijo del Parral*, 22 Jan. 1905, p. 1, AM, caja 1905M.

11. J. Trinidad Hernández y Chávez, "El barretero," *El Hijo del Parral*, 18 Oct. 1903, p. 1, AM, caja 1903C.

12. "Por qué beben vino los operarios," *La Nueva Era*, 16 Jan. 1902, p. 1, AM, caja 1903H. "Maduros" was also the word used in Real del Monte and Pachuca in the nineteenth century to refer to sick mine workers; see Eduardo Flores Clair, *Conflictos de trabajo de una empresa minera, Real del Monte y Pachuca, 1872–1877* (México: Instituto Nacional de Antropología e Historia, 1991), p. 79.

13. More than thirty operarios, Apodaqueña mine, Parral, to José María Botello, 2 July 1911, AM, caja 1911 I.

14. J. Villegas, jefe municipal, Santa Bárbara, to jefe político, Hidalgo District, 7 July 1906, AM, caja 1906T, and Agustín Páez, jefe municipal, Santa Bárbara, to jefe político, 11 Feb. 1908, AM, caja 1908C.

15. Presidente municipal, Santa Bárbara, to jefe político, 13 May 1904, AM, caja 1904O. On the United States Mining Company, see Ignacio Sandoval, presidente municipal, Villa Escobedo, to jefe político, 11 Dec. 1904, AM, caja 1904C. For Los Azules, see Páez, 17 July 1908, AM, caja 1908N.

16. On the consequences of this settlement pattern and official responses to it, see Presidente municipal, Santa Bárbara, to jefe político, 16 Oct. 1903, AM, caja 1903I; Páez to jefe político, 9 May 1907, AM, caja 1907A; and Informe Oficial, Páez, 31 Dec. 1909, AM, caja 1909A.

17. Informe Oficial Rendido por el C. Jefe Municipal de Villa Escobedo, *Boletín Oficial del Distrito Hidalgo,* Año 3, número 96, 26 Jan. 1908, p. 3, AM, caja 1908A.

18. J. J. Gutiérrez, presidente municipal, Santa Bárbara, to jefe político, 13 Nov. 1900, AM, caja 1900SUSY.

19. Leonidez Sapien, Parral, to C. Pres. de la Junta Calificadora, 7 Jan. 1908, AM, caja 1908R.

20. Crew, *Town in the Ruhr,* p. 65. Laite, "Capitalist Development and Labour Organisation," p. 92. Statistics on Phelps-Dodge are from Brown, *Hard-Rock Miners,* p. 10.

21. Rodolfo Valles, jefe político, to Miembros de la Asamblea Municipal, 2 July 1906, AM, caja 1906N.

22. 28 vecinos, Parral, to Secretario, Secretaría del Gobierno del Estado, Ramo de Fomento, 13 March 1908, AM, caja 1908B; 22 petitioners, Parral, to Secretario, Secretaría del Gobierno del Estado, Ramo de Fomento, 17 March 1908, AM, caja 1908B; 44 operarios and artesanos, Parral, to Secretario, Secretaría del Gobierno del Estado, Ramo de Fomento, 23 March 1908, AM, caja 1908B.

23. 44 operarios y artesanos to Governor, 23 March 1908, AM, caja 1908B.

24. "Los productos de las cosechas," El Correo, 5 March 1902, p. 1, Reel 1; "Las angustias del pueblo," El Correo, 12 July 1902, p. 1, Reel 1; "A traves del estado: Parral," El Correo, 3 July 1902, Reel 1. The presidente municipal of Huejotitan stressed that better prices for fruit and vegetables could be obtained in San Francisco del Oro, Santa Bárbara, and Minas Nuevas in Boleta para recoger datos para producciones agrícolas (Año de 1901), AM, caja 1902B.

25. J. S. de Anda, "Los pobres y la clase media," El Hijo del Parral, 10 Dec. 1905, p. 1, AM, caja 1906G.

26. "La carestía del trigo," *La Nueva Era,* 18 June 1905, p. 2, AM, caja 1905D. Also, see "No debe haber monopolio," *El Hijo del Parral,* 28 Nov. 1909, p. 1, AM, caja 1909A.

27. From Boletos para recoger datos para producciones agrícolas (Año de 1901), AM, caja 1902B.

28. Páez to jefe político, 7 Sept. 1907, AM, caja 1907D.

29. Rodrigo Chávez, Parral, to jefe político, 30 June 1910, AM, caja 1910Q. For another example of the fluctuation of property prices, see presidente municipal, Santa Bárbara, to jefe político, 27 June 1903, AM, caja 1903I.

30. Rodolfo Valles, jefe político, to C. C. Miembros de la Asamblea Municipal, 2 July 1906, AM, caja 1906N.

31. 29 vecinos, Parral, to jefe político, 10 June 1903, AM, caja 1903M.

32. Thirteen vecinos de la Avenida de la Estación, Parral, to jefe político, 11 July 1905, AM, caja 1905A.

33. Ego, "La higiene pública," *El Hijo del Parral,* 10 April 1904, p. 1, AM, caja 1904F.

34. Parker, *Mules, Mines and Me in Mexico,* p. 36.

35. Ingersoll, *In and under Mexico,* p. 119. Ramón Eduardo Ruiz concludes that these same conditions prevailed in mining camps throughout Sonora, in *The People of Sonora and Yankee Capitalists,* pp. 85–90.

36. Ignacio Sandoval, jefe municipal, Villa Escobedo, to jefe político, 1 Jan. 1906, AM, caja 1906T; Agustín Páez, jefe municipal, Santa Bárbara, to jefe político, 2 Dec. 1909, AM, caja 1909A.

37. Memoria que rinde el C. José Muñoz, jefe municipal, Santa Bárbara, Año de 1905, 5 Jan. 1906, AM, caja 1906C; Ignacio Sandoval, jefe municipal, Villa Escobedo, to jefe político, 1 Jan. 1906, AM, caja 1906T; Jorge Maul, jefe municipal, Villa Escobedo, to jefe político, 31 Dec. 1908, AM, caja 1908Q; and Informe Oficial, Rendido por el C. Agustín Páez, jefe municipal, Santa Bárbara, 31 Dec. 1909, AM, caja 1909A.

38. Luis Terrazas, Gobernador, to jefe político, Hidalgo District, 12 April 1904, AM, caja 1900A (*sic*). See also J. Cortazar, Secretario, Secretaría del Gobierno del Estado, Ramo de Gobernación, to jefe político, Hidalgo District, 6 July 1903, AM, caja 1903C, and J. Cortazar to jefe político, 1 May 1905, AM, caja 1905Q.

39. Páez to jefe político, 1 Nov. 1909, AM, caja 1909A; Páez to jefe político, 2 Dec. 1909, AM, caja 1909A; and Páez to jefe político, 7 Dec. 1909, AM, caja 1909A.

40. Páez to jefe político, 3 Feb. 1908, AM, caja 1908C.

41. El Corresponsal, "Correspondencia del Parral," *El Correo,* 21 March 1905, p. 1, Reel 4 ("Sabido es por todos, que este lugar siempre ha tenido fama de mal sano . . ."). On mining company operations affecting the water supply, see Twenty-five residents, Barrio de las curtidarias,

Parral, to jefe político, AM, caja 1901E, and Secretaría del Gobierno del Estado, Ramo de Fomento, to jefe político, Hidalgo District, 5 Dec. 1907, AM, caja 1907ñ.

42. Doheny, "Smelter at Aguas Calientes," Doheny Interviews, Occidental College, and "Cananea. Labor," Doheny Interviews, Occidental College.

43. Catherine Hall, "The Tale of Samuel and Jemima: Gender and Working-class Culture in Nineteenth-Century England," in *E. P. Thompson: Critical Perspectives,* ed. Harvey J. Kaye and Keith McClelland (Philadelphia: Temple University Press, 1990), pp. 96–99.

44. Agustín Páez, jefe municipal, to jefe político, 1 Nov. 1910, AM, caja 1910P.

45. M. Martínez, jefe municipal, Villa Escobedo, to jefe político, 11 Oct. 1910, AM, caja 1910M; and Informe que rinde el jefe municipal de Villa Escobedo, M. Martínez, 1910 (31 Dec. 1910), AM, caja 1910U.

46. Benjamín Arguían to jefe político, 30 Oct. 1910, Inspección de Estadística, número 14, AM, caja 1910M.

47. Averiguación con motivo de la muerte de Elijio Torres, San Franciso del Oro, 9 Nov. 1925, AJ, Hidalgo del Parral, caja 1925L.

48. Genara García, Parral, to C. Pres. y Vocales de la Junta Calificadora de Ingresos Municipales, 6 Jan. 1905, AM, caja 1905P. For another woman who owned a small business, see Josefa Santiestevan, Parral, to jefe político, 20 Aug. 1906, AM, caja 1906M.

49. Registro de las cantinas y expendios de licores que existen en esta Villa, Villa Escobedo, 26 Sept. 1906, AM, caja 1906A. Women also owned cantinas in Parral; see Expediente de los negocios pertenecientes á la Municipalidad del Parral y que corresponden al mes de junio, año 1904, AM, caja 1904G; and Contra Jesús Rubio por lesiones, iniciaran 3 Sept. 1899, AJ, caja 1899L.

50. Secretaría de Fomento, Colonización e Industria, Dirección General de Estadística, Estadística Industrial, Año 1904, Municipalidad Zaragoza; presidente municipal, Valle de Zaragoza, to jefe político, Jan. 1904, AM, caja 1904E.

51. Criminal contra José Polanco y cómplices por robo, Parral, 3 Jan. 1899, AJ, 1899R; and Criminal seguida de oficio contra Anastasio y Luciano Sánchez por lesiones inferida á Juan Enriques, 17 Sept. 1899, Minas Nuevas, AJ, caja 1899L.

52. Criminal contra Joaquín Balandran por el aborto de la Señora Jesús Cabrera, Santa Bárbara, 21 May 1902, AJ, caja 1902L.

53. Secretaría del Gobierno del Estado, Ramo de Fomento, núm. 1660, to jefe político, Distrito Hidalgo, 6 April 1908, AM, caja 1908L.

54. María de la Luz Acosta de Romero, Santa Bárbara, to jefe político, 31 July 1909, AM, caja 1909D.

55. Lusana López, Parral, to jefe político, 2 Feb. 1909, AM, caja 1909E.

56. M. V. Corbalín, Balleza, to jefe político, Parral, 30 June 1909, AM, caja 1909F.

57. Criminal contra M. F. por el delito de rapto perpetrado en la joven B. T., Villa Escobedo, 11 July 1905, AJ, caja 1905V.

58. Ibid.

59. Averiguación criminal en contra de F. R. acusado del delito de amenazas, cometidas á F. V., Parral, 28 Feb. 1906, AJ, caja 1906J.

60. Informe Oficial, Rendido por el C. Agustín Páez, jefe municipal de Santa Bárbara, 31 Dec. 1909, AM, caja 1909A; and Informe que rinde el Jefe Municipal de Villa Escobedo, M. Martínez, 1910 (31 Dec. 1910), AM, caja 1910U. For a discussion of illegitimacy rates in Parral over the long term, see Robert McCaa, "Women's Position, Family and Fertility Decline in Parral (Mexico), 1777–1930," *Annales de Démographie Historique* (1989).

61. Criminal en contra de los que resultan responsables al delito de homicidio perpetrado en la persona de la Señora L. E., Santa Bárbara, 15 Feb. 1909, AJ, caja 1909H.

62. Criminal contra Margarita A., por el delito de lesiones, Parral, 17 Oct. 1906, AJ, caja 1906L.

63. Averiguación criminal contra C. R. por delito de lesiones inferidas a su esposa María Isabel M., Villa Escobedo, 15 March 1909, AJ, 1909L.

64. Averiguación con motivo de la muerte de Hipólito Aguirre, Parral, 20 Sept. 1912, AJ, caja 1912L.

65. Criminal contra Manuel R. por lesiones inferidas á Felicitas A., Santa Bárbara, 22 Feb. 1906, AJ, caja 1906L.

66. Averiguación criminal contra C. R. por delito de lesiones inferidas a su esposa María Isabel M., Villa Escobedo, 15 March 1909, AJ, 1909L.

67. Contra M. R., por lesiones, Parral, 28 April 1908, AJ, caja 1908L.

68. These themes are developed more fully in William E. French, "'Progreso forzado': Workers and the Developmentalist Ideology," in Beezley, Martin, and French, *Rituals of Rule, Rituals of Resistance,* pp. 191–212.

69. José Velasco, "Por el honor," *El Hijo del Parral,* 15 Feb. 1903, p. 1, AM, caja 1903K. For a discussion of honor in Porfirian Mexico, see González Navarro, *La vida social,* in Cosío Villegas, *Historia moderna de México,* vol. 4, p. 421.

70. Presidente municipal, San Francisco del Oro, to jefe político, Parral, 13 April 1906, AM, caja 1906C.

71. Enrique de la Garza, jefe municipal, Rosario, to jefe político, 6 Aug. 1905, AM, caja 1905M, and Enrique de la Garza to jefe político, 10 Sept. 1905, AM, caja 1905M. For a discussion of the *serrano* conception of honor and its relationship to the land, see Ana María Alonso, "'Progress' as Disorder and Dishonor: Discourse of Serrano Resistance," *Critique of Anthropology* 8: 1 (1988), p. 22.

72. J. G. Peristiany, quoted in James Farr, *Hands of Honor: Artisans and Their World in Dijon, 1550–1650* (Ithaca: Cornell University Press, 1988), p. 181.

73. "Temas: Libertad de profesiones," *El Correo,* 17 Jan. 1902, p. 1, Reel 1; see also "A traves del estado: Parral," *El Correo,* 6 Aug. 1902, p. 2, Reel 1.

74. "Brujas en Parral," *La Nueva Era,* 5 March 1903, p. 6, AM, caja 1903A.

75. Criminal en contra de Lorenza Esparza y socios por el delito de injurias, Santa Bárbara, 19 June 1908, AJ, caja 1908V.

76. "To the Mountains: Palmore Teachers Visit Some of the Santa Eulalia Mines," *CE,* 7 Dec. 1901, p. 9.

77. Daniel Roche, *The People of Paris: An Essay in Popular Culture in the Eighteenth Century,* trans. Marie Evans (Leamington Spa: Berg Publishers, 1987), p. 167.

78. The term *cacique* was used by petitioners both before and after the Porfiriato. A number of *vecinos* wrote the new governor in 1911 that "the abuses of the 'caciquillos' are still abundant in this unfortunate state"; see Vecinos de Hidalgo del Parral to C. Gobernador, Chihuahua, 6 April 1911, AM, caja 1911I.

79. Crescencio Sáenz, in Secretaría del Gobierno del Estado, Ramo de Fomento, to jefe político, Hidalgo District, 24 June 1908, AM, caja 1908B.

80. Alan Knight uses the concept of "folk liberalism" in "Revolutionary Project, Recalcitrant People: Mexico, 1910–40," in *The Revolutionary Process in Mexico: Essays on Political and Social Change, 1880–1940,* ed. Jaime E. Rodríguez O. (Los Angeles: UCLA Latin American Center Publications, 1990), p. 233.

81. James C. Scott, *Weapons of the Weak: Everyday Forms of Peasant Resistance* (New Haven: Yale University Press, 1985), p. 338. See Scott's critique of the concept of "hegemony" in ibid., pp. 304–50.

82. E. P. Thompson, "Eighteenth-Century English Society: Class Struggle without Class," *Social History* 3: 2 (May 1978), p. 158. American workers in the first half of the nineteenth century held beliefs drawn from republicanism, including those of commonwealth, virtue, independence, citizenship, and equality. Sean Wilentz concludes that workers, when faced with changes in the social relations of production, began to reinterpret their shared ideal and to struggle over the meaning of these terms; see his *Chants Democratic: New York City and the Rise of the American Working Class, 1788–1850* (New York: Oxford University Press, 1984), p. 14.

83. Rodney D. Anderson, *Outcasts in Their Own Land: Mexican Industrial Workers, 1906–1911* (DeKalb: Northern Illinois University Press, 1976), p. xx.

84. E. P. Thompson, "The Moral Economy of the English Crowd," *Past and Present* (1971). Perhaps the best-known example of the use of the concept is James C. Scott, *The Moral Economy of the Peasant: Subsistence and Rebellion in Southeast Asia* (New Haven: Yale University Press, 1976). On Morelos, see Knight, Mexican Revolution, vol. 1, pp. 158, 162, 164, 305, and 314. Thompson discusses much of this subsequent literature in "The Moral Economy Reviewed," in his *Customs in Common* (London: The Merlin Press, 1991).

85. Andrés Domínguez, in Ejecutoria dictada en el toca a la apelación interpuesta en la causa instruida en contra de Jorge Pérez y Andrés Domínguez, por el delito de robo, Parral, 24 de octubre de 1925, AJ, caja 1925R.

86. Yncidente de descarselación de Miguel Vargas y cómplices, bajo fianza, Santa Bárbara, 20 March 1905, AJ, caja 1905V.

87. Averiguación en contra de quienes resulten responsables por el delito de robo que sufrió La Palmilla, Parral, 2 Nov. 1911, AJ, caja 1911R.

88. W. Schumacher, ASARCo, Santa Bárbara, to R. F. Manahan, El Paso, 26 July 1913, Suitland, Washington National Record Center (hereafter cited as WNRC), Record Group 76, Box 221, Docket 2312; W. M. Drury, Summary of the Situation at the Various Mining Units in Mexico, 3 Sept. 1913, WNRC, Record Group 76, Box 221, Docket 2312; and W. M. Drury, Mining Department, El Paso, to S. W. Eccles, Vice President, ASARCo, New York City, 12 June 1914, WNRC, Record Group 76, Box 234, Docket 2533.

89. Criminal contra Pomposo Rico y socios por el delito de robo, Santa Bárbara, 30 Jan. 1913, AJ, caja 1913R.

90. Criminal en contra de Tomás Rodríguez por el delito de robo de herramientas y metales á la mina denominada La "Capitaneña," Santa Bárbara, 22 Dec. 1910, AJ, caja 1910R.

91. A description of the *gambusino* system provided by workers may be found in Criminal contra Ygnacio Moreno por sospechas de robo. Principio, 1 Sept. 1899, Juzgado Menor de Batopilas, AJ, caja 1899R.

92. See the statements of Ygnacio Moreno, operario de minas, and Juan Navarrete, operario de minas, in ibid.

93. Averiguación con motivo del robo perpetrado en la mina de San Juanico, apareciendo responsables Santos Bravo, Ysabel Montoya y Dionisio Chico, 14 Dec. 1902, AJ, 1902R.

94. Leonardo Cabriales, barretero, in En la Carcel Pública de esta Ciudad, pongo a su disposición al reo Leonardo Cabriales, a quien remite el C. Comisario de Policía de Palmilla, por el delito de robo de que se queja el Sr. Leslie Webb, Parral, 31 August 1920, AJ, 1920R. For examples of mine robberies in Hidalgo District before 1910, see Criminal: con motivo a robo de explosivos sucedido á la Guggenheim Exploration

minas Tecolotes y anexas, en este lugar, Santa Bárbara, 5 Feb. 1901, AJ, caja 1901R; Criminal: con relación a robo de 14 caja pólvora a la mina Hesperides, Santa Bárbara, 25 March 1901, AJ, caja 1901R; Averiguación sobre el robo que se cometió en la mina San Patricio, Villa Escobedo, 16 Aug. 1905, AJ, caja 1905R; Averiguación con motivo del robo en la mina llamada "Bretaña," Villa Escobedo, 26 Oct. 1905, AJ, caja 1905R; Criminal contra José Torres por delito de robo, Parral, 26 Nov. 1906, AJ, caja 1906R; Criminal en contra de Antonio Ontiveros Cisneros por el delito de robo, Parral, 18 Jan. 1906, AJ, caja 1906R; Criminal: Averiguación practicada con motivo del robo ejecutado en la Mina "Providencia" la noche del 27 May 1906, Parral, AJ, caja 1906R; Criminal en contra Carlos Páez por robo, 13 Sept. 1906, Santa Bárbara, AJ, caja 1906R.

95. Ejecutoria dictada en el toca a la apelación interpuesta en la causa instruida en contra de Jorge Pérez y Andrés Domínguez, por el delito de robo, Parral, 24 Oct. 1925.

96. Criminal en contra Carlos Páez por robo, 13 Sept. 1906, Santa Bárbara, AJ, caja 1906R.

97. Averiguación instruida por lesiones contra el prófugo Antonio Ramos, Santa Bárbara, 2 Jan. 1910, AJ, caja 1910L.

98. For two examples of blaming robberies on workers, see Criminal con motivo del robo hecho en la Oficina del Señor W. G. Brock, en las Minas denominadas "Cata Rica" y "Cuevecillas," 2 Jan. 1906, Parral, AJ, caja 1906R, and Criminal: Averiguación practicada con motivo del robo ejecutado en la Mina "Providencia" la noche del 27 May 1906, Parral, AJ, 1906R.

99. Scott, *Weapons of the Weak,* pp. 265 and 296.

100. Pedro Corral's statement in Criminal: Contra Feliciano Corral por robo de un hectolitre de frijol, Santa Bárbara, 19 Oct. 1899, AJ, caja 1899R.

101. For a discussion of absenteeism and the rejection of work categories assigned to workers by managers, see Sariego and Santana Paucar, "Transición tecnológica . . . ," pp. 20–21.

102. Ibid., p. 19.

103. Juan Luis Sariego Rodríguez, "La condición del proletariado minero a principios del siglo," in *Arqueología de la industria en México,* coordinación Victoria Novelo (Coyoacán: Museo Nacional de Culturas Populares, SEP Cultura, 1983), p. 26. For workers making their rounds in the morning to pick up work, see the statement of Fortunato Uviña, operario, in Criminal contra Feliciano Corral por robo de un Hectolitro de Frijol, Santa Bárbara, 19 Oct. 1899, AJ, caja 1899R.

104. Averiguación levantada con motivo de un cartucho de dinamita estallado en la casa habitación del C. Jefe Municipal de esta Villa, Santa Bárbara, 29 May 1905, AJ, caja 1905V.

105. Averiguación con motivo de los lesiones que sufrió Fernando Enríquez en la mina "Tecolotes," Santa Bárbara, 24 Jan. 1906, AJ, caja 1906L; Averiguación con motivo a la muerte del Sr. Praxedis Portillo, sucedida en la mina denominada "Alfareña," Santa Bárbara, 15 Nov. 1912, AJ, caja 1912L; and Averiguación con motivo de la muerte de Francisco Montes, Santa Bárbara, 2 Dec. 1912, AJ, caja 1912L.

106. Averiguación con motivo de las lesiones que sufrió Fernando Enríquez en la mina "Tecolotes," Santa Bárbara, 24 Jan. 1906, AJ, caja 1906L.

107. See statement by Miguel Monares, operario, in Averiguación levantada con motivo de un cartucho de dinamita estallado en la casa habitación del C. Jefe Municipal de esta Villa, Santa Bárbara, 29 May 1905, AJ, caja 1905V.

108. Ibid.

109. Twenty-eight jornaleros, Parral, to Gobernador, Chihuahua, in Secretaría del Gobierno del Estado, Ramo de Fomento, 13 March 1908, AM, caja 1908B.

110. León Proa, Santa Bárbara, to jefe político, Parral, 2 July 1903, AM, caja 1903I.

111. Striking carpenters' demands in F. Villegas, jefe municipal, Santa Bárbara, to jefe político, Hidalgo District, 4 Aug. 1906, AM, caja 1906T; the operario candidate is discussed in M. Cavazos, jefe municipal, Santa Bárbara, to jefe político, 23 Nov. 1911, AM, caja 1911F.

112. Anderson, *Outcasts in Their Own Land,* p. 68. See the petition signed by more than one hundred workers sent to Abraham González, Governor of Chihuahua, 1 Aug. 1911, AM, caja 1911S.

113. Rodríguez, cited in Marcelo N. Rodea, *Historia del movimiento obrero ferrocarrilero en México (1890–1943)* (México: 1944), pp. 120 and 125–26. Workers' response to Porfirio Díaz is in ibid., p. 309. Michelle Perrot stresses that the image of the French working class in the nineteenth century was also constructed reactively; see her "On the Formation of the French Working Class," in Katznelson and Zolberg, *Working-Class Formation,* p. 96.

114. Jesús Vargas, "Los obreros de Chihuahua: Sus experiencias de organización (1880–1940)," unpublished manuscript in possession of the author. Vargas provides a list of mutual-aid societies in the state, in ibid., pp. 32–33.

115. "Conferencias en la Sociedad Juárez de Obreros," *El Correo,* 19 Feb. 1904, p. 1, Reel 3. For the stated goals of these societies, see "El mutualismo," *El Correo,* 18 Jan. 1903, p. 2, Reel 2.

116. "Protesta de la Sociedad Juárez de Obreros," *El Correo,* 10 Sept. 1904, p. 2, Reel 3.

117. Sociedad Cooperativa de Obreros, Parral, to jefe político, 22 July

1904, AM, caja 1904D; and José Murillo, Sociedad Cooperativa de Obreros, Escuela Nocturna para Adultos, to jefe político, 6 Dec. 1909, AM, caja 1909E.

118. Vargas, "Los obreros de Chihuahua, pp. 11–12.

119. F. Villegas, jefe municipal, Santa Bárbara, to jefe político, 25 Aug. 1906, AM, caja 1906T.

120. "Locales y personales," El Correo, 14 Jan. 1902, p. 2, Reel 1.

121. "Sociedad mutualista," El Correo, 17 March 1903, p. 2, Reel 2.

122. "Ecos de Villa Escobedo," El Padre Padilla," 15 Nov. 1905, p. 1, AM, caja 1906T.

123. "Cuestión obrera," El Correo, 1 March 1907, p. 2, Reel 6; see also "Escuela nocturna para obreros," El Correo, 2 May 1902, p. 2, Reel 1.

124. "Para los obreros," El Correo, 20 April 1907, p. 2, Reel 6.

125. "Unión de carpinteros mexicanos," El Correo, 19 Aug. 1904, p. 1, Reel 3; "La Unión de carpinteros mexicanos," El Correo, 4 Jan. 1905, p. 2, Reel 4; and Sociedad Mutualista de Empleados, Parral, to Director, Boletín Oficial, 1 Dec. 1907, AM, caja 1907H.

126. "¡Importante á los adultos!," La Nueva Era, 18 Aug. 1901, p. 2, AM, caja 1902G.

127. M. B. del Río, Liga Anti-Alcohólica "Ocampo," Parral, to jefe político, 16 March 1908, AM, caja 1908J.

128. Eulalio Porras, "Ecos parralenses," El Hijo del Parral, 28 enero 1900, p. 1, AM, caja 1900F.

129. "Vejaciones a mexicanos," El Correo, 8 June 1907, Reel 6. Mexican masons working in the Esmeralda Mine of ASARCo hated Mexican paymasters (rayadores) as much as their American equivalents. They also complained of a Mexican master mechanic who treated "peones" like criminals. See "En la American Smelting," El Correo, 10 Dec. 1906, p. 1, Reel 5; and "El Parral necesita de un instituto minero," La Nueva Era, 16 Nov. 1899, AM, caja 1900E.

130. Knight, Mexican Revolution, vol. 1, pp. 146–50.

131. "Cananea. Labor," Doheny Papers, p. 20.

132. D. E. Woodbridge, "Labor Data of Northern Mexico Mine," MMJ, July 1913, p. 49.

Chapter 6

1. Averiguación Acusado Guadalupe Rocha, 1 Aug. 1910, Parral, AJ.

2. Ibid.

3. "¿Donde está Guillermo Baca?," El Correo, 27 June 1911, 1: 2.

4. See the testimony of these individuals in Averiguación con motivo de la consignación hecha por la Jefatura Política de los Acuşados Manuel Becerra, Narcisso Baca, Atanasio Michel y Guadalupe Rocha, Guillermo

Baca y Miguel Baca Ronquilla, 27 June 1910, AJ.

5. "El Sr. Madero en Parral," *El Correo,* 20 Jan. 1910, 4: 1.

6. See the testimony of Atanasio Michel and Pedro Gómez, in Averiguación con motivo de la consignación hecha por la Jefatura Política de los Acusados Manuel Becerra, Narcisso Baca, Atanasio Michel y Guadalupe Rocha, Guillermo Baca y Miguel Baca Ronquillo, 27 June 1910, AJ.

7. See the testimony of Narcisso Baca, Jesús Pérez, and others, in ibid.

8. Testimony of Pedro López, in ibid.

9. Ibid.

10. On the Madero revolt, see Knight, *Mexican Revolution,* vol. 1, pp. 40–77 and 171–246.

11. Antonio Rodríguez, San Isidro de las Cuevas, to jefe político, Parral, 24 Nov. 1910, AM, caja 1910H.

12. Nicolas Hinojo, jefe municipal, Valle de Olivas, to jefe político, Parral, 18 Dec. 1910, AM, caja 1910J.

13. Guillermo Porras, Secretaría del Estado de Chihuahua, Ramo de Gobierno, to jefe político, Parral, 27 Dec. 1910, Parral, AM, caja 1910B.

14. Agustín Páez, jefe municipal, Santa Bárbara, to jefe político, Parral, 1 March 1911, AM., caja 1911B.

15. R. Sapien, ex-presidente municipal, San Francisco del Oro, to jefe político, Parral, 12 Jan. 1911, AM, caja 1910P.

16. Informe que rinde el jefe municipal de Villa Escobedo, M. Martínez, 1910 (31 Dec. 1910), AM, caja 1910U.

17. François-Xavier Guerra makes this argument in "La révolution mexicaine: d'abord une révolution minière?," *Annales* 36: 5 (Sept.–Oct. 1981), pp. 785–814. See also the response by Alan Knight, "Révolution mexicaine: révolution minière ou révolution serrano?," *Annales* 38: 2 (Mar.–Abril 1983), pp. 449–59.

18. M. Martínez, jefe municipal, Villa Escobedo, to jefe político (confidencial), 21 Jan. 1911, AM, caja 1911L.

19. Páez to jefe político, 22 Jan. 1911, AM, caja 1911B.

20. Martínez to jefe político, 8 Jan. 1911, AM, caja 1911C.

21. "Regístranse mas huelgas," *El Correo,* 5 July 1911, 1: 1; "Las costureras están en huelga," *El Correo,* 7 July 1911, 1: 1; and Petición de las obreras," *El Correo,* 13 July 1911, 2: 3. On the support offered by González to workers between June and November of 1911, see William H. Beezley, *Insurgent Governor: Abraham González and the Mexican Revolution in Chihuahua* (Lincoln: University of Nebraska Press, 1973), pp. 99–105.

22. "Petición de empleados," to Sr. D. Martín Falomir, *El Correo,* 30 June 1911, 2: 4.

23. "Ayer se registró una nueva huelga en esta ciudad," *El Correo,* 2 July 1911, 1: 4. Also see "Workers Plan Gigantic Union," *EPMT,* 8 July

1911, 1: 3; "General Orozco in Chihuahua," *EPMT,* 5 July 1911, 1: 3, Reel 53; and "Women Strike in Chihuahua," *EPMT,* 10 July 1911, 1: 3, Reel 53.

24. "Los vecinos de Santa Eulalia," *El Correo,* 6 July 1911, 2: 3.

25. "Las tiendas de Raya en Santa Eulalia," *El Correo,* 17 July 1911, 1: 3; "Noticias de Santa Eulalia," *El Correo,* 27 July 1911, 4: 4; and "Solucionado lo de Santa Eulalia," *El Correo,* 2 Aug. 1911, 1: 1.

26. "Remitido," *El Correo,* 16 July 1911, 2: 3; and "Mineros descontentos," *El Correo,* 18 July 1911, 4: 3.

27. Vecinos de Hidalgo del Parral ál Gobernador, Chihuahua, 6 April 1911, AM, caja 1911I.

28. Averiguación Acusado José Guadalupe Rocha, 1 Aug. 1910, AJ.

29. Beezley, *Insurgent Governor,* p. 109.

30. "Los vecinos de Santa Eulalia," *El Correo,* 6 July 1911, 2: 3.

31. "Excitativa," *El Correo,* 7 July 1911, 4: 1.

32. "Americans Are Leaving Mexico" (editorial), *EPMT,* 2 Aug. 1911, 4: 1, Reel 53.

33. N. B. González to jefe político provisional, Parral, 15 Aug. 1911, AM, caja 1911S.

34. N. B. González, El Comicionado, Borjas, Ramal del Parral, y más de cien firmas, á Sr. Abraham González, Gobernador del Estado, 1 Aug. 1911, AM, caja 1911S.

35. González to Gobernador, 1 Aug. 1911, AM, caja 1911S.

36. González to jefe político provisional, Parral, 15 Aug. 1911, AM, caja 1911S.

37. González to Gobernador, 1 Aug. 1911, AM, caja 1911S.

38. Apodaqueña mine workers mentioned "justice" five times in a two-page letter; see thirty operarios, Apodaqueña mine, Parral to José María Botello, 2 July 1911, AM, caja 1911I.

39. M. Cavazos, jefe municipal, Santa Bárbara, to jefe político, Parral, 23 Nov. 1911, AM, caja 1911F.

40. Hyslop to Calvert G. Schobell, H.B.M. Vice-Consul, Chihuahua, 16 August 1911, Hyslop Papers, Box 2, FF36.

41. Petition from nineteen workers, Villa Escobedo, to jefe municipal, 30 July 1911, located in Santos Esparza, jefe municipal, Villa Escobedo, to jefe político, Parral, 3 Aug. 1911, AM, caja 1911S.

42. Bazile Davidson, Superintendente, to Sr. Don Santiago I. Long, Gerente del Alvarado Mining and Milling Company, Parral, 9 Aug. 1911, AM, caja 1911S.

43. Davidson to Long, 9 Aug. 1911, AM, caja 1911S, and Santos Esparza to jefe político, Parral, 3 Aug. 1911, AM, caja 1911S.

44. Jesús M. Yáñez, Camargo, to Gral. José de la Luz Soto, Parral, 24 Oct. 1911, AM, caja 1911H; Yáñez, Boquilla, to de la Luz Soto, Parral,

28 Oct. 1911, AM, caja 1911H; and 34 petitioners, Balleza, to jefe político, Parral, 12 July 1911, AM, caja 1911O.

45. Reglamento de Juego, 28 Oct. 1912, Abraham González and Braulio Hernández, AM, caja 1912N. Beezley describes the morality campaign, in *Insurgent Governor,* pp. 103–5.

46. R. R. Escarcega, jefe político, Distrito Mina, Guadalupe y Calvo, Chihuahua, to General José de la Luz Soto, Comandante Militar de Hidalgo del Parral, 11 Nov. 1911, AM, caja 1911Q.

47. Arnoldo de la Rocha, El Sub-teniente y jefe de armas, Guadalupe y Calvo, to C. Gral. José de la Luz Soto, Parral, 10 Nov. 1911, AM, caja 1911Q.

48. M. Cavazos, jefe municipal, Santa Bárbara, to jefe político, Parral, 19 July 1911, AM, caja 1911G; Cavazos to jefe político, 23 Aug. 1911, AM, caja 1911S; and Cavazos to jefe político, 29 Aug. 1911, AM, caja 1911S.

49. Juan Chávez, jefe municipal provisional, San Antonio del Tule, Circular 1, 19 Dec. 1911, AM, caja 1911L.

50. Julián Baca, síndico, Villa Escobedo, to jefe político, Parral, 15 Dec. 1911, AM, caja 1911B.

51. M. Guzmán, Secretario, Santa Bárbara, to jefe político, Parral, 4 Feb. 1912, AM, caja 1912O.

52. 23 petitioners, Villa Escobedo, to Ayuntamiento, 7 March 1912, AM, caja 1912D; and Santos Esparza, presidente municipal, Villa Escobedo, to Gral. José de la Luz Soto, Parral, 13 Jan. 1912, AM, caja 1912P.

53. On Orozco as a variant of *serrano* revolt, see Knight, *Mexican Revolution,* vol. 1, pp. 289–309. Michael Meyer provides a detailed description of events leading up to Orozco's decision to rebel against Madero, in his *Mexican Rebel: Pascual Orozco and the Mexican Revolution 1910–1915* (Lincoln: University of Nebraska Press, 1967), pp. 38–52.

54. Donald B. Gillies, President, San Toy Mining Company, Cd. Chihuahua, to Edward Hoopes, Pittsburgh, 6 Feb. 1912, in Washington, National Archives, Record Group (hereafter cited as NA, RG) 59, St. Dec. File, Box 3898C, 312.115C. Gillies thought very highly of Interim Governor Aureliano Gonzáles, whom he described as a "peach," a "man on the job" enforcing "law and order in every instance."

55. Donald B. Gillies, San Toy Mining Company, Chihuahua, to Edward Hoopes, Pittsburgh, 7 Feb. 1912, NA, RG 59, Box 3898C, 312.115D.

56. See the testimony of Jesús L. Alvarez and Angel Delgado, in Criminal con motivo de la muerte de los Señores Arnulfo y Fidel Martínez, Parral, 28 Sept. 1912, AJ, caja 1912L.

57. Eduardo Sander, comerciante, Parral, to C. Tesorero Municipal, 6

Nov. 1912, AM, caja 1912F.

58. E. C. Bryan, Parral, to Hon. W. J. Bryan, Secretary of State, 25 Aug. 1913, in Washington, NA, RG 59, Box 3712, 312.11/2446.

59. A. R. Fletcher, Supt., Minas Veta Grande y Anexas, Villa Escobedo, to James I. Long, U.S. Consular Agent, Parral, 24 Oct. 1912, NA, RG 59, Box 3698D.

60. "Maderistas Did Not Loot Parral," *EPMT,* 9 April 1912, 1: 4, Reel 56.

61. "American Smelting and Refining Company," *EMJ,* 12 April 1913, p. 773.

62. "Millions for Mexican Miners," *EPMT,* 18 Oct. 1912, 5: 3, Reel 58.

63. Sam Gill, President, Parral and Durango Railroad Co., Pittsburgh, Pa., to P. C. Knox, Secretary of State, 25 July 1912, NA, RG 59, 312.115P241/3.

64. W. P. Schumacher, Superintendent, Minas Tecolotes y Anexas, Santa Bárbara, to Mining Department, American Consular Agent, Parral, 17 March 1913, in Suitland, Maryland, WNRC, RG 76, Mexican Claims Commission, Awarded Claims, 1924–1938, Box 221, Docket 2312.

65. Ibid.; and R. F. Manahan, Assistant General Manager, Santa Bárbara, to W. M. Drury, General Manager, Mining Department, ASARCo, Mexico City, 10 March 1913, WNRC, Box 221, Docket 2312.

66. W. M. Drury, Mining Department, ASARCo, Mexico, "Summary of the Situation at the Various Mining Units in Mexico," 3 September 1913, WNRC, Box 221, Docket 2312. See also Edward Brush and S. W. Eccles, Vice-Presidents, ASARCo, to William J. Bryan, Secretary of State, 15 July 1913, WNRC, RG 76, Box 130, GCC U.S. and Mex., Ag. No. 435.

67. W. M. Drury, "Summary of the Situation at the Various Mining Units in Mexico," 3 September 1913, at WNRC, RG 76, Box 221, Docket 2312; and "Parral District Paralyzed," *EPMT,* 17 Aug. 1913, 1: 3, Reel 62.

68. Frederick Simpich, U.S. Consul, Nogales, Sonora, to U.S. Secretary of State, Washington, 24 April 1913, NA, RG 59, Box 3793E. See the Memorandum.

69. Wm. Loeb, Jr., ASARCo, New York, to William J. Bryan, Secretary of State, 10 Sept. 1913, NA, RG 59, 312.115Am3/65.

70. American mining manager in Parral camp to A. J. McQuatters, President, Alvarado Mining and Milling Co., 14 Aug. 1913, entitled Copy of a Document left with the Latin American Division by the Private Secretary of Senator Oliver on August 22, and located in NA, RG 59, Box 3711, 312.11/2130.

71. Ibid.

72. W. P. Schumacher, Superintendent, Minas Tecolotes y Anexas, Unit of the American Smelters Securities Company, WNRC, RG 76, Box 221, Docket 2312.

73. E. C. Bryan, Parral, to W. J. Bryan, Secretary of State, 25 Aug. 1913, NA, RG 59, Box 3712, 312.11/2446.

74. Peckham to Secretary of State, Washington, 20 December 1913, quoting from a letter sent from Harold McLeod Cobb, Superintendent, Guanacevi Mining Company, Mexico, to Edward H. Clark, New York, in NA, RG 59, Box 3793G, 312.115H121/2.

75. Edward Brush and S. W. Eccles, Vice-Presidents, ASARCo, to William J. Bryan, Secretary of State, Washington, 15 July 1913, WNRC, RG 76, Box 130d, GCC US and Mex, Ag No. 435.

76. A. M. Hamilton, Superintendent, Velardeña Plant, ASARCo, Asarco, Durango, to H. R. Wagner, General Manager, ASARCo, Mexico D.F., 12 June 1913, WNRC RG 76, Box 217, Docket 2280.

77. "General Pancho Villa" (editorial), *EPMT,* 1 Dec. 1913, 6: 1. On the revival of trade, see "Chihuahua Enjoys Revival of Trade," *EPMT,* 10 April 1914, Reel 66.

78. John N. Steele, General Counsel, ASARCo, to S. C. Neale, Washington, 19 November 1914, NA, RG 59, 312.115Am3/95. ASARCo experienced other losses of bullion from its operations in Durango in late 1913; see Rafael Díaz G., Asarco, Durango, to C. L. Baker, Asst. General Manager, ASARCo 17 Dec. 1913.

79. C. L. Baker, General Manager, ASARCo, Mexican Department, El Paso, Tex., to Z. L. Cobb, Collector of Customs, El Paso, NA, RG 59, Box 3898, 312.115Am3/115.

80. Charles Qualey, Manager, Yoquivo Development Company, El Paso, Tex., to Marion Letcher, American Consul, Chihuahua, 19 December 1913, NA, RG 59, Box 3698E, 312.115Y8/4.

81. J. O. Crocket to H. I. Miller, El Paso, 28 April 1914, Box 13, McNeely Collection, University of Texas at El Paso. On the Cumbre tunnel, see Karl V. Eck, as dictated to Joseph N. Quail, 19 Sept. 1919, El Paso, in Albert Bacon Fall Papers.

82. Sam Gill, President, Parral and Durango Railroad Co., Pittsburgh, Pa., to William J Bryan, Secretary of State, Washington, 2 November 1914, NA, RG 59, Box 3698E, 312.115P241/30.

83. W. M. Drury, Mining Department, El Paso, to S. W. Eccles, Vice President, ASARCo, New York City, 12 June 1914, WNRC, RG 76, Box 234, Docket 2533.

84. Walter M. Brodie, "Present Mining Conditions in Mexico," *EMJ,* 18 July 1914, p. 126.

85. Edward Brush, Vice-President, ASARCo, to Robert Lansing, Secretary of State, 30 July 1915, NA, RG 59, Box 3729, 312.11/6394.

86. Henry O. Flipper, El Paso, to Albert Bacon Fall, 15 August 1914, Fall Papers.

87. William K. Meyers, "Pancho Villa and the Multinationals: United States Mining Interests in Villista Mexico, 1913–1915," *Journal of Latin American Studies*, 23: 2 (May 1991), p. 347.

88. Edward Brush, Vice President, ASARCo, to Robert Lansing, Secretary of State, Washington, 30 July 1915, NA, RG 59, Box 3729, 312.11/ 6394.

89. For a discussion of attempts by Villista officials to confiscate mines see Meyers, "Pancho Villa and the Multinationals," pp. 350–59.

90. Walter M. Brodie, "Present Mining Conditions in Mexico," *EMJ*, 18 July 1914, pp. 126–27.

91. R. F. Manahan, Asst. General Manager, Mexico, ASARCo, to C. F. Galan, Chihuahua, 28 May 1917, WNRC, Box 221, Docket 2312.

92. Letcher, Chihuahua, to Secretary of State, 21 Sept. 1915, NA, RG 59, 312.11/6693.

93. Edward Brush to Lansing, 30 July 1915, NA, RG 59, Box 3729, 312.11/6394.

94. S. W. Eccles, New York, ASARCo, to George J. Benedict, San Diego, Calif., 21 Sept. 1915, ASARCo Archive, File No. 245–10–4.

95. According to C. R. Watson, Chairman of the Executive Committee of the Mine and Smelter Operators' Association, the following companies belonged to the association: Alvarado Consolidated Mining Co., Cusi Mining Co., Buena Tierra Mining Co., Yoquivo Development Co., Rio Tinto Copper Co., Cocheno Mining Co., San Toy Mining Co., San Francisco Mines of Mexico, Montezuma Lead Co., ASARCo, Batopilas Mining Co., El Potosí Mining Co., Mines Company of America, Segovia Mining Co., Minas San Juan y Anexas, Peñoles Mining Co. See C. R. Watson to All Members, El Paso, 14 Oct. 1915, and Henry Bornhoff, Asst. General Manager, to F. E. Stevenson, Secretary, Mine and Smelter Operators' Association, El Paso, 22 Sept. 1915, in Albert Bacon Fall Papers.

96. C. F. Galan, Agent of ASARCo, Chihuahua, to Secretary of State, Washington, 11 Oct. 1915, NA, RG 59, 312.115Am3/104.

97. C. L. Baker, ASARCo, to Willard S. Morse, New York, 29 Oct. 1915, NA RG59, Box 3898C, 312.115Am3/109, and C. L. Baker to Morse, 26 Nov. 1915, 312.115Am3/110.

98. A. M. Hamilton, Superintendent, ASARCo, Asarco, Durango, to H. R. Wagner, General Manager, Mexico, 14 Feb. 1912, WNRC, Box 218, Docket 2280.

99. Superintendent, ASARCo, Asarco, Durango, to C. L. Baker, General Manager, El Paso, 17 Jan. 1916, WNRC, Box 217, Docket 2280, and Julio Sinner, Santa Bárbara, to R. F. Manahan, Asst. General Manager, ASARCo, El Paso, 29 Dec. 1916, WNRC, Box 221, Docket 2312.

100. W. M. Drury, General Manager, Mexico, to S. W. Eccles, Vice-President, ASARCo, New York, 30 December 1916, WNRC, Box 221, Docket 2312.

101. For an analysis of Villa at this juncture, see Knight, *Mexican Revolution,* vol. 2, pp. 330–60.

102. Octaviano López, Cusi Mining Company, Cusihiuriáchic, Chihuahua, to E. P. Ryan, Supt., Cusi Mining Company, El Paso, 23 May 1916, WNRC, Docket 513. Mexican representatives of the Cusi Co. worked closely with General Pershing in May 1916, providing guides and information on troop movements. In exchange, Pershing sent two hundred men and a machine gun to Cusi when the company was threatened by Cruz Domínguez; see Octaviano López, Cusi Mining Co., Cusihuiriáchic, to E. P. Ryan, El Paso, Tex., 7 May 1916, WNRC, RG 76, Docket 513.

103. Marion Letcher, American Consul for Chihuahua, to Secretary of State, 20 Jan. 1916, 312.115C96/73, and Sworn Statement of Henry Hollis, President, Cusi Mining Company, 1 March 1937, WNRC, Docket 513. Cusi officials blamed Pablo López, Francisco Beltran, and "other Villa followers"; see Cusi Mining Company to Secretary of State, Washington, 11 Feb. 1917, in WNRC, File 513.

104. Mine and Smelter Operators' Association to Secretary of State, 13 January 1916, NA, RG 59, 312.11/7198.

105. Cusi Mining Co. to Secretary of State, 11 Feb. 1917, WNRC, RG 76, File 513. As officials of the company declared, "All employees at mine are Mexicans."

106. See the long report made by Julio Sinner, Santa Bárbara, to R. F. Manahan, Assistant General Manager, ASARCo, 29 Dec. 1916, WNRC, RG 76, Box 221, Docket 2312.

107. Deposition of Dr. Thomas Flannigan, Eagle Pass, Tex., 19 Dec. 1916, NA, RG 59, 312.11/8315.

108. Ibid.

109. W. M. Drury, Mexican Mining Department, ASARCo, to William Loeb, ASARCo, New York, 15 June 1916, NA, RG 59, Box 3898C, 312.115Am3/145, and Jesús Canal, ASARCo representative, Dolores mine, Matehuala Unit, to E. E. Reyer, Superintendent, El Paso, 30 May 1916, NA, RG 59, 312.115Am3/145.

110. Superintendent, ASARCo, Asarco, to C. L. Baker, General Manager, ASARCo, El Paso, 17 Jan. 1916, WNRC, RG 76, Box 217, Docket 2280.

111. Letter to C. L. Montague, Manager, Cusi Mining Company, El Paso, 26 Feb. 1917, WNRC, RG 76, File 513.

112. Collector Zach Cobb of the U.S. Treasury Department considered the stealing of ore from "American-owned" mines in Mexico to be worse in September 1916 than at any previous time. A record of his ef-

forts to halt this trade is found in Cobb to Frank L. Polk, State Department, 9 Sept. 1916, NA, RG 59, Box 3735, 312.11/8125, and Cobb to Secretary of State, 22 Sept. 1916, 312.115Y8/19. On the stealing of ore in Parral in 1916, see E. F. Knotts, El Paso, to Albert Bacon Fall, 29 May 1916, Fall Papers.

113. Sinner to Manahan, 29 Dec. 1916. On this occasion, Sinner reported that although the houses were plundered, the pay office, mill, zinc plant, power plant, shops, and assay office of ASARCo were all untouched.

114. R. Calderón, Cusi Mining Co., Cusihuiriáchic, to C. L. Montague, General Manager, Cusi Mining Co., El Paso, 4 March 1917.

115. General Manager, Mining Department, Monterrey, Nuevo León, to W. C. Potter, Chairman, Executive Committee, Southwestern Department, ASARCo, 5 April 1910, ASARCo Archive, Drawer 11, File 245–5.

116. W. M. Drury, Mexican Mining Department, to S. W. Eccles, Vice President, ASARCo, 28 Jan. 1914, ASARCo Archive, File 245–3–12, Subject: Chihuahua, Cía. Minera de Naica. Drury discusses a letter sent to him by Eccles, 16 Dec. 1913.

117. C. L. Baker, General Manager, ASARCo, Mexico, to Edgar L. Newhouse, Vice President, ASARCo, New York, 23 Nov. 1916, ASARCo Archive, File 245–3–12, Subject: Chihuahua, Cía. Minera de Naica.

118. Ibid. Baker reminded company executives in late 1916: "However, we have a great deal at stake in Mexico and sooner or later we are going to be able to work and make large profits there." Others concluded that the German company had some special arrangement with Mexican political authorities not enjoyed by American companies; see Lansing, State Department, to U.S. Embassy, Mexico City, 14 June 1916, NA, RG 59, Box 3795, 312.115/310a.

119. Board of Directors, New York, to W. S. Morse, El Paso, 13 Jan. 1916, ASARCo Archive, File 245–6.

120. W. M. Drury, General Manager, to Willard S. Morse, 19 Jan. 1916, ASARCo Archive, File 245–6.

121. Hardy to J. Kruttschnitt, 26 Feb. 1917, ASARCo Archive, File 245–16–13, Subject: Sonora—Quintera mine, Alamos Dist. W.M. Drury to S.W. Eccles, 30 Dec. 1916, ASARCo Archive, File 245–12–2, Subject: La Blanca, Cerralvo, Nuevo León and Drury to H.A. Guess, 23 March 1917, File 245–18–3, Subject: Zacatecas—La Noria, near Sombrerete.

122. W. M. Drury to S. W. Eccles, Vice President, ASARCo, 17 May 1917, ASARCo Archive, File 245–5–3, Subject: Coahuila—Cont. Mng. Co.—Panuco. All ASARCo officials were in agreement on this point; see also R. F. Manahan, Assistant General Manager, Mexico, to C. F. Galan, Chihuahua, 28 May 1917, WNRC, Box 221, Docket 2312.

123. Gill, President, Parral and Durango Railroad, to Robert Lansing, Secretary of State, 26 Jan. 1917, NA, RG 59, Box 3698E, 312.115P241/40.

124. Gill to Lansing, 15 Oct., 1917, NA, RG 59, Box 3698E,

312.115P241/47.

125. Affidavit of Henry L. Hollis, President, Cusi Mining Company, 1 March 1937, Mexican Claims, Awarded Claims, 1924–38, Docket 513. See pps. 20–26 for conditions in Chihuahua in 1917.

126. R. F. Manahan, Asst. General Manager, ASARCo, to C. F. Galan, Chihuahua, 26 May 1917, WNRC, Box 221, Docket 2312.

127. Wm. Loeb, Jr., ASARCo, to Frank L. Polk, Counselor, State Department, 9 July 1917, NA, RG59, Box 3898C, 312.115 Am3/171, and Carlos Galan to J. R. Woodul, Asst. to General Manager, ASARCo, 5 July 1917, 312.115 Am3/171.

128. C. L. Baker to Gen. Venustiano Carranza, President of the Mexican Republic, n.d. [one week after the arrest of Galan], NA, RG 59, 312.115 Am3/171.

129. Both of these are discussed in Haff to Frank L. Polk, Department of State, 1 May 1917, and C. E. Mills, General Manager, Cananea Consolidated Copper Company, to W. D. Thornton, 20 July 1917, both in NA, RG 59, Box 3794, 312.115/293. For a discussion of the decrees and legislation pertaining to mining between 1910 and 1920 see Juan Luis Sariego Rodríguez, Luis Reygadas, Miguel Angel Gómez and Javier Farrera, *El estado y la minería mexicana,* pp. 59–63.

130. W. M. Drury to S. W. Eccles, Vice President, ASARCo, 17 May 1917, ASARCo Archive, File 245–5–3, Subject: Coahuila-Cont. Mng. Co.-Panuco.

131. W. M. Drury to H. A. Guess, ASARCo, New York, 10 April 1917, ASARCo Archive, File 245–16–13, Subject: Sonora—Quintera Mine, Alamos District.

132. Cobb, Office of the Collector, Treasury Department, to Secretary of State, 11 May 1917, NA, RG 59, Box 3794, 312.115/296.

133. Cobb to Frank L. Polk, Counselor, State Department, 18 May 1917, 312.115/297. On the theft of ore in Hidalgo District, see Cobb to Secretary of State, 3 July 1917, 312.115/351, and Letter to F. T. Anderson, 1 Sept. 1917, WNRC, RG79, Box 221, Docket 2312.

134. Stewart, American Consul, Chihuahua, to Secretary of State, 12 Oct. 1918, NA, RG 59, 312.115/347. Stewart also reported that Enríquez was practically deposed as governor by General Murguía in early October 1918. Mining companies contributing to the monthly payment were El Potosí Mining Co., ASARCo, Buena Tierra Mining Co., Cusi-Mexicana Mining Co., Cusi Mining Co., San Francisco Mines of Mexico, and Alvarado Mining and Milling Co.

135. Wm. Loeb, Jr., Managing Director, ASARCo, to Robert Lansing, Secretary of State, 27 November 1918, NA, RG 59, Box 3898C, 312.115Am3/184.

136. The threat is discussed in Willard S. Morse, Executive Committee, ASARCo, to Boaz Long, Department of State, 6 Feb. 1919, NA, RG

59, Box 3898C, 312.115 Am3/199. On the destruction of mines belong-
ing to the company, see L. C. Neale, Attorney, ASARCo, to Frank L.
Polk, Secretary of State, 29 Jan. 1919, NA, RG 59, Box 3898C, 312.115
Am3/202.

137. Neale to Polk, 312.115Am3/202, and Morse to Long, NA, RG
59, 312.115Am3/199. Home Forces formerly had been called *Defensas
Sociales.*

138. J. G. E., Jefe de las Armas, Parral, to Generals Castro and Martínez
in Chihuahua, 27 Dec. 1918, WNRC, Box 221, Docket 2312. For conditions in Hidalgo District at this time, see also Gill, President, Parral and
Durango Railroad Co., to Lansing, 15 Oct. 1918, NA, RG 59, Box 3698E,
312.115P241/52, and Gill to Lansing, 17 Feb. 1919, NA, RG 59, Box
3698E, 312.115P241/65.

139. J. A. Wright, Cusi Mining Co., to Secretary of State, 3 Feb. 1919,
NA, RG 59, 312.115C96/181.

140. American Consul, Torreón, Coahuila, to Secretary of State, 23
June 1919, NA, RG 59, 312.11/8722.

141. J. de Beraza, Oficial Ayudante del Dpto. Trabajo, to Sr. Dn. Esteban
Flores, Jefe Interino del Depto. del Trabajo, 10 Oct. 1920, in Archivo
General de la Nación, Fondo Trabajo, Vol. 211, Exp. 15, F. 100. I thank
Jesús Vargas, professor at the Centro de Investigaciones del Estado de
Chihuahua, for this material. Beraza's exact words were: "Existe el
antecedente de que la mayor parte de los trabajadores está formada de
revolucionarios de todos colores y por bandidos que han bajado de la
sierra, por lo que la inmensa mayoría cuenta con armas y parque."

142. G. Jones to Albert Bacon Fall, 12 April 1920, Fall Papers. Jones
comments as follows: "Villa's men that were disbanded by him last year
and sent to work for American mines are being called back and from all
information obtained they are also conscripting a number of men."

143. For the demands of the skilled workers, see petición signed by 48
workers to the Compañía Tecolotes y Anexas, S.A., 26 Sept. 1920. The
resolution of the strike is discussed in Beraza to Sr. Don Esteban Flores,
Jefe Interino del Departamento del Trabajo, 6 Nov. de 1920, both in
Trabajo, Vol. 211, Expediente 15, F. 100.

144. The celebrations are discussed in Beraza to Flores, 6 Nov. 1920,
Trabajo.

145. El Presidente de la Unión Libre de Trabajadores Mineros, Santa
Bárbara, al Sr. General Dn. Francisco Villa, Canutillo, 7 Oct. 1920,
Trabajo.

Chapter 7

1. Confidential Report of Harry B. Ott, American Vice Consul, Chihuahua, entitled "The Safety and Protection of American Lives and Property in the Region of Parral, Chih., Mexico," dated 27 March 1924, NA, RG 84, Confidential Files 1922–28.

2. J. Kruttschnitt to H. A. Guess, 1 June 1920, ASARCo Archive, File 245–15–1, Subject: Sinaloa.

3. W. M. Drury to Fairman, 22 May 1923, ASARCo Archive, File 245–3–19, Subject: Chihuahua: Esmeralda Mine, Parral.

4. Ott, "Safety and Protection of American Lives and Property," NA, RG 84. Ott considered the Municipal Guard to be part of the problem rather than part of the solution.

5. For a list of Americans held for ransom in 1921, see "Memorandum of Lawless Outbreaks and Bandit Activity in the Parral District, State of Chihuahua, Mexico," Drury to Wm. Loeb, Jr., ASARCo, New York, 3 Oct. 1921, NA, RG59, Box 3793B, 312.115Am3/225. On Manuel Chao and Villistas, see Ott, "Safety and Protection of American Lives and Property," NA, RG 84.

6. Ott, "The Safety and Protection of American Lives and Property," NA, RG 84.

7. Secretaría de Industria, Comercio y Trabajo to Compañía Tecolotes, Santa Bárbara, 11 Oct. 1920, AGN, Fondo Trabajo, Vol. 211, Expediente 15.

8. This was the interpretation of ASARCo officials in Mexico. See W. M. Drury to H. A. Guess, 18 April 1922, ASARCo Archive, File 245–3, Subject: Chihuahua, 1913–33. The McQuatters deal is more fully discussed in Mark Wasserman, *Persistent Oligarchs: Elites and Politics in Chihuahua, Mexico, 1910–1940* (Durham: Duke University Press, 1993), pp. 76–77.

9. Drury to Guess, 18 April 1922. See also Drury to Fairman, 24 April 1922: "During the past few months we have been very much concerned because of the proposed radical labor laws. The present legislature there is now discussing this subject, and Heaven knows what the outcome will be. Should laws be enacted as they are now proposed, it will be a very serious blow to the mining industry in that state." (ASARCo Archive, File 245–3–19 Subject: Chihuahua: Esmeralda Mine, Parral).

10. H. A. Guess, Memo to Senator Guggenheim, 24 April 1922, ASARCo Archive, File 245–3–19, Subject: Chihuahua: Esmeralda Mine, Parral.

11. "The Chihuahua State Labor Law," *EMJ*, 1922, pp. 414–17.

12. El Presidente Municipal, Parral, Circular, 17 April 1923, in Año de 1923, Mes de Abril, Contenido: Citatorias, Circulares y actas de esta P.M., en el mes y año mencionados, AM, caja 1923.

13. El Inspector to C. Pres. Municipal, Parral, 2 July 1923, in Año de 1923, Mes de Julio, Contenido: Oficios girados por las Oficinas del Poder Ejecutivo Federal y sus dependencias, Parral, AM, caja 1923.

14. "The Chihuahua State Labor Law," *EMJ*, 1922, p. 416.

15. El Inspector to C. Pres. Municipal, Parral, 4 July 1923, in Año de 1923, Mes de Julio, AM, caja 1923.

16. ASARCo purchases in the Parral district between May 1922 and May 1923 are discussed in W. M. Drury to Fairman, 22 May 1923, ASARCo Archive, File 245-3-19, Subject: Chihuahua: Esmeralda Mine, Parral. Wasserman concludes that by the late 1920s, the mining companies had the upper hand as these laws were circumvented with the tacit support of state and national governments; see his *Persistent Oligarchs*, p. 39. This was clearly not the case in 1922 and 1923. In their discussion of the mining legislation passed in the 1920s, Sariego Rodríguez, Luis Reygadas, Miguel Angel Gómez and Javier Farrera conclude that, despite the beginnings of nationalist reform, the structure of property and the functioning of the mining sector remained essentially unaltered in the 1920s; see their *El estado y la minería mexicana,* pp. 25 and 68-74.

17. See the eight political tracts submitted as evidence in Criminal instruida en contra de los que resulten responsables del delito de alteración de listas Electorales en las Elecciones de Ayuntamiento en la Municipalidad de Santa Bárbara de este Distrito, 3 Jan. 1923, AM, caja 1923J.

18. "A los Habitantes de la Municipalidad de Santa Bárbara: El Club Morelos y el Partido Cooperatista Chihuahuense" and "¡Abajo los 75 Centavos Traidores!," both in ibid.

19. The direct quote is interesting: "Debemos de ser francos, el Club Morelos compuesto por sentenares de ciudadanos, no permitiremos jamás la nulidad de las elecciones y que acienda [*sic*] al poder uno a gusto de las Compañías Norte Americanas ni a gusto de unos cuantos comerciantes que solamente luchan por no pagar contribuciones quienes, son los eternos enemigos del Gobierno actual y del Pueblo Mexicano." Club "Morelos," 9 Dec. 1922, in Criminal instruida en contra de los que resulten responsables del delito de alteración de listas Electorales en las Elecciones de Ayuntamiento en la Municipalidad de Santa Bárbara de este Distrito, 3 Jan. 1923, AM, caja 1923J.

20. Ibid.

21. "¡Señores Partidarios de Eduardo Modesto Flores, estáis VENCIDOS!" and "El Momento Solemne. La gran batalla del Sufragio," both in ibid.

22. Criminal instruida en contra del President Municipal de Villa Escobedo, señor Gonzalo Montoya, por el delito de abuso de autoridad, denunciado por José Herrera y cometido en la persona de José Moriel, Tesorero de la Unión de Obreros "Benito Juárez," 1 Dec. 1922, AJ, caja 1922V. On Julian Baca and his constituency, see "El Presidente Munici-

pal se niega a obedecer una Orden Judicial Arbitrariamente encarcela al Tesorero de la Unión B. Juárez," *El Correo de Parral,* 19 Oct. 1922, p. 1.

23. For the program of the Tricolor party, see "Al pueblo de V. Escobedo," *El Correo de Parral,* 19 Nov. 1922, p. 2.

24. Querella contra del Sindicato Confederado "Ricardo Flores Magón," Santa Bárbara, 8 Aug. 1923, AJ, caja 1923V. The message read: "Pueblo Obrero, alerta, odiad al tirano Nemesio Tejeda, zángano maldito; que desprecia iniucuamente al elemento obrero desheredado de este pueblo maldecid a este miserable 'ballena' recibe cobarde 'tiburon' el escupitajo eterno del elemento sindicalizado. Sindicato Confederado 'Ricardo Flores Magón,' salud y revolución social."

25. La Comisión, Sindicato de Trabajadores Mineros "Benito Juárez," to H. Ayuntamiento, Parral, 23 April 1923, AM, caja 1923.

26. Agapito Gómez, merchant, to C. C. Presidente y demás miembros del H. Ayuntamiento, Hidalgo del Parral, 5 Aug. 1920, in Expediente de Correspondencia del H. Ayuntamiento del mes de agosto 1920, AM, caja 1920.

27. One hundred fifty vecinos to C. C. Presidente y Miembros del H. Ayuntamiento, 21 Aug. 1920, in Expediente de Correspondencia del H. Ayuntamiento, mes de agosto 1920, AM, caja 1920.

28. Eight residents to C. Presidente Municipal y Miembros del I. Ayuntamiento, 6 Aug. 1920, in Expediente de Correspondencia del H. Ayuntamiento del mes de agosto 1920, AM, caja 1920.

29. Circular, Parral, 1 April 1923, in Año de 1923, Mes de Abril, Contenido: Citatorias Circulares y actas de esta P.M., en el mes y año mencionados, AM, caja 1923.

30. Inspección de Sanidad, Parral, AM, caja 1920.

31. Seven brothel owners to C. Presidente y Vocales del I. Ayuntamiento, Parral, 15 May 1923, Año de 1923, Mes de Mayo, Contenido: Ocursos dirigidos al H. Ayuntamiento y dictamines é iniciativas de los C. C. Municipes, mes y año mencionados, AM, caja 1923.

32. Fifteen vecinos to C. C. Presidente y Miembros del H. Ayuntamiento, Parral, 17 May 1923, Año de 1923, Mes de Mayo, Contenido: Ocursos dirigidos al H. Ayuntamiento y dictamines é iniciativas de los C. C. Municipes, mes y año mencionados, AM, caja 1923.

Conclusion

1. See Knight, "Working Class and the Mexican Revolution."

2. Scott uses this term in his *Domination and the Arts of Resistance: Hidden Transcripts* (New Haven: Yale University Press, 1990).

3. Katznelson, "Working-Class Formation." Katznelson's model of class is applied here in Chapter 5.

4. Bergquist, *Labor in Latin America*. See his first chapter, "Modern Latin American Historiography and the Labor Movement," for an explanation of his model, and his final chapter, "On the Limits of This Study and the Promise of the Approach," for its application to Mexico.

5. See the articles in the Katznelson and Zolberg, *Working-Class Formation*.

6. Wilentz, *Chants Democratic*, pp. 383–86.

Bibliography

Primary Sources

Archives, Collections, Papers

Austin, Texas
University of Texas at Austin
    Benson Latin American Collection
        Ferrocarril Noroeste de México
        Thomas Wentworth Peirce, Jr., Papers
            Corralitos
            Candelaria Mining Company

El Paso, Texas
University of Texas at El Paso
    McNeely Collection
        James E. Hyslop Collection
        Mexican North Western Railway Papers
    Max Weber Collection

Hidalgo del Parral, Chihuahua, Mexico
Preventiva
    Archivo Municipal
    Archivo Judicial

Los Angeles, California
Occidental College
    Edward L. Doheny Research Fund Collection

Suitland, Maryland
Washington National Record Center
    Record Group 76
        General Claims Commission, U.S. and Mexico
        Mexican Claims Commission

Tucson, Arizona
American Smelting and Refining Company
  American Smelting and Refining Company Archive

Washington, D.C.
National Archives
  Record Group 59: State Decimal File (312)
  Record Group 84: Records of the American Consular
                Post in Chihuahua City, Mexico, 1918–1925

Mexico City, Mexico
Archivo General de la Nación
  Trabajo

South Pasadena, California
Henry E. Huntington Library and Art Gallery
  Albert Bacon Fall Papers

Newspapers and Periodicals

Boletín Oficial del Distrito Hidalgo
El Paso Morning Times
El Correo de Chihuahua (Ciudad Chihuahua)
El Correo de Parral (Hidalgo del Parral)
El Hijo del Parral (Hidalgo del Parral)
La Nueva Era (Santa Bárbara)
Mexican Mining Journal
Engineering and Mining Journal
Chihuahua Enterprise
El Padre Padilla

Secondary Sources

Books and Articles

Adelman, Jeremy. "Against Essentialism: Latin American Labour His-
    tory in Comparative Perspective. A Critique of Bergquist." *La-
    bour/LeTravail* 27 (Spring 1991).
——. *Essays in Argentine Labour History, 1870–1930.* London: Mac-
    Millan Press, 1992.
Almada, Francisco R. *Resumen de historia del estado de Chihuahua.*
    México: Libros Mexicanos, 1955.

Alonso, Ana María. "'Progress' as Disorder and Dishonor: Discourse of Serrano Resistance." *Critique of Anthropology* 8: 1 (1988).

Anderson, Rodney D. *Outcasts in Their Own Land: Mexican Industrial Workers, 1906–1911.* DeKalb: Northern Illinois University Press, 1976.

Arrom, Silvia Marina. *The Women of Mexico City, 1790–1857.* Stanford, Calif.: Stanford University Press, 1985.

Avila, Dolores, Inés Herrera and Rina Oritz, eds. *Minería regional mexicana: Primera reunión de historiadores de la minería latinoamericana (IV).* México: Instituto Nacional de Antropología e Historia, 1994.

Basurto, Jorge. *El proletariado industrial en México 1850–1930).* México: Universidad Nacional Autónoma de México, 1975.

Beezley, William H. *Insurgent Governor: Abraham González and the Mexican Revolution in Chihuahua.* Lincoln: University of Nebraska Press, 1973.

——. *Judas at the Jockey Club and other Episodes of Porfirian Mexico.* Lincoln: University of Nebraska Press, 1987.

Beezley, William H., Cheryl E. Martin, and William E. French, eds. *Rituals of Rule, Rituals of Resistance: Public Celebrations and Popular Culture in Mexico.* Wilmington, Del.: Scholarly Resources, 1994.

Bergquist, Charles. "Latin American Labour History in Comparative Perspective: Notes on the Insidiousness of Cultural Imperialism." *Labour/LeTravail* 25 (1990).

——. *Labor in Latin America: Comparative Essays on Chile, Argentina, Venezuela, and Colombia.* Stanford, Calif.: Stanford University Press, 1986.

Bernstein, Marvin D. *The Mexican Mining Industry, 1890–1950: A Study of the Interaction of Politics, Economics, and Technology.* Albany: State University of New York, 1965.

Bourdieu, Pierre. *Outline of a Theory of Practice,* trans. Richard Nice. Cambridge: Cambridge University Press, 1977.

Boyer, Paul. *Urban Masses and Moral Order in America, 1820–1920.* Cambridge: Harvard University Press, 1978.

Brading, David. *The First America: The Spanish Monarchy, Creole Patriots, and the Liberal State, 1492–1867.* Cambridge: Cambridge University Press, 1991.

Braverman, Harry. *Labor and Monopoly Capital: The Degradation of Work in the Twentieth Century.* New York: Monthly Review Press, 1974.

Brown, Ronald C. *Hard-Rock Miners: The Intermountain West, 1860–1920.* College Station: Texas A. & M. Press, 1979.

Buffington, Robert. "Revolutionary Reform: The Mexican Revolution and the Discourse on Prison Reform." *Mexican Studies/Estudios Mexicanos* 9: 1 (Winter 1993).

Cardoso, Ciro, ed. *México en el siglo XIX (1821–1910): Historia económica y de la estructura social.* México: Editorial Nueva Imagen, 1983.

Carr, Barry. *El movimiento obrero y la política en México, 1910–1929.* México: Ediciones Era: Colección Problemas de México, 1981.

Coatsworth, John H. "Railroads, Landholding and Agrarian Protest in the Early Porfiriato." *Hispanic American Historical Review* 54 (1974).

Connelly, Mark Thomas. *The Response to Prostitution in the Progressive Era.* Chapel Hill: University of North Carolina Press, 1980.

Corbin, Alain. *Women for Hire: Prostitution and Sexuality in France after 1850,* trans. Alan Sheridan. Cambridge: Harvard University Press, 1990.

Cornford, Daniel A. *Workers and Dissent in the Redwood Empire.* Philadelphia: Temple University Press, 1987.

Corrigan, Philip, and Derek Sayer. *The Great Arch: English State Formation as Cultural Revolution.* Oxford: Basil Blackwell, 1985.

Cosío Villegas, Daniel, ed. *Historia moderna de México: El Porfiriato, La vida económica.* Vols. 4 and 6. México: Editorial Hermes, 1957 and 1965, respectively.

Crew, David. *Town in the Ruhr: A Social History of Bochum, 1860–1914.* New York: Columbia University Press, 1979.

Dannenbaum, Jed. *Drink and Disorder: Temperance Reform in Cincinnati from the Washington Revival to the WCTU.* Urbana: University of Illinois Press, 1984.

Derickson, Alan. *Workers' Health, Workers' Democracy: The Western Miners' Struggle, 1891–1925.* Ithaca: Cornell University Press, 1988.

Eakin, Marshall C. *British Enterprise in Brazil: The St. John d'el Rey Mining Company and the Morro Velho Gold Mine, 1830–1960.* Durham: Duke University Press, 1989.

Farr, James. *Hands of Honor: Artisans and Their World in Dijon, 1550–1650.* Ithaca: Cornell University Press, 1988.

Fell, James E., Jr. *Ores to Metals: The Rocky Mountain Smelting Industry.* Lincoln: University of Nebraska Press, 1979.

Fishback, P. V. "Did Coal Miners 'Owe Their Souls to the Company Store'? Theory and Evidence from the Early 1900s." *Journal of Economic History* 46: 4 (December 1986).

Flores Clair, Eduardo. *Conflictos de trabajo de una empresa minera, Real del Monte y Pachuca, 1872–1877.* México: Instituto Nacional de Antropología e Historia, 1991.

Franco, Jean. *Plotting Women: Gender and Representation in Mexico.* New York: Columbia University Press, 1989.

French, William E. "Business as Usual: Mexico North Western Railway Managers Confront the Mexican Revolution." *Mexican Studies/ Estudios Mexicanos* 5: 2 (Summer 1989).

García, Mario T. *Desert Immigrants: The Mexicans of El Paso, 1880–1920.* New Haven: Yale University Press, 1981.

García, Trinidad. *Los mineros mexicanos.* México: Editorial Porrúa, 1970.

Gerth, H. H., and C. Wright Mills, eds. *From Max Weber: Essays in Sociology.* London: Kegan Paul, 1947.

Gibson, Mary. *Prostitution and the State in Italy, 1860–1915.* New Brunswick: Rutgers University Press, 1986.

Giddens, Anthony. *Capitalism and Modern Social Theory: An Analysis of the Writings of Marx, Durkheim and Max Weber.* Cambridge: Cambridge University Press, 1971.

Goddard, Jorge Adame. *El pensamiento político y social de los católicos mexicanos, 1867–1914.* México: Universidad Nacional Autónoma de México, 1981.

González y González, Luis. *San José de Gracia: Mexican Village in Transition,* trans. John Upton. Austin: University of Texas Press, 1972.

González Rodríguez, Sergio. *Los bajos fondos: El antro, la bohemia y el café.* México: Cal y Arena, 1989.

Greaves, Thomas, and William Culver, eds. *Miners and Mining in the Americas.* Manchester: Manchester University Press, 1985.

Gruber, Helmut. "Sexuality in 'Red Vienna': Socialist Party Conceptions and Programs and Working-Class Life, 1920–34." *International Labor and Working-Class History* 31 (Spring 1987).

Guerra, Francois-Xavier. "La révolution mexicaine: d'abord une révolution minière?" *Annales* 36: 5 (Sept.–Oct. 1981): 785–814.

Guerrero, Julio. *La génesis del crimen en México.* México: Editorial Porrúa, 1977.

Gutman, Herbert G. *Work, Culture, and Society in Industrializing America: Essays in American Working-Class and Social History.* New York: Vintage Books, 1977.

Haber, Stephen H. *Industry and Underdevelopment: Industrialization of Mexico, 1890–1940.* Stanford, Calif.: Stanford University Press, 1989.

Hall, Jacquelyn Dowd, James Leloudis, Robert Korstad, Mary Murphy, Lu Ann Jones, and Christopher B. Daly. *Like a Family: The Making of a Southern Cotton Mill World.* Chapel Hill: University of North Carolina Press, 1987.

Hanagan, Michael, and Charles Stephenson, eds. *Proletarians and*

Protest: The Roots of Class Formation in an Industrializing World. New York: Greenwood Press, 1986.

Hart, John Mason. *Revolutionary Mexico: The Coming and Process of the Mexican Revolution.* Berkeley: University of California Press, 1987.

Heyman, Josiah McC. *Life and Labor on the Border: Working People of Northeastern Sonora, Mexico, 1886–1986.* Tucson: University of Arizona Press, 1991.

Hill, Christopher. *Society and Puritanism in Pre-Revolutionary England.* London: Secker and Warburg, 1964.

Holden, Robert H. "Priorities of the State in the Survey of the Public Land in Mexico, 1876–1911." *Hispanic American Historical Review* 70: 4 (November 1990).

Holmes, Douglas R. *Cultural Disenchantments: Worker Peasantries in Northeast Italy.* Princeton, N.J.: Princeton University Press, 1989.

Holmes, Douglas R., and Jean H. Quataert. "An Approach to Modern Labor: Worker Peasantries in Historic Saxony and the Friuli Region over Three Centuries." *Comparative Studies in Society and History* 28: 2 (April 1986).

Ingersoll, Ralph McA. *In and under Mexico.* New York: Century Company, 1924.

Joyce, Patrick, ed. *The Historical Meanings of Work.* Cambridge: Cambridge University Press, 1987.

Joyce, Patrick. *Work, Society and Politics: The Culture of the Factory in Later Victorian England.* Brighton: Harvester Press, 1980.

Kaplan, Steven Laurence, and Cynthia J. Koepp, eds. *Work in France: Representations, Meaning, Organization and Practice.* Ithaca: Cornell University Press, 1986.

Katz, Friedrich, ed. *Riot, Rebellion, and Revolution: Rural Social Conflict in Mexico.* Princeton, N.J.: Princeton University Press, 1988.

Katznelson, Ira, and Aristide R. Zolberg, eds. *Working-Class Formation: Nineteenth-Century Patterns in Western Europe and the United States.* Princeton, N.J.: Princeton University Press, 1986.

Kaye, Harvey J., and Keith McClelland, eds. *E. P. Thompson: Critical Perspectives.* Philadelphia: Temple University Press, 1990.

Knight, Alan. *The Mexican Revolution.* 2 vols. Cambridge: Cambridge University Press, 1986.

———. "The Peculiarities of Mexican History: Mexico Compared to Latin America, 1821–1992." *Journal of Latin American Studies* 24 (Quincentenary Supplement 1992).

———. "Révolution mexicaine: révolution minière ou révolution serrano?" *Annales* 38: 2 (Mar.–Abril 1983).

——. "The Working Class and the Mexican Revolution, c. 1900–1920." *Journal of Latin American Studies* 16 (May 1984).

Ladd, Doris M. *The Making of a Strike: Mexican Silver Workers' Struggles in Real del Monte, 1766–1775*. Lincoln: University of Nebraska Press, 1988.

Landes, Joan B. *Women and the Public Sphere in the Age of the French Revolution*. Ithaca: Cornell University Press, 1988.

Lankton, Larry D. "The Machine under the Garden: Rock Drills Arrive at the Lake Superior Copper Mines, 1868–1883." *Technology and Culture* 24: 1 (January 1983).

Lankton, Larry D., and Jack K. Martin. "Technological Advance, Organizational Structure, and Underground Fatalities in the Upper Michigan Copper Mines, 1860–1929." *Technology and Culture* 28: 1 (January 1987).

Lara y Pardo, Luis. *La prostitución en México*. México: Librería de la Vda. de Ch. Bouret, 1908.

Lloyd, Jane-Dale. *El proceso de modernización capitalista en el noroeste de Chihuahua (1880–1910)*. México: Universidad Iberoamericana, 1987.

Long, Norman, and Bryan Roberts, eds. *Miners, Peasants and Entrepreneurs: Regional Development in the Central Highlands of Peru*. Cambridge: Cambridge University Press, 1984.

Lumholtz, Carl. *Unknown Mexico: A Record of Five Years' Exploration among the Tribes of the Western Sierra Madre; in the Tierra Caliente of Tepic and Jalisco; and among the Tarascos of Michoacán*. 2 vols. London: Macmillan and Company, 1903.

Lynch, Katherine A. *Family, Class, and Ideology in Early Industrial France: Social Policy and the Working-Class Family, 1825–1848*. Madison: University of Wisconsin Press, 1988.

Macedo, Miguel. *La criminalidad en México: Medios de combatirla*. México: Secretaría de Fomento, 1897.

Marcosson, Isaac F. *Metal Magic: The Story of the American Smelting and Refining Company*. New York: Farrar, Straus and Company, 1949.

McCaa, Robert. "Women's Position, Family and Fertility Decline in Parral (Mexico), 1777–1930." *Annales de Démographie Historique* (1989).

McCreery, David. "'This Life of Misery and Shame': Female Prostitution in Guatemala City, 1880–1920." *Journal of Latin American Studies* 18: 2 (November 1986).

McHugh, Cathy L. *Mill Family: The Labor System in the Southern Cotton Textile Industry, 1880–1915*. New York: Oxford University Press, 1988.

Merriman, John M., ed. *Consciousness and Class Experience in Nine-teenth-Century Europe.* New York: Holmes and Meier, 1979.

Meyer, Michael. *Mexican Rebel: Pascual Orozco and the Mexican Revolution, 1910–1915.* Lincoln: University of Nebraska Press, 1967.

Meyer, Stephen. *The Five Dollar Day: Labor Management and Social Control in the Ford Motor Company, 1908–1921.* Albany: State University of New York Press, 1981.

Meyers, William K. "Pancho Villa and the Multinationals: United States Mining Interests in Villista Mexico, 1913–1915." *Journal of Latin American Studies* 23: 2 (May 1991).

Monsiváis, Carlos. "La mujer en la cultura mexicana." In *Mujer y sociedad en América Latina,* ed. Lucía Guerra-Cunningham. Irvine: University of California, Editorial Pacífico, 1980.

Nelson, Daniel. *Managers and Workers: Origins of the New Factory System in the United States, 1880–1920.* Madison: University of Wisconsin Press, 1975.

Neuschatz, Michael. *The Golden Sword: The Coming of Capitalism to the Colorado Mining Frontier.* New York: Greenwood Press, 1986.

Parker, David S. "White-Collar Lima, 1910–1929: Commercial Em-ployees and the Rise of the Peruvian Middle Class." *Hispanic American Historical Review* 72: 1 (February 1992).

Parker, Morris B. *Mules, Mines and Me in Mexico, 1895–1932.* Tuc-son: University of Arizona Press, 1979.

Piore, Michael J. *Birds of Passage: Migrant Labor and Industrial Soci-eties.* Cambridge: Cambridge University Press, 1979.

Pollard, Sidney. *The Genesis of Modern Management: A Study of the Industrial Revolution in Great Britain.* Cambridge: Harvard University Press, 1965.

Price, Richard. *Labour in British Society: An Interpretative History.* London: Croom Helm, 1986.

——. "Theories of Labour Process Formation." *Journal of Social History* (Fall 1984).

Radkau, Verena. *"Por la debilidad de nuestro ser": Mujeres del pueblo en la paz porfiriana.* México: Centro de Investigaciones y Estudios Superiores en Antropología Social, Secretaría de Educación Púb-lica, 1989.

Ramos Escandón, Carmen. "Gender Construction in a Progressive Society: Mexico, 1870–1917." *Texas Papers on Mexico,* no. 90-07. Austin: Mexican Center, Institute of Latin American Studies, University of Texas, 1990.

Ramos Escandón, Carmen, ed. *Presencia y transparencia: La mujer en la historia de México*. México: El Colegio de México, 1987.

Reid, Donald. "Industrial Paternalism: Discourse and Practice in Nineteenth-Century French Mining and Metallurgy." *Comparative Studies in Society and History* 27: 4 (1985).

———. "Labour Management and Labour Conflict in Rural France: The Aubin Miners' Strike of 1869." *Social History* 13: 1 (January 1988).

———. *The Miners of Decazeville: A Genealogy of Deindustrialization*. Cambridge: Harvard University Press, 1985.

Roche, Daniel. *The People of Paris: An Essay in Popular Culture in the Eighteenth Century*, trans. Marie Evans. Leamington Spa: Berg Publishers, 1987.

Rodea, Marcelo N. *Historia del movimiento obrero ferrocarrilero en México (1890–1943)*. México: 1944.

Rodríguez O., Jaime E., ed. *The Revolutionary Process in Mexico: Essays on Political and Social Change, 1880–1940*. Los Angeles: University of California at Los Angeles, Latin American Center Publications, 1990.

Ross, Ellen, and Rayna Rapp. "Sex and Society: A Research Note from Social History and Anthropology." *Comparative Studies in Society and History* 23 (January 1981).

Roumagnac, Carlos. *Los criminales en México: Ensayo de psicología criminal*. México: Tipografía "El Fenix," 1904.

Ruiz, Ramón Eduardo. *The People of Sonora and Yankee Capitalists*. Tucson: University of Arizona Press, 1988.

Sabel, Charles F. *Work and Politics: The Division of Labor in Industry*. Cambridge: Cambridge University Press, 1982.

Sahay, Arun, ed. *Max Weber and Modern Sociology*. London: Routledge and Kegan Paul, 1971.

Sanz, M. A. *La mujer mexicana en el santuario del hogar*. México: Lacaud, 1907.

Sariego Rodríguez, Juan Luis. "La condición del proletariado minero a principios del siglo." In *Arqueología de la industria en México*, ed. Victoria Novelo. Coyoacán: Museo Nacional de Culturas Populares, SEP Cultura, 1983.

———. "La cultura minera en crisis. Aproximación a algunos elementos de la identidad de un grupo obrero." In *Coloquio sobre cultura obrera*, ed. Victoria Novelo. Tlalpan, México: Secretaría de Educación Pública, Centro de Investigaciones y Estudios Superiores en Antropología Social, 1987.

———. *Enclaves y minerales en el norte de México: Historia social de los mineros de Cananea y Nueva Rosita, 1900–1970*. México: Centro de Investigaciones y Estudios Superiores en Antropología Social, 1988.

Sariego Rodríguez, Juan Luis, Luis Reygadas, Miguel Angel Gómez, and Javier Farrera. *El estado y la minería mexicana: Política, trabajo y sociedad durante el siglo XX.* México: Secretaría de Energía, Minas e Industria Paraestatal, Fondo de Cultura Económica, 1988.

Sariego Rodríguez, Juan Luis and Raúl Santana Paucar. "Transición tecnológica y resistencia obrera en la minería mexicana." *Cuadernos políticos* 31 (1982).

Scott, James C. *Domination and the Arts of Resistance: Hidden Transcripts.* New Haven: Yale University Press, 1990.

——. *The Moral Economy of the Peasant: Subsistence and Rebellion in Southeast Asia.* New Haven: Yale University Press, 1976.

——. *Weapons of the Weak: Everyday Forms of Peasant Resistance.* New Haven: Yale University Press, 1985.

Scott, Joan Wallach. *Gender and the Politics of History.* New York: Columbia University Press, 1986.

Shepherd, Grant. *The Silver Magnet: Fifty Years in a Mexican Silver Mine.* New York: E. P. Dutton and Co., 1938.

Shuber, Adrian. *The Road to Revolution in Spain: The Coal Miners of Asturias, 1860–1934.* Urbana: University of Illinois Press, 1987.

Stallybrass, Peter, and Allon White. *The Politics and Poetics of Transgression.* London: Methuen, 1986.

Stearns, Peter N. *Paths to Authority: The Middle Class and the Industrial Labor Force in France, 1820–48.* Urbana: University of Illinois Press, 1978.

Stepan, Nancy Leys. *"The Hour of Eugenics": Race, Gender and Nation in Latin America.* Ithaca: Cornell University Press, 1991.

Thompson, E. P. *Customs in Common.* London: The Merlin Press, 1991.

——. "Eighteenth-Century English Society: Class Struggle without Class." *Social History* 3: 2 (May 1978).

——. *The Making of the English Working Class.* New York: Vintage Books, 1966.

——. "The Moral Economy of the English Crowd." *Past and Present* (1971).

——. "Time, Work-Discipline, and Industrial Capitalism." *Past and Present* 38 (1967).

Valverde, Mariana. "The Love of Finery: Fashion and the Fallen Woman in Nineteenth-Century Social Discourse." *Victorian Studies* 32: 2 (Winter 1989).

Vaughan, Mary Kay. "Primary Education and Literacy in Nineteenth-

Century Mexico: Research Trends, 1968–1988." *Latin American Research Review* 25: 1 (1990).
——. *The State, Education, and Social Class in Mexico, 1880–1928.* DeKalb: Northern Illinois University Press, 1982,
——. "Women, Class, and Education in Mexico, 1880–1928." *Latin American Perspectives* 12–13 (1977).
Velasco Avila, Cuauhtémoc, Eduardo Flores, Edgar Gutiérrez, and Alma Parra. *Estado y minería en México (1767–1910).* México: Secretaría de Energía, Minas e Industria Paraestatal, Fondo de Cultura Económica, 1988.
Viquiera Albán, Juan Pedro. *¿Relajados o reprimidos? Diversiones públicas y vida social en la ciudad de México durante el Siglo de las Luces.* México: Fondo de Cultura Económica, 1987.
Voekel, Pamela. "Peeing on the Palace: Bodily Resistance to Bourbon Reforms in Mexico." *Journal of Historical Sociology* 5: 2 (June 1992).
Viotti da Costa, Emilia. "Experience versus Structures: New Tendencies in the History of Labor and the Working Class in Latin America —What Do We Gain? What Do We Lose?" *International Labor and Working Class History* 36 (Fall 1989).
Walkowitz, Judith R. *City of Dreadful Delight: Narratives of Sexual Danger in Late-Victorian London.* Chicago: University of Chicago Press, 1992.
Wasserman, Mark. *Capitalists, Caciques, and Revolution: The Native Elite and Foreign Enterprise in Chihuahua, Mexico, 1854–1911.* Chapel Hill: University of North Carolina Press, 1984.
——. *Persistent Oligarchs: Elites and Politics in Chihuahua, Mexico, 1910–1940.* Durham: Duke University Press, 1993.
Weeks, Jeffrey. *Sex, Politics, and Society: The Regulation of Sexuality since 1800.* New York: Longman, 1981.
Wilentz, Sean. "Against Exceptionalism: Class Consciousness and the American Labor Movement, 1790–1920." *International Labor and Working Class History* 26 (Fall 1984): 1–24.
——. *Chants Democratic: New York City and the Rise of the American Working Class, 1788–1850.* New York: Oxford University Press, 1984.
Wyman, Mark. *Hard Rock Epic: Western Miners and the Industrial Revolution, 1860–1910.* Berkeley: University of California Press, 1979.
Young, Otis E., Jr. *How They Dug the Gold: An Informal History of Frontier Prospecting, Placering, Lode-Mining and Milling in Arizona and the Southwest.* Tucson: Arizona Pioneers' Historical Society, 1967.

Unpublished Materials

Rohlfes, Laurence. "Police and Penal Correction in Mexico City, 1876–1911: A Study of Order and Progress in Porfirian Mexico." Ph.D. diss., Tulane University, 1983.

Vargas, Jesús. "Los obreros de Chihuahua: Sus experiencias de organización (1880–1940)." Unpublished manuscript in possession of the author.

Index

About the Book and Author

A Peaceful and Working People
Manners, Morals, and Class Formation in Northern Mexico

WILLIAM E. FRENCH

The mining boom that began in northern Mexico in the 1890s set in motion fundamental social change. On the one hand it uprooted many workers, and the concerns of gobernment officials, middle class reformers, and company managers coalesced into laws and programs to control the restless masses. But changes in the mining economy and political cullture also precipitated class consciousness among merchants and artisans as well as skilled and unskilled workers.

This study of the Hidalgo mining district in Chihuahua from the 1890s to the 1920s examines class formation, in particular its relation to social control, popular values, and preindustrial traditions. In arguing that class identity stemmed less from the nature of one's work than from the beliefs one held, this work brings together the disparate themes of moral reform, the cult of domesticity, the moral economy of mine workers, vice, new mining technology, and the management policy of mine owners during the Mexican Revolution.

This volume provides a new understanding of the dynamics of labor and class amid modernization unleashed during the Porfirian era and in the upheaval of the Mexican Revolution.

"A groundbreaking analysis of Porfirian Mexico."—Professor William H. Beezley, Penrose Professor of History, TCU

William E. French is associate professor and graduate chair in the Department of History at the University of British Columbia, Vancouver.